Mind, Metaphysics, and Value

in the Thomistic
and Analytical Traditions

THOMISTIC STUDIES

Daniel J. McInerny, General Editor

Sponsored by the Center for Thomistic Studies
Houston, Texas

Mind, Metaphysics, and Value

in the Thomistic and Analytical Traditions

edited by

JOHN HALDANE

University of Notre Dame Press
Notre Dame, Indiana

A record of the Library of Congress Cataloging-in-Publication Data
is available upon request from the Library of Congress.

ISBN 0-268-03467-2

CONTENTS

INTRODUCTION

John Haldane

It is always appropriate to begin the work of a single author with an introduction explaining the motivations, character, and content of the remainder of the book. In the case of an edited collection of solicited essays the policy has dangers, particularly if the editor takes it upon himself to describe the work of the diverse hands he has commissioned. Such a volume is more like a buffet contributed to by several chefs, than an extended meal prepared by a single cook. Readers are not required to begin at one end and proceed to the other; rather they have the option of picking elements in a sequence of their own choosing, according to their own tastes and interests, but, one hopes, completing the full menu in due course.

It may be apt, however, to say something about the general aim of this collection, and in doing so confess my own motivation and hope. Having been educated by the Jesuits, I left school with a sense of the importance which the Catholic tradition has long attached to philosophy and of the contributions it has made to it. However, my later university education in the subject was entirely secular and conducted in a largely ahistorical manner. Additionally, it was exclusively within the analytical tradition and at a time when, as is still largely the case, that school laid great emphasis on the philosophies of logic, language, and mind. I had, and have, no complaint about this. Indeed, I regard that education as a very good preparation for philosophical work. Like any formation, however, it has its failings in respect of both omission and commission.

So far as the latter is concerned, there is a tendency of analytical philosophy to proceed as if it, uniquely, were free of prejudices. Like Mr. Valiant for Truth it sees itself as advancing heroically against confusion and error, though increasingly the image is less that of a knight than of a scientific researcher cutting through to the core of things, exposing their inner construction and operations. What this imagery fails to record are the possibilities that the activity is unreasonably prejudiced in its assumptions and methods, and that the latter may do unwarranted damage to the objects upon which they are exercised. Anticipating the phenomenological movement by more than half a century, Professor James Ferrier, first of Edinburgh and then of St Andrews, challenged the analytical philosophy of his day, namely, empiricist naturalism:

> [I]f it should appear that this science [of the human mind] carries in its conception such a radical defect that all the true and distinctive phenomena of man necessarily elude its grasp, and that it is forever doomed to fall short of the end it designs to encompass, then our adoption of its method could only lead us to the poorest and most unsatisfactory results. . . . The human mind, not to speak it profanely, is like the goose that laid golden eggs. The [empiricist] metaphysician resembles the analytic poulterer who slew it to get at them in a lump, and found nothing for his pains. . . . Cut into the mind metaphysically, with a view to grasping the embryo truth, and of ascertaining the process by which all these bright results are elaborated in the womb, and every trace of 'what has been' vanishes beneath the knife; the breathing realities are dead, and lifeless abstractions are in place. . . .
>
> Language itself, and consequently the very nature of thought, render impracticable anything like a true and real *science* of the human mind . . . if mind can be conceived as an object of research, its vital distinguishing and fundamental phenomenon, namely consciousness, necessarily becomes invisible, inasmuch as it adheres tenaciously to the side of the inquiring *subject;* and that if it be again invested with this phenomenon, it becomes from that moment inconceivable as *object.*[1]

It is perhaps unsurprising to learn that the main source of Ferrier's preferred conception of philosophy was Hegel, whose metaphysical doctrines were appealing to his own poetic and transcendentalist sensibility. Ferrier, however, made no secret of his commitments and dispositions. Indeed, he tested the adequacy of philosophies against them, to see which might make space for, if not necessarily confirm, his pre-philosophical intuitions and judgements. There is in this the danger of remaining with one's prejudices; but that is less likely if one recognises them for what they are, namely, antecedent commitments—and ones which may, after all, be correct. The opposite danger is that of assuming that the inquirer looks upon things with an innocent and neutral eye, or of thinking that any prejudices are purely personal and separable from the practice of analysis and argumentation.

The point has often been made that one of the merits of studying the history of philosophy, particularly that of a period culturally and intellectually remote from one's own, is that it encourages the realisation of just how parochial and prejudiced one's assumptions and ways of thinking may be. This thought introduces what is probably the chief omission of analytical philosophy, namely, a proper study and appreciation of other perspectives, particularly historical ones and especially the more distant of these. A well-known American philosopher in one of the country's most highly ranked departments, in what is also one of its oldest universities, for a time took to espousing the maxim (in emulation of an antidrug slogan) "Just Say 'No' to History of Philosophy." For those who have eyes to see, this is more revealing than witty. Certainly it can be the case that students of the history of a subject cease, if they ever began, to practice the subject itself, and disappear instead into texts. On the other hand it is at least philistine to have no interest in the history of one's subject, and without an appreciation of past insight and error one is handicapped in one's own efforts. Philosophical collaboration extends in time as well as in space.

Predisposition and general curiosity has led me and others raised in the analytical tradition to look beyond its sometimes narrow confines, and I can still recall something of the thrill of discovering the worlds of scholasticism and Thomism. Such have been their marginalisation within the main forums of English-language philosophy that, unless they were peculiarly fortunate, anyone wishing to study them would most likely have to do so by their own efforts, seeking out books and articles. In my own case even the resources of the main library of the University of London proved quite limited, and I soon became indebted to the Catholic Central Library then located behind Westminster Cathedral. Things are improving, however: there is greater interest in the history of philosophy; increased questioning of the presumed innocence of analytical inquiry; more extensive publication of hitherto inaccessible works and of associated commentary; and a general pluralisation of philosophy. The last of these can take the form of damaging fragmentation and lead to a superficial eclecticism of the sort criticised by John Paul II in *Fides et Ratio*. But it can also take a healthy form leading to the recognition of parallels and resemblances hitherto impossible to observe.

With such thoughts and experiences in mind I have been interested in fostering interactions and exchanges between analytical and scholastic, but especially Aristotelian-Thomistic, philosophies. For the most part this effort has been committed to producing philosophical writings in which the different strands are worked together. Yet philosophy is a collective activity, and apart from one's own need for colleagues from whom to learn and with whom to discuss, there is the broader need to establish and maintain communications across intellectual divides in the hope that they will thereby be narrowed. (I doubt that it is desirable, let alone feasible, that they should ever be closed.) To this end I have been involved in several editing projects designed to demonstrate and encourage such interactions.[2] Happily, thanks to the contributors, these have borne fruit both in their contents and in the responses to them. Moreover, with longer-standing examples of such interaction, among which must be included the genuinely pioneering work of Elizabeth Anscombe, Peter Geach, and Anthony Kenny, and the fine scholarship and argumentation associated with the Cornell group, with the late Norman Kretzmann at the centre of it, the time is overdue for a broad movement bringing together the interests, knowledge, and expertise of traditional Thomists, analytical philosophers, and others appreciative of both traditions.

This volume is a further contribution to developing that broad intellectual community. The essays range widely across the fields of metaphysics, epistemology, philosophy of mind and action, and theory of value, with most linking analytical and Aristotelian-Thomistic ideas and some focusing on Aquinas in particular. The papers are certainly of high quality, but what is particularly pleasing, and hitherto unusual in North American publishing in the areas of medieval philosophy, scholasticism, and Thomism, is the fact that for the most part the authors are based in Europe. Furthermore, many are at universities in which scholasticism had an historical presence, in some cases a prominent and distinguished one: David Braine (Aberdeen), Fergus Kerr (Edinburgh), Stefaan Cuypers (Leuven), Richard Cross and Gerard Hughes (Oxford: Oriel and Campion, respectively), and John Haldane (St Andrews). In addition to these are Christopher Hughes and Martin Stone (King's London), David Oderberg (Reading), and from the United States Jonathan Jacobs (Colgate), Gyula Klima (Fordham), and Christopher Martin (St. Thomas, Texas). Add to this the fact that most of the contributors are in their forties or younger and there is reason to hope that this collection may signal a new phase in the continuing international history of Thomism.

I am very grateful to the contributors for making their essays available for the purpose and for their patience in awaiting publication. Also to be thanked is the Center for Thomistic Studies at the University of St. Thomas for providing, through *Thomistic Papers*, the means of their presentation. I am especially grateful to Terry Hall of the Center for overseeing the initial process of bringing them to print and to Daniel McInerny for his support of the project.

University of St Andrews

Notes

1. J. F. Ferrier, "An Introduction to the Philosophy of Consciousness" (1838–39), in Sir Alexander Grant and E. L. Lushington, eds., *Philosophical Works of the Late James Frederick Ferrier* (Edinburgh: Blackwood, 1875), vol. 3, *Philosophical Remains*, pp. 16–17, 21–23.

2. See *The Philosophical Quarterly*, vol. 43, 1993, *Special Issue: Philosophers and Philosophies*. This arose from a *Philosophical Quarterly* prize essay competition on the theme of 'Scholasticism: Old and New' which is also the title of the editorial. The issue features the prize-winning essay by Richard Gaskin on "Conditionals of Freedom and Middle Knowledge" and other papers on the transcendentals, Scotus, Scotism, Leibniz, Hume, and Anselm and includes contributions from Elizabeth Anscombe, Frederick Copleston, David Hamlyn, D. P. Henry, Lynn Joy, Anthony Kenny, James Ross, and C. J. F. Williams. Also *The Monist*, vol. 80, 1997, issue on *Analytical Thomism* with contributions from Brian Davies, Jonathan Jacobs and John Zeis, John Lamont, Sandra Menssen and Thomas Sullivan, Robert Pasnau, Hilary Putnam, Eleonore Stump, and Stephen Theron. Readers may also be interested in the special issue of *New Blackfriars*, vol. 80, 1999, *Thomism and the Future of Catholic Philosophy*, edited by Fergus Kerr with contributions from John Haldane, Timothy Chappell, Dagfinn Follesdal, Bas van Frassen, John Greco, Bonnie Kent, Christopher Martin, Ralph McInerny, Hayden Ramsay, Nicholas Rescher, Thomas Sullivan, Charles Taylor, and Linda Zagzebski.

CHAPTER ONE

Aquinas after Wittgenstein

Fergus Kerr

Anthony Kenny once suggested that 'the points on which Aquinas dif-
fered from his medieval critics are precisely the points on which
Wittgenstein, in his later philosophical writing, was at variance with
positivist thought'.[1] On several important issues, 'Aquinas was opposed
by Scotus in a way remarkably similar to the way in which Wittgenstein was opposed to the positivists'.[2]

The first similarity is that Aquinas and Wittgenstein agree about
which problems need *not* be raised: 'For neither of them is there a real
problem about how one passes from the private world revealed by
introspection to the publicly observable world'. Wittgenstein, admittedly, had to argue, repeatedly and with ingenuity, to show that there
is no genuine problem here, whereas for Aquinas, 'living before Descartes', no such problem even occurred.

Secondly, neither Aquinas nor Wittgenstein had to attend to 'the
problem of induction'. Living before Hume, Kenny no doubt means,
Aquinas had not imagined inductive inferences to be the result of custom or habit and thus not rationally justifiable. Contrary to what
Kenny says, however, Wittgenstein paid a good deal of attention to the
problem of induction. Repeatedly, in the later writings, he seeks to
undermine both scepticism about inductive reasoning and founda-
tionalist proposals to vindicate it.

These 'negative coincidences' prove nothing, Kenny concludes. He
sets himself the task of showing, in some detail, that there are, on the

other hand, four topics about which Aquinas and Wittgenstein may be regarded as being on the same side against Scotists and logical positivists respectively. Aquinas favoured analogy, Scotus believed in univocity; Wittgenstein deployed 'family likeness' over against verificationism. Scotus misunderstood Aristotelian hylomorphism; Wittgenstein mocked logical atomism.[3] For Scotus the mind had direct knowledge of particulars; Wittgenstein attacked the notion of the primacy of ostensive definition. Finally, for Aquinas intellectual knowledge was an *active* process, whereas Scotus regarded it as *receptive*, like sense-perception; logical-positivist epistemology made a similar mistake, while Wittgenstein strove to eliminate sense-datum theories.

Christopher Williams replied by defending these allegedly Scotist/positivist positions, though without questioning Kenny's aligning of Aquinas's hylomorphism with Wittgenstein's mockery of atomism.[4] Sketchy as they were, each of Kenny's suggestions opens a 'post-Wittgensteinian' perspective on Aquinas which would repay attention. Mainly, however, what invites examination is the very first claim, which Williams does not reject, that, for Aquinas, *there is no real problem about how one passes from the private to the public world.*

I

Aquinas did not have any problem about bridging the gap between the individual's inner world and the public world in quite the form that Wittgenstein's private-language arguments seek to remove.[5] If the upshot of these arguments is that the possibility of thinking and knowing about anything presupposes the existence of public objects, then Aquinas lines up with Wittgenstein. For one thing, he takes it for granted that he should first discuss how we have thoughts and knowledge of material things before he turns to the question of knowledge of our own minds and their contents.[6]

On the other hand, contrary to what Kenny says and Williams accepted, Aquinas has indeed to argue for this position. He locates it over against three objections which, taken together, amount to a characteristically 'Cartesian' picture of the knowing subject's self-transparency. Translating into his own jargon Augustine's insistence that 'the mind knows itself through itself because it is incorporeal', Aquinas allows that it seems plausible to say that the mind knows itself by its own essence (*per suam essentiam*).[7] Secondly, since angels have direct knowledge of themselves and we humans belong to the class of mind-endowed entities as they do, it seems likely that we too have such self-transparency. Thirdly, since (as Aquinas believed) the human mind is not tied to any particular bodily organ, it lacks materiality and so falls into the category of objects for which 'what thinks and what is thought are identical'.[8]

Against that, Aquinas contends that it is 'connatural for our intellect in the present life to look to material, sensible things'—'our intellect understands itself according as it is made actual by *species* abstracted from sensible realities by the light of the agent intellect'. This means, in turn, that 'our intellect knows itself, not by its own essence, but by means of its activity, *non per essentiam suam sed per actum suum.*'[9] In effect, we see the contents of our minds from finding ourselves engaged in a variety of intelligent activities; not by introspection of mental events that are allegedly 'private', but by remembering and reflecting on the things that we do in the public world.

We see what the human mind is like, and what its capacities are, from the sort of activities that it goes in for. That is Aquinas's view. Our capacities to perform any particular intelligent activity are potentialities that are always actualised only by some *object*. While the notion of an object is clearly analogical, it is natural for Aquinas to characterise our various intellectual capacities in terms of their actualisation by objects in the real world outside our minds. He starts, so to speak, from objects in the world outside and their effects on us, and moves back from our engagement with these objects to identify the mental powers which such engagement manifests.

What Augustine says is right, Aquinas holds, but only if we take him as meaning that 'the mind knows itself by means of itself in that ultimately, though by means of its acts, it arrives at a knowledge of itself'. Contrary to what Augustine might seem to mean, the knowledge that the human mind has of itself is not immediately self-evident, 'arrived at through nothing else'. Rather, knowledge of the nature, contents, and existence of one's own mind is inseparable from knowledge of the operations which are those of the human being as a rational (and social) animal. In principle, therefore, self-knowledge depends on what we *do*.

For Aquinas, introspection, like examination of conscience, was an activity of reflection on one's behaviour, motivation, attitudes, etc., an activity which, though perhaps ordinarily conducted in solitude, could always be shared with a counsellor or friend. The role assigned by moralists to conscience is filled, not with an inner voice or special moral sense, but by the practical reason. Aquinas even thinks of conscience, etymologically, as *con-scientia:* 'knowledge with another', as something that is in principle shareable, not something essentially 'private'.

Thus, Aquinas and the later Wittgenstein are on the same side against the idea that our own minds are accessible to us by some kind of direct inward perception, rather than in a way which is in principle accessible to others. But Aquinas certainly had to argue for his quasi-Wittgensteinian view against a powerful and influential alternative which was on the face of it not unlike the 'Cartesian' conception of the self-transparent subject. He develops his view dialectically, very much in terms of rival theories that he rejects.

Aquinas steers his way between the materialist epistemologies of the pre-Socratics and the neo-Platonic Aristotelianism of Avicenna and Averroes. His knowledge of the pre-Socratics comes from Aristotle's account of their belief that there was nothing in the world except material reality.[10] He plays off this radical materialism against the Platonic doctrine that we have direct knowledge, not of the material things around us, but of their immaterial Forms.

Aquinas's knowledge of materialism did not come only from ancient texts. On the only occasion in all his work where he very uncharacteristically denounces a thinker as 'extremely stupid', he means David of Dinant, according to whom God would simply be *materia prima.*[11] He presumably heard about David's pantheist materialism from Albert the Great, from whose arguments against it all our knowledge of David's work derives. His writings were burnt in Paris in 1210, in the context of the proscription of Aristotle's works on natural philosophy, then regarded as a threat to Christian doctrine. This was still a sensitive question in Aquinas's day. He probably never read David's works, for anyone who possessed a copy that survived the fire was *ipso facto* a heretic! Driven off the public agenda, pantheistic materialism continued underground, to surface again in due course.[12]

Aquinas's attention, however, is mainly devoted to discussing the neo-Platonism of Augustine. We have knowledge of material things (*corpora*), not just of things which are in the mind (*quae sunt per essentiam suam in anima*), which he thinks of as Augustine's view.[13] On the contrary, it is not by way of its own substance that the human mind has knowledge of material things,[14] for a mind to have knowledge of things *per essentiam suam* would be characteristic of God alone. Aquinas's resistance to Augustine's conception of how the mind works springs ultimately from a desire to protect the radical difference between God and creaturely minds: 'God alone understands everything by means of his own essence—not so the human soul or even an angel'.

One after the other, Aquinas rejects the theses that we human beings have knowledge of things by means of innate ideas; or by ideas that come from heaven, as it were, dropped by Platonic forms; or by the divine ideas; or by way of something other than pure sense-experience; or by concepts without sense experience.[15] He finds himself, once again with reference to Augustine, arguing against the thesis that the human mind has knowledge of itself *per suam essentiam,* a possibility that he clearly takes very seriously.

Augustine's basic assumption is that the human mind is primarily a centre of self-awareness, of presence to self, since it knows itself simply by being itself:

> if anyone says that in terms of general and specific notions the mind believes itself to be such as it has experienced others to be . . . he is talking very great nonsense. How can the mind know another mind if it does not know itself? You cannot say the mind knows other minds and is ignorant of itself in the same sort of way as the bodily eye sees other eyes and does not see itself.[16]

Aquinas seldom accentuates—indeed mostly he minimises—differences with Augustine, but his picture of the mind's attaining knowledge of itself as a result of its various intelligent engagements with objects in the world is very different from Augustine's insistence that the root of the soul's self-knowledge is neither knowledge of sense-perceptible objects nor of Platonic intelligibles, but *of ourselves*—ultimately, of course, in *God*.

Self-knowledge for Augustine means knowing *that* one exists; it does not mean having a clear idea of *what* we are. His view might well lead to scepticism but for the fact that we come to recognise the existence, though not the nature, of God through introspection. The discovery of God within the soul, one may say, takes the place of the discovery of reality behind appearances in Plato. 'Where for Plato the dimly perceived existence of Forms establishes objectivity', as John Rist says, 'for Augustine the dimly perceived memory of God *within* supplies this objectivity'. Thus, for Augustine, unlike Descartes, there is no problem of bridging the gap between one's mind and other minds or the external world: 'we find them, with our selves, in God'.[17] Augustine believed that, by the power of introspection, we could reach, to some degree, a vision of God, within ourselves though beyond ourselves. This was then, and to some extent remains, an immensely powerful and influential alternative to Aquinas's proto-Wittgensteinian conception of the dependence of our inner life on our involvement with things in the public world.[18]

Aquinas repeatedly argues in favour of his own conception of mediated self-awareness over against Augustine's introspectionist doctrine. But he is also concerned, more generally and without reference to any specific author, to highlight the difference between the minds that we human beings have and the minds that angels and God must have. While not employing his proto-Wittgensteinian arguments against a quasi-Cartesian notion of subjectivity, his discussion of human knowledge is nevertheless haunted by something very like a 'Cartesian' dream of total transparence to self. Human beings (Aquinas seems to have thought) are repeatedly tempted to think that their minds are as transparent to themselves as God's mind is to God. In effect, Augustine's neo-Platonic conception of the human mind needs to be modified by a strong dose of Aristotelianism in order to protect the distinctiveness of God.

Aquinas seems to fear that the introspectionist philosophy of mind in the theologies of his day was tacitly dominated by an ideal of knowledge which could be instantiated only by the divine mind. The ultimate perfection of mind is its own operation, Aquinas thinks: 'for it is not the sort of activity that goes out to something else and to the completion of that, say the constructing of a building'. Rather, 'it remains in the agent as its actuality and perfection'.[19] In that case, the first thing which is known by the mind is *its own act of knowing*, but the only mind that is identical with its own mental act is the divine mind: 'for God to understand his own understanding is the same thing as to understand his own essence, for his essence is his understanding'.[20]

Thus, Aquinas has a proto-Wittgensteinian conception of how subjective experience depends on our engagement with objects in the public world, but his concern (quite unlike Wittgenstein's) is to secure proper recognition of the *difference* between *our* minds and the *divine* mind. The 'Cartesian' self-transparent subject whom he finds (so to speak) in Augustine's introspectionist doctrine seemed dangerously close to an idolatrous displacement of God's own unique self-awareness. If we characterise scepticism, with Stanley Cavell, as perpetual dissatisfaction with the cognitive situation of the human mind, as, in effect, a demand for divine knowledge, it is not implausible to suggest that Aquinas was out to remove this temptation.[21]

II

One way in which Wittgenstein sought to undermine the doctrine of epistemological privacy is to recall how we *learn* the uses of words. 'The *speaking* of language is part of an activity, or of a form of life' (*Investigations* §23): to learn to speak is to be initiated into a variety of activities or forms of life, such as giving and obeying orders, describing a thing, reporting an event, speculating about an event, making up a story, guessing a riddle, making a joke, and so on. We think learning language consists in giving names to objects (§26); but prior to that it is a matter of being brought up, trained, for example, to ask what a thing is called (§27). Wittgenstein is fascinated with the question of the pupil's capacity to learn (§143–§157). In effect, he reminds us of the indispensability of *learning:* of being initiated into human forms of life, which are the a priori conditions required for knowing anything.[22]

If that is right, then it may be wondered, in a post-Wittgensteinian perspective, whether Aquinas is altogether immune to the charms of the fantasy of knowing what is the case without having to learn it from anyone. In particular, for example, he resists the thought that the child Jesus could have learnt anything from anyone (*Summa Theologiae* 3a, 12, 3). Aquinas is a theologian, trying to make sense of Scripture. Traditionally, it was believed that, from the moment of his incarnation, the world's redeemer had knowledge not only of his own mission and identity but, more controversially, of everything that any human being could know—everything, at least, that has a bearing on salvation. This theological thesis,[23] far from displaying pious determination to endow Christ with every conceivable prerogative, actually springs from New Testament texts where Jesus appears 'omniscient' (John 16:30; cf. 16:19). Such texts are difficult to reconcile with the assertion by Jesus that not even the Son knows when the Day of Judgement will be (Mark 13:32). That 'ignorance', Aquinas insists, ingeniously and even disingenuously, means only that the Son is unwilling to reveal the date, but of course knows it all along (*S.T.* 3, 10, 2 ad 1). As his references here to Arius, Eunomius, Chrysostom, Origen and others show, Aquinas is well aware of the history of this delicate question.

Aquinas devotes four questions in the *Summa* to Christ's knowledge. That already indicates his concern. He also records a change of mind. In the only text in the *Summa* in which he refers to himself—'although elsewhere I may have written otherwise'—we are assured that Christ had *acquired* (as well as *infused*) knowledge. In his early commentary on the *Sentences* Aquinas claimed that, from the beginning of his existence, Christ had supernaturally infused ideas which gave him knowledge of everything. Allowing Christ to learn anything from the world that he did not already know, implied a certain potentiality and thus imperfection in Christ (a revealing implication). In the *Summa*, however, Aquinas changed his view: Christ's perfection is now seen to require that his *intellectus agens* should have a real job to do. Hence we have to say that 'some intelligible *species* were received in the passive intellect of Christ as a result of the action of his active intellect'—'which means he had acquired or, as some people call it, experimental knowledge' (*S.T.* 3a, 9, 4).

The argument against Christ's having any acquired or experimental knowledge is that anything that Christ had he must have had *at its best*. But he did not have acquired knowledge at its best because he did not learn to read, which is how knowledge is best acquired—John 7: 15: 'How is it that this man knows his letters when he has never studied?'

In effect, it appears, Christ had knowledge *without ever having to learn*. That thesis would make anyone persuaded by the later Wittgenstein's reminders of how we come to know anything suspicious of Aquinas's conception of knowledge. Yet, for Aquinas, it is a perfectly natural and innocuous thought. Citing Aristotle, he tells us that, of the two ways of gaining knowledge, by discovering for oneself and by learning from others, discovery, *inventio*, ranks first, learning, *disciplina*, comes second: 'That man is best who sees the truth himself; good too is he who hearkens to wise counsel' (1095b 10: actually a quotation from Hesiod). It is more appropriate for Christ to acquire knowledge by *inventio* rather than by *disciplina*. After all, he was sent by God to be the universal teacher.

Aquinas considers strong objections to the thesis he will defend. The boy was 'found in the Temple sitting among the teachers, asking them questions and replying' (Luke 2:46): asking and answering questions is learning, and so he was learning something from others (*ab hominibus*). As Origen says, however, 'The Lord asked questions, not in order to learn anything but to teach those he questioned. For the ability to ask, as well as to answer wisely comes from the same wellspring of knowledge'.

Secondly, it may seem 'nobler' to receive knowledge from a teacher than to acquire it through the senses. The *species intelligibiles* are fully realised, *in actu*, in the mind of the teacher, whereas in things they are only in the condition of possibility, *in potentia*. This seems a powerful and attractive line of argument. We might think, for example, that the world of sense-perceptible things has always already become a *human* world, a world established in a *culture*. In particular, if we were to think of a cultural tradition as the process by which the natural world to which we belong becomes the social world that belongs to us, it seems not just inescapable but actually enriching, pleasurable, and in every way desirable, that we should learn from others, from the systems of knowledge that we inherit, as well as from our families, social customs, etc. Christ acquired knowledge from the sense-perceptible world, as has already been agreed (previous article: *S.T.* 3a, 12, 2)—how much more, one might think, he could have gained by learning from *people*. But it was not appropriate to his cognitive status, in virtue of the union of his human nature with the divine nature, that he should be taught anything by any human being whatsoever:

> In learning from a person one does not get knowledge immediately from the intelligible *species* in his mind but by the medium of words that register on the senses; these act as signs of intellectual concepts. Just as words formed by man are signs of his intellectual knowledge so the creatures made by God are signs of his wisdom. . . . Therefore, as it is more dignified to be taught by God than by man so it is more dignified to get knowledge from the material creation than from the teaching of men.

Far from being attracted by the thought that Christ acquired knowledge by being initiated like everyone else into the cultural tradition which makes the natural world accessible to us in the first place, Aquinas prefers to think of him as having direct and unmediated knowledge of the world of things.

This thesis runs into theological difficulties. As Hans Urs von Balthasar says,[24] a theological a priori seems to conflict with an elementary truth of human nature; if a child is not awakened to a sense of its own identity through being addressed by others it could not become human at all: 'Thomas' proposition is at odds with the logic of the Incarnation'. Quoting Maurice Nédoncelle, von Balthasar insists on the principle of 'reciprocity of consciousnesses': no human being is aware of his or her own identity independently of being indebted to others.[25] Quite Wittgensteinian. For von Balthasar, however, this shows the relevance of Mariology in Christology: without the tradition which his mother was able to pass on to him, 'simultaneously with the bodily gift of mother's milk and motherly care', the one in whom the Word of God had become incarnate would not have really become flesh.

There would appear to be three difficulties about Aquinas's conception of knowledge: (1) finding things out for oneself is given a priority over learning things from others in a way which seems to make us radical autodidacts, or at least to isolate Christ as such an implausibly self-taught human being; (2) words seem to be regarded as getting in the way of what would otherwise be the self-manifestation of mental contents; and (3) knowledge seems, at least in principle and in the case of Christ, to be derivable directly from the natural world without the mediation of cultural traditions such as the natural sciences.

The first is not so difficult. Denying that Christ could have been anyone's pupil (even his mother's!) might seem to be a failure of nerve,[26] one more concession to the resiliently docetic tendency in classical Christology. But we need to recall that, for Aquinas, the concept of learning is tied to a very precise concept of teaching, involving real causality in the teacher and dependence in the pupil.[27] Aquinas distinguishes between teaching and indoctrination. In the last resort, learning, and thus knowing, always involves a spontaneous act of appropriation on the part of the pupil, no one can be *caused* to learn by any external agent; one *causes oneself* to learn.

Aquinas is well aware of alternative views. The dominant view in Paris at the time was the Averroist claim that one does not bring about a piece of knowledge in someone else's mind from what one knows but rather that one communicates to the other the knowledge that one has by influencing him to order the *phantasmata* in his mind in such a way that he is appropriately disposed to understand. This view is correct, Aquinas allows, in the sense that knowledge in the pupil and in the teacher is one and the same; they have knowledge of the same thing (*eadem rei veritas*). But the Averroist believed in a single passive intellect for us all. We all have the same intelligible *species*, differing only with regard to the *phantasmata*. In effect, one's thoughts (*species*) are the thoughts of a supra-individual mind, transcending the human individual, who as an animal has perceptions of visible objects (*phantasmata*). The mind that understands, thinks, and knows, is regarded as separate from the human being who perceives, imagines, and moves about in the world of natural objects.

For Aquinas, the Averroist view represented one more type of dualism. The objection here is that no one learns from anyone else; but only because none of us has a mind of his own, all the knowing, thinking, etc., that goes on takes place in the supra-individual intellect.[28] On the other hand, Aquinas reminds us, there is the Platonists' view, according to which knowledge is innate in our minds from the beginning through participation in the separately existing forms; it is just that the mind is obstructed by union with the body from being able easily to attend to the objects of its knowledge. The pupil acquires no new knowledge from the teacher but this is because the pupil is merely stirred by the teacher to attend to what he already knows.

Neither view satisfies Aquinas. The receptive intellect of a human being is in a state of pure potentiality with regard to things that are intelligible, as Aristotle says. The teacher brings the pupil from a state of potentiality to one of actuality. Elucidating this, Aquinas notes that of the effects that come from an external source, some come from the external source alone, while others come sometimes from an external source and sometimes from an internal one. Knowledge is something that one acquires both from an internal source and from an external one.

Consider the case of one who acquires knowledge through his own research, and then the case of one who is taught:

For there is in everyone a kind of source of knowledge, namely the light of the active intellect, through which certain universal principles of all kinds of knowledge are known naturally from the start. When anyone applies these universal principles to particular cases, the memory and experience of which he gets through the senses, then he acquires knowledge by his own research of things of which he was ignorant, thus proceeding from the known to the unknown. So anyone teaching leads the learner on from what he already knows to knowledge of what he did not know before.

'All teaching and all learning comes about on the basis of pre-existing knowledge', as Aristotle says. There are two ways of doing this. The teacher may put certain means before the pupil: less universal propositions which the pupil is invited to judge on the basis of the more general ones he has already mastered; or concrete examples. Or the teacher may set out the relationship of principles to conclusions when the learner is not bright enough to see the connections. But the main cause of one's knowing anything is the internal light of the mind (*interius lumen intellectus*).

Let us return now to Wittgenstein. Consider the quotation from Augustine (*Confessions* I, viii) in the famous first paragraph of the *Investigations*:

when people gave a name to an object and when, following the sound, they moved their body towards that object, I would see and retain the fact that that object received from them this sound which they pronounced when they intended to draw attention to it. More-over, their intention was evident from the gestures which are, as it were, the natural vocabulary of all races, and are made with the face and the inclination of the eyes and the movements of other parts of the body, and by the tone of voice which indicates whether the mind's inward sentiments are to seek and possess or to reject and avoid. Accordingly, I gradually gathered the meaning of words, occurring in their places in different sentences and frequently heard; and already I learnt to articulate my wishes by training my mouth to use these signs.[29]

Wittgenstein finds in this account of how Augustine learnt to speak a particular picture of the essence of language, a description certainly of a system of communication but not of the whole of language (§2). Or, rather, Augustine would be describing the child's learning language as if the child 'already had a language, only not this one' (§32). It would be like what happens when one visits a foreign country and begins to learn the language by guessing what the natives mean when they point to things as they speak.

Much has been made of Wittgenstein's attack on the 'Augustinian picture of language'.[30] While most commentators take it for granted that Wittgenstein is right in finding a certain 'philosophical concept of meaning' in this picture of 'a language more primitive than ours' (§2), others think that what Wittgenstein quotes is 'trivial, prosaic, well-nigh unobjectionable': 'It is just a harmless elaboration of the observations that early in life children learn what things are called and learn to express their wants and needs verbally'.[31]

However that may be, the story perhaps should be kept in its context. What Augustine has been claiming is that his elders did not teach him to speak; *he taught himself:* 'It was not that grown-up people instructed me by presenting me with words in a certain order by formal teaching, as later I was to learn the letters of the alphabet. I myself acquired this power of speech with the intelligence which you gave me, my God'.

Augustine might have been about to concede a difference between learning to read and acquiring language. We might well want to bring in something about the natural language of gesture, facial expression, tone of voice, etc., and agree that a child's learning its first language, its mother tongue, is not a matter of formal instruction. Wittgenstein certainly emphasises the indispensability of natural reactions to gestures, for example in learning to count (§185). He will say that language is 'an extension of primitive behaviour'; indeed that language *is* behaviour.[32] Along such lines we might develop a polemic against 'Cartesian' mentalism.

Augustine's point, however, is not that he was initiated into language by such informal, 'natural', training, but rather that he needed no one to teach him to speak. He himself strove to express the intentions of his heart by groans and various sounds and various movements of his limbs, *by the mind that God had given him.* For Augustine, no one teaches another language or *anything else.*

Far from being an extraordinary view, this insistence that no one can be taught by another has a very long pedigree in Western philosophy. In his *De Magistro*, Augustine shows that there is no teacher who teaches a man knowledge except God. As Scripture says: 'One is your teacher, Christ' (Matt. 23:10).

More to the point, philosophically, it depends what one means by *knowledge.* Reflecting the continuing influence of Plato and Aristotle on the philosophical assumptions of the time, Augustine, like Aquinas nine hundred years later, meant that no man can teach another to *understand* something. No doubt knowledge as information can be transmitted from one human being to another, but knowledge as the understanding of any such information remains a task that each one has to work at alone.

It is a very simple point. It is one thing to know, say, that certain propositions constitute the proof of a theorem (the kind of example that Plato and Aristotle would likely have in mind), and quite another to understand the connection. You cannot understand something except *for yourself*. Any knowledge which falls short of this is simply not in the fullest sense knowledge because the one who claims to have it does not see all the connections.

Augustine's concentration, in the famous scene of learning, on words for objects that are pointed out, may be twisted into a theory of meaning, but as it stands and on the face of it, he is simply saying that learning to speak begins with the interplay between visible objects and visible adults because these are the things the child can see for himself. His task is to discover, and that can only be for himself, that certain of the sounds that adults make are connected with things that he already knows. *It is actually a Wittgensteinian point*. Nothing others say, or do, and no fact about the world around, can determine one to understand. No one can achieve my understanding for me, not just for the trivial reason that it is mine, but because to put the relevant connections into my head goes beyond what is possible on any occasion of so-called instruction.

The difference here, between Wittgenstein and Aquinas, is theological. Augustine, inheriting the Platonic tradition, believed that mind in the form of *mens* or *memoria* was needed for transforming sounds into meanings, information into knowledge, and so on. Mind, for Augustine, was God-given. For Aquinas too, human beings are created by God with minds; and these minds participate in the light which is ultimately the light of divine illumination, only they do so, in Aquinas's view, in an indirect and mediated way, in this life.

As Myles Burnyeat suggests, in a splendid paper, Wittgenstein perhaps deliberately left out the two sentences about *mens* and *memoria* and the invocation of the deity.[33] In the rule-following considerations Wittgenstein discusses the conceptual differences between obeying a kind of inspiration and following a rule (§232). He imagines children who could calculate, each in his own way, each for himself, but as a kind of *composing;* they would listen to their inner voice and obey it (§233). Indeed, as he is prompted to ask, could we not calculate exactly as we do, and yet have at every step the feeling of being guided by the rules as by magic? Perhaps feeling astonished that we get the same results? 'We might even give thanks to the Deity for this agreement' (§234). Perhaps he is suggesting, as Burnyeat proposes, that we now have to see what belongs to the physiognomy of what we call in everyday life 'following a rule' (§235); but now in purely human terms, without appealing to any God-given *memoria*.

The case of Christ's incapacity to receive knowledge from other people is surely only an instance of the ancient thesis that no human being can acquire from another knowledge in the sense of knowledge *understood*. Far from being some implausible epistemological thesis, this points us back to the familiar difference between being able to copy a set of signs and being able to understand them: the difference between indoctrination and understanding. Aquinas and Wittgenstein would be on the same side in this matter. What the comparison shows, rather, is that, where Aquinas refers to the 'light of reason', Wittgenstein speaks of natural 'reactions', as if his selective quotation of the Augustine passage were intended to displace a theological picture of divine illumination by a thoroughly naturalistic account in our understanding of learning and teaching.

A doubt about how vulnerable Aquinas's position is to late-Wittgensteinian considerations about our being taught by others is thus removed. He means nothing out of the ordinary; indeed he means something that Wittgenstein himself went to considerable lengths to recall. There is a difference between being instructed by others and understanding what they mean: knowledge as information understood rather than merely as information memorised involves being able to see the connections for oneself. Nothing *guarantees* that understanding will take place. On the contrary, a pupil's capacity to learn may come to an abrupt and unexpected end, so Wittgenstein would think. The difference between Wittgenstein and Aquinas lies elsewhere. Wittgenstein brings us back to natural reactions on the pupil's part; Aquinas, with Augustine and indeed Plato, rests his conception of knowledge on our being in the light, a light in which every being endowed with reason is always already at home, however obscured the light may be for a variety of reasons (sin, emotional disturbance, etc.).

Given some Wittgensteinian considerations, then, we find that Aquinas certainly endorses the view that the private world depends on the public. But, contrary to Kenny's contention, he has to fight for this view over against neo-Platonist alternatives, very powerful in his day, which amount to versions of the age-old impulse to disparage the cognitive situation of human beings in comparison with divine self-knowledge. Secondly, with his thesis that no human being can learn from another, Aquinas might seem remote from anything that Wittgenstein would have endorsed. It turns out, however, that, with a long-standing tradition, he means that no one can make another *understand*. Thus, he is not saying anything significantly different from what Wittgenstein held. That we could have knowledge of nature independently of being initiated into a culture, remains a puzzle, though perhaps no one before Vico explicitly recognised the indispensability of tradition in the constitution and communication of knowledge. Philosophically, on the matters discussed here, Aquinas would have been happy to agree with Wittgenstein—up to a point. In the end, of course, Aquinas would not have separated theology from philosophy. For better or worse, that must keep his philosophy far apart from Wittgenstein's.

Notes

1. *Downside Review*, vol. 77 (1959), pp. 217–35.
2. Ibid., p. 218.
3. E.g., *Philosophical Investigations* (Oxford: Blackwell, 1968), §47.
4. *Downside Review*, vol. 78 (1960), pp. 203–12.
5. Assuming that Wittgenstein's remarks about the impossibility of a private language *are* an argument, and that it is directed at something called 'Cartesianism', and that this has something to do with the historical Descartes—all of which is, of course, arguable!
6. *Summa Theologiae* 1a, 84–87.
7. *S.T.* 1a, 87, 1 obj.1; Augustine, *De Trinitate* ix, 3.
8. Aristotle, *De Anima* III, 4, 430a3.
9. *S.T.* 1a, 87, 1.
10. *S.T.* 1a, 84, 1.
11. *S.T.* 1a, 3, 8.
12. Ernst Bloch, *Avicenna und die Aristotelische Linke* (Frankfurt am Main: Suhrkamp Verlag, 1952), remains the best study.
13. *S.T.* 1a, 84, 1 obj 1.
14. *S.T.* 1a, 84, 2.
15. *S.T.* 1a, 84, 3 to 7.
16. *De Trinitate* ix, 3, introduction, translation, and notes by Edmund Hill, O.P. (New York: New City Press, 1991), p. 272.

17. J. M. Rist, *Augustine: Ancient Thought Baptised* (Cambridge: Cambridge University Press, 1994), p. 88.

18. 'An "inner process" stands in need of outward criteria', so to speak: *Investigations*, par. 580.

19. *S.T.* 1a, 87, 3, citing Aristotle, *Metaphysics* VIII, 8, 1050a35.

20. What Aquinas understands by the word *intelligere* is difficult to decide: he sometimes takes it etymologically as meaning 'reading that which is within' (*intus-legere*), but he seems to mean any and every kind of intellectual activity: understanding, knowing, thinking.

21. Stanley Cavell, 'The Availability of Wittgenstein's Later Philosophy', in *Must We Mean What We Say? A Book of Essays* (New York: Charles Scribner, 1969), pp. 60–61; and frequently since.

22. E.g., Stanley Cavell, *This New Yet Unapproachable America: Lectures after Emerson after Wittgenstein* (Albuquerque, N.M.: Living Batch Press, 1989), pp. 6off.

23. H. Riedlinger, *Geschichtlichkeit und Vollendung des Wissens Christi*, QD 32 (Freiburg am Breisgau: Herder, 1966).

24. *Theo-Drama: Theological Dramatic Theory*, vol. 3: *Dramatis Personae* (San Francisco: Ignatius Press, 1992), pp. 173–76.

25. *La réciprocité des consciences* (Paris: Aubier, 1942).

26. Liam Walsh, *Summa Theologiae*, Blackfriars edition (London: Eyre & Spottiswoode, 1974), vol. 49, p. 146.

27. *S.T.* 1a, 117, 1, vol. 15.

28. These Averroist doctrines in epistemology have much in common with post-structuralism (out of Saussure, Nietzsche, Heidegger, Foucault, et al.), according to which the 'subject-position' is nothing more than a transient epiphenomenon of the prevailing 'discourse'.

29. Henry Chadwick's translation, for a change: *Confessions* (Oxford: Oxford University Press, 1992), pp. 10–11.

30. G. P. Baker and P. M. S. Hacker, *Wittgenstein: Meaning and Understanding* (Oxford: Blackwell, 1980), p. 34.

31. Warren D. Goldfarb, "I Want You to Bring Me a Slab: Remarks on the Opening Sections of the Philosophical Investigations," *Synthese*, vol. 56 (1983), pp. 265–82; p. 268.

32. *Zettel* §545.

33. M. F. Burnyeat, "Wittgenstein and Augustine's *De Magistro*," *Proceedings of the Aristotelian Society Supplementary Volume*, vol. 61 (1987), pp. 1–24.

CHAPTER TWO

The Active and Potential Intellects

Aquinas as a Philosopher in His Own Right

David Braine

Introduction

Plainly, Aquinas was both a philosopher and a theologian.

The natural starting point in considering Aquinas's philosophy and philosophical method lies firstly with those of his disputed questions which concern topics that he clearly regarded as primarily philosophical, and secondly with his commentaries on Aristotle. His various series of disputed questions stretch from the two earliest, *De Veritate* (Paris, 1256–59) and *De Potentia* (Rome, 1265–66), up to those given in Paris in 1272.

Starting with his disputed questions is especially instructive because it immediately introduces one to the main method of Aquinas's university teaching. On each topic the starting point for Aquinas, acting as *magister*, is to seek objections to the thesis he intends to maintain. It is as if the high point of academic life required a lecturer to chair a class of postgraduates and fellow teachers, and ask for objections to the thesis he intended to maintain, typically sixteen to twenty objections (in the extreme case, thirty-one). One could imagine each participant producing at least one objection, some producing more than one, some producing supplementary argument, others trying to produce strengthened versions of objections already made. Finally the lecturer himself might add objections of his own before commencing to reply. Then the real business would begin, the *magister* announcing some seemingly knockout reasons for his thesis, and then proceeding to an exposition of the whole topic, making it clear why and in what sense his thesis must hold; then, finally, answering in order each of the objections.

The philosophical meat lies primarily in the expositions, commonly quite extensive, central to each article, but sandwiched between objections and replies to objections. Within each *Quaestio* or group of articles on related topics, some particular articles turn out to be of greater strategic importance; these are the ones in which Aquinas chooses to review the history of the thought of previous philosophers occupied with the same topic-area. A beautiful example of this is presented in Quaestio III of the *QD. De Potentia,* in which, after clarifying terminology (in articles 1–3), he proceeds (in 4–8) to philosophical demonstration that no being other than God can create, that nothing can exist which is not created by God, that there can be only one root (*principium, archē*) of creation (rather than evil having a separate origin), that God's working is involved internally in all the operations of nature, and that this working is not a creating (i.e., natural things are still operative themselves, even though this operation has God's working underlying it, cf. q. 5, art. 1). This style of presentation, beginning with a survey of the views of previous philosophers, commenting on their naturalness and yet showing why they are not satisfactory, is one nicely pioneered by Aristotle, e.g. in *Physics,* Books I–IV, as each new topic arises, and most famously in the first book of the *Metaphysics.*

At other times, instead of presenting an historical perspective, we find Aquinas using his expository section within a strategically placed article to present an overview of a whole philosophical area, the kind of overview one meets at the beginning of some of Aristotle's works, for instance the start of the *Nicomachean Ethics.*

In addition to these numerous disputed questions on topics which he would have regarded as primarily philosophical, we have his commentaries on the principal works of Aristotle and some few other philosophical works, and his early opuscula. These things should be our starting-points for understanding Aquinas as a philosopher.

I. Texts and Methods

The *Sentences* of Peter Lombard had become effectively the basic set text for theology students in the thirteenth century, so that the first job of a budding teacher of Christian theology was to comment on this standard collection of 'Sayings'. Unsurprisingly, therefore, his *Commentary on the Sentences* (Paris, 1252–56) constitutes Aquinas's first main presentation of Christian doctrine. Equally unsurprisingly, he found this a rather unsatisfactory format in which to make his own systematic presentation. As he says in the prologue of the *Summa Theologica,*

> [Students of Christian doctrine] have not seldom been hampered
> by what they have found written by other authors, partly because
> of the mutiplication of useless questions, articles and arguments,
> and partly because the things they need to know are not taught
> according to the order of the subject matter, but according as the
> plan of the book concerned might require or the occasion of the
> argument offer—partly too because of weariness and confusion
> produced by frequent repetition.

Accordingly, in the same prologue Aquinas regards his role as precisely that of 'treating of whatever belongs to the Christian religion', 'in such a way as to avoid these defects', 'in a way conducive to teaching beginners, and not just the proficient'.

In the *Summa* he attempted to accomplish this aim as far as possible by reorganising materials available to him from already completed works. This plan was a huge task, involving the production of quite fresh discussions and their integration with articles which are often abridgements of existing disputed questions, violently pruning the number of objections considered, leaving behind only those containing amplifications vital for clarity, and presenting summaries of conclusions reached in his commentaries. All of this is set within a carefully planned systematic scheme ordered according to subject matter. At any stage we are liable to find that he has incorporated some quite new topic, especially in Parts II and III where we meet with entirely new discussions of striking freshness and economy of presentation, e.g. of topics in Christology.

Accordingly, we should be very hesitant in our handling of the *Summa* as a philosophical source. True, where there are matters not obvious to people of his time, as in discussing the 'names of God' or explaining the ambiguities of the word *ousia*, he brings all his philosophical acumen into service and follows the general principle that in matters open to reason the argument from authority is the weakest. For this reason, in his own *Respondeo* (as distinct from the things he states *Sed contra*) he avoids appeal to Revelation, except where it is strictly necessary. He puts his main effort into dealing with matters disputed or obscure amongst the theologians, and very little into sharpening philosophical arguments where he would have anticipated no dispute from Aristotelian readers. In his day, the ontological argument was highly disputed amongst theologians, but other arguments to God seemed obvious.

Aquinas's unconcern in the *Summa* with philosophical points for their own sake, and his rigidity in avoiding repetition, have the result that we often find key logical clarifications tucked away in some much later discussions of quite unrelated topics, making them rather unsuited to philosophical readers, except in passages which present almost direct abridgements either of particular articles selected from the huge corpus of disputed questions or of some particular sections of certain of the commentaries on Aristotle.

II. The Special Character of the *Summa Contra Gentiles*

The *Summa Theologica* was not the first of Aquinas's experiments in seeking a better way of presenting philosophical and theological topics in systematic order. His first experiment was in what we now call the *Summa Contra Gentiles*, written between 1259 and 1264, and devised to help Dominican missionaries deal with the 'errors of the infidels' in Spain and North Africa.[1] Presented under the guise of an exposition of wisdom (*sapientia*), occupied in 'meditating and speaking forth the divine truth' and 'refuting opposing error',[2] it seeks to make clear the advantage of appealing to philosophical reason rather than revelation, whenever such appeal is possible.[3] He himself seems to have given no title to the work and it was never delivered live to any audience, being written intermittently, beginning in Paris and continuing in Naples and Orvieto. It combined the freedom to give an ordered exposition, free of the disputation structure, with the readiness to state and answer objections typical of disputations. This strongly reinforces its character as much more a philosophical work than its greater successor, the

Summa proper, and is beautifully exhibited in his discussion of whether the natural universe is necessarily without a beginning or eternal (Book II, chs. 31–38), and again in the treatment of the relationship between the human intellect and the body (Book II, chs. 56–90).

This last section is particularly apposite to our present purpose, namely that of exhibiting how Aquinas, far from being a slavish copyist of Aristotle or Augustine in his philosophy, presents permanently valuable original philosophical views of his own. The example I have chosen to consider is the distinction between the 'active and the potential intellect'. In what might appear the most obscure, and perhaps damaged, chapters of Aristotle's *De Anima,* it is certain that a 'potential' intellect (open to the reception and storing of forms, *possibilis*) and an 'active' intellect are distinguished. However, Aquinas was presented with four rival accounts of what these were, and in general how human beings function intellectually. Perhaps William and Martha Kneale were right in saying that Aquinas is practically always Aristotle's most reliable and sure interpreter, but this was not obvious to the medieval readers of Alexander of Aphrodisias, Avicenna, and Averroes, and not in the least obvious in Paris, Rome, or Oxford in the 1200s. Effectively, what we have in Aquinas is an account of the intellect of striking originality in its detailed development, and by its structure avoiding the impossibilities of both Platonist and empiricist accounts, the latter typified in Locke and Hume, and exemplified in the 'psychologism' rejected by Frege.

III. The Status of *Species*

Beginning with a *tabula rasa* view of the human intellect, Aquinas's first puzzle is to identify what is required for us to be able to use general concepts in judgements. He takes the view that, for each such general concept, there has to be some process or act (he calls it abstraction, but the name is of no importance to the structure of his theory) by means of which the human being acquires certain standing intellectual capacities from its experience of sensible particulars, in particular acquiring the capacity to use the general concept concerned. For reasons which I will make clear later, he identifies the possession of the standing intellectual capacity in question with the intellect's possession of the relevant 'intellectual' (*intelligibilis* or *intellectiva*) *species*.

Clearly, such a capacity must allow the use of the general concept concerned without restricting it in its application, and no features of whatever has become present in the intellect (e.g., this so-called *species*) must interfere with or limit the exercise of the capacity for judgement involved. Clearly also, this capacity or this 'species' has the status only of a means by which (*quo*) or according to which (*secundum quod*) the relevant actual judgements or understanding are exercised. Accordingly, it is not itself the object of such judgement or understanding, or an object of the mind in any way at all in the course of such judgement or understanding.

It is vital to notice the gulf which we here identify between Aquinas's use of the adjective 'intentional' and the use of this term in Brentano. In Brentano, and following him the whole phenomenological tradition, the intentional is that which the mind is directed towards in a mental act: 'intentional' is used as an adjective to pick out things which are objects in the sense of being objects of the mind[4]—whereas for Aquinas that which has *esse intentionale* is precisely never an object in its own right but only a means by which the mind is made able to attend to other things as objects. For Aquinas, the *species* becomes a topic or subject of thought only when the philosopher comes to reflect on what is involved in acts of judgement or understanding and their conditions. Even at this second-order or meta-level, when the intellect is reflecting upon its own operation, *species* still have no real or actual existence but only the status of grammatical subjects.[5]

Thus, in Aquinas's theory, it is not the object of insightful knowledge which is universal in its nature, and free from individuating conditions, but the *species*[6] or *forma* (Greek *morphē*, form or shape) of the thing known as it exists in the knower as the means of knowledge. And the difference between Aquinas and both Plato and the empiricists lay not only in these *species* not being objects of the mind (despite the root meaning of the word), but in Aquinas viewing them as having no natural or actual existence, but only an *esse intentionale*—'likenesses' but only with a *similitudo intentionalis*. What Aquinas means by *esse intentionale* will be clarified later.

IV. Rejection of Platonism

In Aquinas's conception, intellectual *species* have no reality or actuality in their own right. We have said that they are not themselves the objects of understanding at the primary level. The only things with any kind of actuality at this level are the particularised accidents (or particular persons as fulfilled intellectually in the way concerned) which consist in the *species* being present with *esse intentionale* within the intellect. The significant point is that *species* are never actual or real objects. Their existence in the intellect consists in the intellect's thereby having the means of understanding real things of a certain kind, e.g. in the case of the intellectual *species* of a cow the means of understanding the nature of cows as cows.

The importance of this is its embodying of Aquinas's rejection of Plato's account of human knowledge, the so-called 'theory of ideas'. This rejection is most fully explained in the *QD. De Anima*. There, for instance, in q. 3, ad 8, he says:

> According to the Platonists the reason why something is under-stood as a one-in-many [i.e., universally] is not to be attributed to the intellect, but to the thing. They argue that, because our intellect knows a thing as one-in-many, it would apparently be empty of any real content unless there were one real nature shared by many indi-viduals. For in that case the intellect would have in itself nothing corresponding to this one-in-many in reality. Hence the Platonists felt obliged to posit Ideas, by participation in which both natural things are given their specific natures, and our intellects made cog-nizant of universals. But according to Aristotle, the fact that the intellect understands a one-in-many in abstraction from individu-ating principles, is to be attributed to the intellect itself. And though nothing abstract exists in reality, the intellect is not void of any real content, nor is it misrepresentative of things as they are; because, of those things which necessarily exist together, one can be truly understood or named without another being understood or named. But it cannot be truly understood or said of things existing in this way, that one exists without the other. Thus whatever exists in an individual which pertains to the nature of its species,[7] and in respect of which it is like other things, can be known and spoken of truly without taking into consideration its individuating principles, which distinguish it from all other individuals [of the same species]. Consequently, by its abstractive power the intellect makes this uni-versal unity itself, not as though it were a unity existing in things themselves, but as an immaterial *repraesentatio*[8] of them.[9]

Thus, when Aquinas speaks of intellectual *species,* the *formae* or *similitudines intentionales,* of the thing known as they exist in the knower, it is not as *objects* of insightful knowledge, but as the *means* making such knowledge possible, things enabling us to exercise our intellect in such knowledge. What precisely do these *species* make possible? To summarise in the most general way, they make possible all applications of general concepts expressible in linguistic form, and so all acts of defining, of composing and dividing, performed by the intellect, and signified by the voice (in words signifying the *ratio* or definition of something, and in assertions [*enuntiationes, enuntiabilia,* cf. *S. Th.* Ia q. 14, art. 14, and Ia IIae q. 90, art. 1 ad 2] signifying or expressing composition or division, that is, affirmation or negation [I, q. 85, aa. 2 & 3]). These will include judgements of the sensory powers, as well as universal judgements.

Here we need to distinguish two things. First, these *species* make the specifically human way of exercising the sensory powers possible, e.g. making it possible for us to perceive things as such and such, i.e. as falling under certain universal concepts. This is the point of Aquinas's remark about "the universal reason which, so to speak, overflows into the cogitative and memorative powers" (*S. Th.* Ia. q. 78, art. 5): he says this because they involve judgements (which, *qua* judgements, necessarily use universal concepts). This is why he contrasts what he calls the estimative power in animals, taking this to be exhibited in emotion and behaviour, but not in judgement, with the corresponding power in man which he calls the cogitative power, or 'particular reason' for reasons now evident.[10]

As affecting the exercise of the sensory powers, their most fundamental expression is in singular judgements such as 'Socrates is pale today'. But the term "particular" has rarely been uniform;[11] it typically has been used to cover 'Some A's are B' statements as well as singular, 'a is B', statements, and naturally enough extended to cover general statements about closed classes, e.g. in 'Somebody pale has just come in', 'Everyone at the party looks ill', or 'The shoes under his bed are dirty', which might well arise as perceptual judgements and pass into history. These statements confine themselves to a closed class of things seen or experienced in one act, rather than extending, e.g., to 'all soldiers' or 'all men (*homines*)', let alone 'men in virtue of their nature', which would have implications for men who might have been and future men.

Second, these *species* make possible all those judgements which are general in a more radical sense, not limited to closed perceived classes, but judgements of what arises simply from the meaning of the general term or predicate concerned or from what belongs to the general nature of the kind of thing being considered or which arise from theoretical thinking about the relations between different events and states of affairs, nature's general conditions, such as go beyond anything straightforwardly perceptual. In particular, in relation to mundane or natural things, they allow an appreciation of what is essential to their natures such as underlie their behaviour and characteristic modes of operation (*essentia* as *physis*) as opposed to what we would mention in our initial expressions of the ordinary meaning of the word for things of the kind concerned ('nominal essence').[12]

V. Rejection of Empiricist Theories

Granted that all this is true, several puzzles still remain: first, why should the *species* thus agreed to be present in the intellect be free of any particular properties irrelevant to this, their main function, and therefore free of particular images or phantasms? Second, why when it comes to actually making judgements and exercising understanding should it be that we still have to turn towards the phantasms or images, i.e. why isn't the possession of the capacity or *species* by itself enough to enable us to actually understand or judge?

This pair of puzzles can be resolved together. The modern reader tends to suppose that intelligible *species* are being brought in by Aquinas in order to serve the same role as ideas in Berkeley and Hume's theories of our use of general terms, and is therefore confused by Aquinas's insistence that the *species* present in the intellect be free of any of the natural or individuating properties of its objects. Berkeley has the theory that our capacity to use a general word depends on our having the idea of some representative instance to which the word applies, and that in using the general word with meaning we exercise a habit or capacity to attend to this representative idea in such a way as allows us to ignore those features of the instance taken which are irrelevant. Hume has a variant theory whereby our meaningful use of general words involves a habit or capacity to judge whether or not the term applies by reference to the applicability or nonapplicability of images or ideas associated with a family of terms broader or narrower than the term under consideration.

The *species* Aquinas speaks of is precisely not a particular idea of a kind Berkeley and Hume are referring to. Rather the possession of the *species* in the intellect is that in virtue of which we can have and exercise the capacities or habits Berkeley and Hume speak of[13]—the capacity to ignore the appropriate irrelevant features of an idea taken as representative and to discriminate between appropriate ranges of image and ranges equally representative of more general terms, or only to terms less general or overlapping. What they refer to as ideas are rather to be identified with the phantasms to which, Aquinas says, the intellect has to turn in exercising the acts of judgement or understanding.

Thus Aquinas's insistence on 'intellectual *species*' as needed as well as these phantasms in order for the phantasms to be of any use, constitutes his rejection of empiricist theory. Someone will object that both Berkeley and Hume held that there had to be habits in the use of the ideas as well as the ideas in order for us to make appropriate judgements using general terms, but Aquinas is telling us that the existence of such habits depends upon some prior activity and capacity on the part of the intellect. This prior activity is precisely what he calls 'abstracting intellectual *species*', the work of the intellect as 'active'. Afterwards, *qua* 'potential' it receives and stores the *species* in such a way as to be available to be used when we make judgements or understand some general term or concept. In this aspect it is *possibilis* in that human beings are not always exercising the *species* they store.

Accordingly, the intellect has three stages of 'activity'; first, the abstraction of *species* by the intellect as active; then the possession of these *species* by the intellect as 'potential'; and finally the conscious activity of thought and understanding. Aquinas's distinction of active and potential intellect, therefore, has nothing to do with our conscious activity, except as a precondition; and it is a precondition arising from man's nature as 'the least of all intellectual substances', a *tabula rasa* dependent on experience of sensible particulars for knowledge, and therefore needing the active intellect in order to form any concept at all.

The level of conscious exercise of understanding lies elsewhere, later, at the level of expression. In Aquinas's view, our store of intellectual *species* make it possible for us to express something, to issue a *verbum*. It might be the definition or account of the nature of something, in this case a *species expressa*, or it might be a judgement, an inquiry, a command, request, or prayer, a wish or an expression of sorrow, joy, or wonder. Neither active nor potential intellect operate at this level. But this is the level at which the wealth contained in the *species* to which they give us possession, is actualised in untrammelled exploration and creative thought, drawing on the powers of discrimination and fresh analogy which these *species* or notions open out.

VI. Aquinas's Notions of Intellectual and Perceptual *Species*, and of *Esse Intentionale*

These explanations leave one modern worry unaffected, namely how Aquinas's argument shows that the intellect has none of the natural properties it may think about. Yet it is on this that Aquinas's main argument that the intellect cannot operate through a bodily organ depends (although it may involve a bodily organ for objects to be presented to it). As he says in Q. 1 of the *De Anima:* "not only does it receive intelligible *species* without matter and material conditions, but it is also quite impossible for it, in performing its proper operation, to have anything in common with a bodily organ, as though something corporeal might be an organ of understanding, as the eye is the organ of sight." This even though judgements are characteristically expressed by bodily organs, e.g. in speech and writing.

So, the intellect must have *species* but these must have no natural properties, must exist but only with *esse intentionale,* must possess a *similitudo* to their objects but only a *similitudo intentionalis!* Aquinas realizes that what the intellect depends upon to think about its objects is no more like its objects than the intention to kick a football is like the kicking of a football, let alone like a football; but what on earth does his alternative explanation mean?

To understand this vocabulary we have to understand Aquinas's theory of perception. In the case of the sense of touch, somewhat as a foot leaves an imprint in the sand so the object of touch leaves an imprint on the immediate organ of touch, shaping the organ to itself, perhaps even so as to allow distinction of textures. In the same act, as an imprint is left we know by it whether the object touched is soft or hard, according to the degree of its active tendency to cause the organ concerned (part of our body) to be moved by it. Beyond this, if the object of touch is moist or hot, the organ of touch will tend to be altered to become more moist or hot than before. As a result, in addition to perception of the properties of the object of touch, there may be sensations in respect of the part of the body concerned. Obviously, parallel effects arise with the cold and the dry. All these, in the understanding of Aristotle and Aquinas, are material properties in the sense of being those most general properties of all bodies in virtue of which they causally interact, so that the *immutatio* suffered by the immediate sense-organ is material.[14]

Taste involves touch inasmuch as it involves experience of moisture, but its proper sensibles are noncausal properties of the liquid medium involved (sweetness, sourness, etc.) so that neither they nor the *immutationes* involved count as material. Smell and hearing involve the air as a medium, but neither Aristotle nor Aquinas conceive the properties experienced (the proper sensibles of smell and hearing) and the *immutationes* involved as being material. Of course, a modern author might want to point out how smell modifies taste, how smell involves local sensations in the respiratory system (e.g. such as to provoke sneezing) and how air is to smell materially as moisture is to taste. Further he would distinguish between (a) the causally operative reality underlying the experience of things as in different degrees hot and cold, viz. varying levels of kinetic energy, and (b) the qualities of hotness and coldness as we experience them themselves, conceiving these latter as related to the physical realities underlying them. This would be logically parallel to the much more complex way that (a) the physical electromagnetic wave-realities underlying our more complex experience of colours are related to (b) this experience of colours itself.

However, it would remain that some sensory properties are, even as we experience them, physical, and some of these involve experiencing the sense-organ as having the same qualities as the object of experience, or at least as generating sensations of some kind, whereas other sensory properties are not causal or material in nature in any of these ways. This is clearly a distinction we still need to make.

The sense of sight presents the clearest case of this. In Aquinas's understanding, the *immutationes* involved in the sense of sight, both those in the air and any other transparent medium intervening between our eyes and the object seen, and the *immutationes* in the pupil as the part of the eye which receives the sensible imprint (*immutatio*), only exist with an *esse spirituale,* or *esse intentionale,* possessing no kind of *esse materiale* or *naturale.* A natural mark is made on the sand, none on the pupil.

To understand Aquinas's meaning, our best clue is found if we consider an example, looking at the roof of a house through a clean colourless transparent window-pane, say. Clearly, the light which comes to us by reflection off the roof that we see is configured in a certain way, both in each stage of its passing through the air, in the window-pane, in the air between us and the window-pane, and in the pupil. Plainly, our perception of the roof depends on this configuration at each stage having some sort of isomorphism ('sameness of form') with the roof relevant to this perception. Equally plainly, however, this configuration of light in air, window-pane, and pupil, is not a material or natural likeness of the sort we find between a foot and its print in the sand, between the warmth we feel a hot stone and our hand holding it to share, or between the shapes of the thing perceived and the image set up on the retina of the eye or on a photographic plate. If there was such an image in the window-pane, it would be this, not the roof, that we were seeing. Aquinas conceives the imprint or *immutatio intentionale* received by the eye as received by the pupil of the eye, existing in the pupil in a manner analogous to the way it exists in the window-pane and the air. In one place, he describes such existence as *esse viale*— '*en route* existence'—existence consisting in directedness, so that one cannot specify what is intermediate except in respect of its goal.[15] Hence, the aptitude of the phrase *esse intentionale*.

VII. Arguments to the Conclusion That Intellect Does Not Have a Bodily Organ

This is the background of the importance Aquinas gives to Anaxagoras' statement that 'it is necessary for mind, since its understanding extends to everything, for it to be unmixed with anything, so that it may command, i.e. know. For what appeared inwardly would prevent and hinder [knowledge of] what was outside. Hence the mind has no nature but this: to be potential [i.e. have its actualization in receiving *species*]' (*De Anima*, III, c. 4, 429a 22). This general conception of the intellect is vital to open-ended enquiry, a conception excluded by Hume and Kant.[16]

In arguing to this conclusion, Aquinas gives most prominence to the argument arising from analogy between the way both intellect and sight depend on *species* whose existence is only *intentionale*, possessed of no natural *similitudo* or isomorphism—not even that most purely formal structural isomorphism which Wittgenstein realized did not exist between propositions and reality.[17] Truthful vision of the colour of external objects is distorted by coloured or cloudy window-panes; material conditions altering the perceptual *species impressa* or imprint on the sense-organ, distort perception; and any natural or material isomorphism between means of perception and object perceived is irrelevant to the possibility of visual or auditory perception. By analogy, Aristotle and Aquinas insisted that the intellectual *species impressa,* abstracted by the intellect as active to be stored by the intellect as potential, must set up no natural or material isomorphism,[18] and the operation of intellect depends on no natural structural isomorphism whatsoever. Knowledge requires that the form or *species* present *naturally* in the thing known be present in the knower but only *intentionally* (i.e. directed towards, a means to, knowledge); it absolutely must not be present in the knower naturally. An isomorphism, or sharing of form, is necessary, but only an intentional isomorphism.[19] It is this which Aquinas conceives understanding to share with vision, the 'most spiritual' of the senses.

Our conception of light may have changed, but the logical features of configurations of light as it passes through space, as it is organised in space, in window-panes or in the pupil of the eye, still provide an instructive model for our thinking about the character of the concepts we use. These are the concepts by means of which we are made free to attend to, and gain knowledge of, the objects to be known without this attention and knowledge being directed towards the concept which are its means, and without this attention and knowledge being shaped, distorted, or limited by them. It is this freedom which makes open-ended enquiry possible, open also in the often unanticipated kinds of answers it can receive. Whether in Aristotle or in Einstein, Newton, or Gödel, we find a strange mingling of the a priori or theoretical with the empirical, of first-order and second-order or otherwise indirect approaches. All this is made possible by our capacity to use a multiplicity of concepts without this amounting to a knowledge of the concepts themselves. Aquinas's account of the active and possible intellects suggests a possible structure which would free us from the prisons in which Plato and the empiricists would place us.

A Note on Light

Aquinas also speaks of light in contrasting a light source with light as it exists in the air when the air is lit up, comparing this with the contrast between God's existence and existence as present in the things to which he gives existence. When a light source first begins to light up a transparent medium such as the air, then if this was not at the beginning of time,[20] it constitutes a change, but not a material one. A period when there was no light in the air is followed by a period when the air is lit: "after causing the form or disposition in the effect, without any fresh change in the effect, the cause preserves that form or disposition; as in the air, when it is lit up anew, we must allow some change to have taken place, while the preservation of the light is without any further change in the air due to the presence of the source of light" (*S. Th.* I, q. 104, art. 2, ad 3). If the light source continues shining, the air continues to be lit up. It is not that the light source is doing nothing, for it continues to light up the air but without this action involving change in anything.

This lighting of the air, keeping it lit up, involves the existence of light as 'a mere *intentio,* incomplete in being, comparable with the way colours exist in the [colourless] air' (*De Potentia,* q. 3, art. 7, ad 3), or, speaking more fully later, as 'the communicating of a certain likeness of form into the medium, according to the likeness of the spiritual intention which is received from a thing into the senses or intelligence, and by this way the sun illuminates the air, and colour multiplies its *species* in [its] medium' (*De Potentia,* q. 5, art. 8, *in corp.*).[21] The source of light makes the transparent light up and be capable of allowing the passage of light through it, so as to be reflected from the things we see so that we can see them, but it no more makes the medium itself into a source of light than a craftsman making an axe gives the axe the power of making other axes: the medium no more possesses light in its own right in the manner of a light source, than created things possess being in their own right in the manner of their creator.

Aquinas contrasts the influences of light and heat sources on continuous media: heating and cooling are unlike lighting in being material processes causally altering the things acted upon. With heat, the action is not instantaneous but by gradual increase, and involves, not the maintenance of a state, but continuous causal action on the medium being heated. If the heat source ceases to act, the medium does not instantaneously cease to be hot, but gradually cools as its heat disperses (whereas, when the light source ceases to act, the air instantaneously ceases to be light). In grasping why, for Aquinas, the difference between the cases of light and heat was so absolute, one has to realize that he conceived of light only as radiant light, filling the unobstructed space instantaneously as if possessed of infinite velocity, and believed there to be no such thing as a vacuum; meantime, not aware of the existence of radiant heat, he naturally treated only of heating by conduction.

Notes

1. James. A. Weisheipl, O.P., *Friar Thomas D'Aquino* (Oxford: Blackwell, 1975), p. 359.

2. *S.C.G.*, Book I, ch. 1.

3. *S.C.G.*, Book I, chs. 2–9.

4. Possessed of 'objective reality' without 'formal reality' (in the sense of Descartes, *Meditations*, III).

5. In Aquinas's terms, *species* is a subject within propositions exhibiting composition and division, i.e. affirmation and negation, of which *esse* is predicated grammatically in the form of the copula, implying no actuality or *actus essendi*.

6. 'Species' translates the Greek *eidos*, like it in deriving from a verb to do with sight, and with the initial meaning of what is seen, as form or shape.

7. I follow the rule of rendering the word "species" in italics only when not used in its modern English meaning of biological or natural species.

8. This word has the primary meaning of 'manifestation'—also in late Latin something which stands for its original. Its use to mean 'portrayal' is secondary.

9. Again in q. 15, he says: 'The fact that our soul in its present condition needs sensible things in order to understand, is the cause of the difficulty encountered in solving the problem raised in this article. . . . in order that the soul's knowledge may be perfect in its kind, bearing directly upon singulars, the soul must acquire a knowledge of truth from singular things. However, the light of the agent intellect is necessary in order that those things may be received in the soul and may exist there in a higher mode than that in which they exist materially. Hence it was necessary that the soul be united to a body for the perfection of its intellectual operation.'

10. Cf. *S.Th.*, I, q. 78, also q. 83, art. 1, on the way reason enters into judgements even about particular acts, and the way human freedom depends on this.

11. Historically, the use of the word "particular" has been confused: the *Prior Analytics* uses the term "particular" to refer to "Some" statements (*kata merou*, or 'according to a part', the statements concerned being considered as about a part of a class, not the whole), perhaps covering singular statements also. Aquinas is strict in referring to *ta kath'hecasta*, as 'singulars', not 'particulars'.

12. It is a very different matter, for example, to define copper as the element with such and such a number of protons in the nucleus of its atoms (its so-called atomic number) in the context of modern theory reflected in the periodic table, and to explain the meaning of the word "copper" as being the substance used to make electric wires, forming part of the composition of bronze, obtainable from ores of this or that character, and values for its tendency when used as a metallic covering of rules to weather to a notable green colour.

13. Frege somewhere refers to abstraction in empiricist theory as the 'celebrated faculty of ignoring'; cf. his review of Husserl's *Philosophy of Arithmetic* in P. Geach and M. Black, eds., *Translations from the Philosophical Writings of Gottlob Frege* (Oxford: Blackwell, 1952), pp. 84–85.

14. This general structure, distinguishing between natural and intentional *immutationes,* as well as between the organ of a sense, considered as a whole, and its immediate organ as what receives the imprint or *immutatio,* e.g. heart and skin in the case of touch, *oculus* and *pupilla* in the case of sight, conveniently fitting with considering brain and skin, and brain and pupil in a modern theory, is well-presented in G. van Riet, *Problemes d'Epistemologie* (Louvain, 1960), ch. 2.

15. This structure of thought is relevant to corpuscular as well as wave theories of light: we only identify which of two slits a photon passed through retrospectively from where it encounters the screen beyond.

16. For a brief summary of the issues involved, see David Braine, *The Reality of Time and the Existence of God* (Oxford: Clarendon Press, 1988), pp. 239–48, cf. 47–52, 66–67, 234–39, 280–84.

17. Cf. David Braine, *The Human Person* (Notre Dame: University of Notre Dame Press, 1992), pp. 402–5.

18. The pupil of the eye sees a red thing, but does not become red (cf. *De Anima,* qq. 2 & 14 (cf. 1); *Comm. De Anima,* §§. 678–85; *S.Th.* Ia q. 75, art. 2, resp, §. 1; *S.C.G.* II, c. 49, §§. 2 (cf. 3) & 5, c. 50, §§. 5 & 6; also Peter Geach, "Aquinas" in G. E. M. Anscombe and P. T. Geach, *Three Philosophers* (Oxford: Blackwell, 1961), p. 96f. Note *Comm. De Anima,* §§. 678–79: as Anaxagoras maintained that the intellect has to be unmixed in order to command (being material would restrict its course of action), so Aristotle maintains that it has to be unmixed in order to know. Cf. *S.C.G.* II, c. 66, §.2, on the connection of intellect with freedom.

19. Aquinas has three other closely related arguments to the same conclusion that the operation of intellect, unlike operations of imagination, memory (when this includes imagining) and perception, has no bodily organ. (1) Freedom from matter is needed not only in order to be able to know all sensible creatures, but also in order to know nonsensible things, *S.C.G.* II, c. 66, §. 4 & c. 49, §. 5. (2) Intellect knows universals, considered without reference to matter and individuating conditions, and this requires *species* to be received

in a completely immaterial way (cf. *De Anima, qq.* 1 & 14; *Comm. De anima,* §§. 92–93 & 724; *S.C.G.* II, c. 46, §§. 4 & 6, c. 50, §. 3, c. 66, §. 3, cf. c. 51, § 4). (3) He states that common sense reflects upon proper sense, but no sensory power or other materially embodied faculty reflects on itself; whereas intellect does reflect upon itself (*S.C.G.* II, c. 66, §.5). The problems involved in one intellect knowing either itself or others, since reflection is upon oneself as a whole or as single subject, are identified in *S.C.G.* II, c. 49, §.8 (§.7).

He has two other arguments of less weight, viz. (a) that, if the intellect had a bodily organ, it would be corrupted by excessive objects (*S.C.G.* II, c. 66, §. 6; *Comm. De Anima,* §§. 686–88, as the eye is injured by the sun or the ear by excessive vibration), and (b) that, the reception of forms into the intellect is not a motion or change in a proper sense, because it is not a process which proceeds in stages (*S.C.G.* II, c. 50, §. 3), an argument applying equally to perception of the continuous as such.

20. If it was at the beginning of time, then it would constitute a coming to be of light in the air out of nothing. This would be a case of creation, not change, inasmuch as there would be no before, no air to be lit or left unlit.

21. He goes on to express the view that 'when the heavenly movement ceases, in this lower world the action of illumination and *immutatio* of the medium by sensible things will continue, but not the action whereby matter is transformed and which results in generation and corruption.' I.e., in his view, when at the end of natural time there comes to be a new heaven and a new earth, it is not that there will be no celestial bodies, no light and no perception, but only that causation will not depend on physical movement and no causation will involve generation and corruption.

CHAPTER THREE

Aquinas and the Mind-Body Problem

Richard Cross

I

Modern solutions of the mind-body problem tend to fall into three groups: (1) those defending some kind of substance-dualism; (2) those defending some kind of physicalism or "hard" (reductive) materialism; and (3) those defending some kind of property-dualism or "soft" (non-reductive) materialism. None of these positions is entirely free of problems. Substance-dualism—which claims that a human being is two substances, body and soul—has difficulty explaining how soul and body can exercise any causal influence on each other. Physicalism—according to which the only properties a human being instantiates are physical and in principle publicly observable—has difficulty explaining the apparently non-physical nature of thought. Property-dualism has difficulty spelling out how its central claim—that a merely physical substance can instantiate non-physical properties—is coherent.

Aquinas was well aware that there are problems with these three theories, and in broad terms he was able to pinpoint what these problems are.[1] According to the kind of substance-dualism which Aquinas rejects, body and soul are two *distinct* substances, such that no part of one is in any sense a part of the other. I shall label this form of substance-dualism "P-substance-dualism" (from Plato, whom Aquinas takes to be a proponent of this sort of substance-dualism). I do not want to be too precise about the definition of P-substance-dualism: merely to distinguish it from a position according to which body and soul are two substances such that part (in some sense) of the soul is a part (in some other sense) of the body. However we label it, this latter account, as we shall see, would describe Aquinas's own position. According to Aquinas, P-substance-dualism has difficulty showing how body and soul can be in any sense directly united to each other, and thus has difficulty giving a plausible account of the *direct* causal interactions of body and soul.[2] Aquinas also saw that mental acts are seemingly non-physical,[3] and hence he would have had no difficulty rejecting physicalism. Finally, he expressly rejected the claim that a merely physical substance could instantiate non-physical properties.[4] Aquinas's detailed arguments do not have much to commend them, and I will not discuss them here: though it seems to me that the basic objections are well taken.[5]

Aquinas attempted to find a solution to the mind-body problem which is different from any of the positions outlined above, and which as far as I can see clearly avoids the objections which I have just raised against these three positions. This does not mean that Aquinas's position is immune to objection; just that it is different enough from P-substance-dualism, physicalism, and property-dualism to avoid the difficulties found in these positions. In what follows, I will try to sketch out just what Aquinas's position is. I will defend it against an objection raised by Anthony Kenny, and I will try to suggest a way in which it could be improved. I will assess the extent to which Aquinas's account is immune to the objections to P-substance-dualism, physicalism, and property-dualism raised above, and the extent to which the account might be workable today.

II

Aquinas holds that all material substances (bodies) are composites of prime matter and substantial form. He understands prime matter to be the potentiality which a body has to change into another substance, and substantial form to be that in virtue of which a body is a substance of some kind, having the essential properties which it has. Substantial form here is not only that in virtue of which a body has the shape and organization that it has, but also in relevant cases that in virtue of which a body is capable of functioning in the kind of way that it does: e.g., by being an agent, or by having parts which causally interact with each other.[6]

It would be easy to make several mistakes about Aquinas's account of prime matter and substantial form. One would be to claim that prime matter is *nothing at all* on this showing. According to Aquinas, prime matter is not a thing in the sense of being able to exist without any form at all. But it is a thing in the sense of being that which is potential to form, or the subject of form.[7] A second mistake, related to the first, would be to claim that a substantial form, standardly, is a *thing in its own right*. Not so, according to Aquinas:

> As the Philosopher [Aristotle] proves in *Metaphysics* 7, what is made, properly speaking, is the composite: for this is properly a kind of subsistent. A form is not said to be a being as something which exists, but as that by which something exists. Therefore a form is not made, properly speaking; for it is what exists that is made. . . .[8]

What Aquinas is driving at is that substantial form is the organizational principle of a material substance, and that standardly it exists only as instantiated in some material composite. This account might perhaps tempt us into making a third mistake: namely, that substantial form is to be understood as a *universal*. Aquinas, on the contrary, holds that any actually existing extra-mental item is individual. A substantial form fits this description.[9] (In fact, Aquinas probably holds that prime matter coupled with extension is a sufficient condition for the individuation of a substantial form.)[10] So when Aquinas claims that standardly a substantial form does not properly speaking exist, he does not mean that it is not an individualized particular; merely that it does not exist in its own right.

Describing substantial form in this way (as a body's organizational principle, or as that in virtue of which a body is a substance of some kind) invites a couple of questions. First, we might wonder what exactly the relation is between substantial form, thus conceived, and the complete set of a body's essential properties. I shall label the complete set of a body's essential properties "CSP".[11] Second, we might wonder whether a substantial form, as an individualized particular, is itself in any sense a property-bearer.

The first of these questions is rather tricky. Aquinas would probably want to claim that talking about CSP fails to be either an adequate or an accurate way of talking about form. This is not to say that a substantial form will not be something very like CSP. It would however, for Aquinas, be inadequate to talk about substantial form as CSP because a substantial form, for Aquinas, is more than just something which includes properties, or which has properties as its parts. It is more like that in virtue of which a body has the essential properties which it has: loosely, it is in some sense the source of a body's essential properties. Describing it thus brings out two important features of substantial form in Aquinas's account: such a form is just one thing, and such a form is supposed to have some explanatory value (it explains why a body has those essential properties which it has).[12]

Neither would it be entirely accurate to describe substantial form as CSP. The reason is that Aquinas's position, rather confusingly, entails that a body has some essential properties which it does not have in virtue of its substantial form. The problem here has its roots in two different Aristotelian ways of talking about substance. According to one of these Aristotelian accounts, found in the *Physics*, a substance is a composite of matter and form. According to the other, found in the *Categories*, a substance is an indivisible particular instantiating an essence. Aristotle's attempt in *Metaphysics* Z to combine these two accounts is ambiguous and can hardly be labeled a success.[13] Aquinas, however, like all the schoolmen, assumed both that Aristotle's two accounts of substance were true and that they were entirely consistent with each other. According to Aquinas, the essence of a body will include reference to the fact that the body is a composite of prime matter and substantial form.[14] A body on Aquinas's account will thus include *materiality* amongst its essential properties: and this property cannot be a part of the body's substantial *form*.[15] For this reason, then, it would be inaccurate to identify substantial form and CSP.

On the other hand, as I have just noted, a substantial form is very like CSP, and the account just given underlines two important features of substantial form. First, a substantial form is something like an *instantiated* property, or a property instance: where such properties, for Aquinas, are necessarily individualized items; second, the substantial form of a material substance is instantiated *in matter*. (The second claim here, of course, entails the first.) The second claim here amounts to the position that substantial form does not itself include matter as a part. The importance of this position will become clear below.

On this account, will an individualized form itself be a property-bearer? The answer will perhaps depend on what kind of thing is allowed to count as a property. I would regard "being the substantial form of a body" as a property, and I will present below evidence that Aquinas would agree with me. In this sense, an individualized substantial form will be a property-bearer. Irrespective of our view on the trivial property "being the substantial form of a body," there seem to be no conceptual reasons why an individualized substantial form could not be a property-bearer. And this concession seems to me to be crucial to the coherence of Aquinas's account of the human soul, to which I now turn.

III

Aquinas's term for the substantial form of a body capable of exercising vital activity is "soul." A human soul is the substantial form of a human body.[16] Thus, a human soul is capable of satisfying, for a human body, all of those conditions which a substantial form satisfies. It is the body's organizational principle, and it is that in virtue of which a human body is the kind of substance which it is. It is also that in virtue of which a human body is capable of functioning in just the way that it does. Equally, since all existing substantial forms are individualized, any existing human soul will be individualized. But Aquinas wants to say something more about the human soul than that it is an individualized substantial form. Aquinas also holds that there is a sense in which a human soul exists in its own right—that it is a *subsistent:*

> Therefore that intellectual principle, which is called the mind or the intellect, has an activity in itself, in which the body does not share. But nothing can act unless it subsists in itself. For activity pertains only to an actual entity. . . .[17]

The activities which the soul has are cognition and volition: and according to Aquinas these are not at all activities of the body.[18] In other words, a human soul, according to Aquinas, is a subsistent in its own right on the grounds that some of its properties are *not* properties of a human body. Thus a human soul is more than just the substantial form of a human body. As Aquinas puts it:

> On account of its perfection, the human soul is not a form that is immersed in bodily matter, or totally contained by it. And thus nothing prevents some of its power from not being the actuality of a body.[19]

On this account, a human soul is an individual with certain properties of its own. (It does not, however, quite count as a substance according to Aquinas [although Aquinas sometimes calls it a substance], since its essence is to be the substantial form of a body: it is essentially a *part* [in the relevant sense] of some whole.)[20]

This position is at first sight fairly odd, but I think that if we look a bit more closely at the way Aquinas spells out his account, we shall see that it is both comprehensible and coherent. Aquinas makes it quite explicit that being the substantial form of a human body is an *essential property* of the human soul: the soul, according to its essence, is the form of a body.[21]

It might be thought that I have jumped too quickly from "essence" to "essential property" here. Aquinas, however, consistently claims that any item belonging to a species which admits of more than one member will be a composite of *suppositum* ([onto]logical subject) and essence:[22] and I think we should have no trouble labeling such an essence an "essential property." In virtue, then, of having "being the substantial form of a human body" as an essential property, a human soul will be (amongst other things) that in virtue of which a human body has the essential properties which it has. In this respect, a human soul is like every other kind of substantial form: it is a form *informing matter,* or a "material" substantial from. But whereas "being the substantial form of a ϕ-like body" is the only property had by material substantial forms other than the human soul, it is not the only property had by a human soul. A human soul has two additional properties: capacities for cognition and volition. In virtue of these capacities, a human soul is capable of *agency*. These capacities are, according to Aquinas, *propria* of a human soul. A *proprium* is a necessary but non-essential (non-defining) property:

A *proprium* does not pertain to the essence of a thing, but is caused from the essential principles of a species.[23]

On this account, the fact that a human soul is capable of agency is in some sense explained by its being the form of a human body. I will return to this below.

Of course, *none* of the human soul's properties are the properties of a human body. But there is still a difference between the property "being the substantial form of a human body" and the property "having certain causal capacities." In the case of the former of the human soul's properties, the property is that in virtue of which a human soul is the source of a body's essential properties. In the latter case, the property has no *direct* connection with the human body at all. We need to get quite clear here about what Aquinas might have in mind. It is crucial to understand that the capacities for cognition and volition are not at all capacities in which the body has any share. Aquinas notes that cognition and volition are not the operations of any bodily organ:

> Neither however is what is said by the philosophers—that the intellect is separated from the body—removed by the fact that the intellectual substance is united to the body as form. For in the soul we need to consider both its essence and its power. According to its essence it gives existence to such a body; but according to its power it brings about its own activities. If therefore the activity of the soul were completed through some bodily organ, it would be necessary that the power of the soul which is the principle of that activity is the actuality of that part of the body through which the activity is completed: just as sight is the actuality of the eye. If however its activity is not completed through a bodily organ, its power will not be the actuality of some body. And because of this the intellect is said to be separated.[24]

Equally, he argues that the human soul acts "of itself,"[25] and that the human soul (and *not* the human body) is the subject of human cognitive and appetitive capacities.[26] Not surprisingly, the human soul, thus described, can exercise efficient causality over the human body.[27] Aquinas, although he holds that some human activities are not activities of a human body, is nevertheless clear that all human activities— whether bodily or not—should be ascribed properly to the whole human being. (Recall here that the whole human being is more than *just* a human body.) He reasons that activities of any part (for example, cognitive and appetitive activities of the human soul) can be ascribed properly to the whole human being.[28]

The discussion thus makes it clear that Aquinas does not regard the human body as *all* that a human being is. A human being is more than just body, since a whole human being will include both body (i.e., composite of prime matter and substantial form) and that part of the soul which on Aquinas's showing is not part of the body (i.e., its cognitive and appetitive capacities). Aquinas's account clearly has more in common with substance-dualism than with property-dualism or physicalism: and we might want to classify it as a kind of substance-dualism distinct from P-substance-dualism. In the next section of this essay, I will consider the extent to which Aquinas's account can avoid the problems associated with P-substance-dualism.

Aquinas's position looks to me to be both comprehensible and coherent. To show incoherence, we would have to show that a human soul could not instantiate the kinds of properties which Aquinas believes it to instantiate. I do not see clearly how this could be done. One possible way would be to argue that such a soul, howsoever united to prime matter, could not satisfy the *unity* requirement necessary for any kind of hylomorphic composition. Aquinas puts this requirement as follows:

> Two things are required for something to be the substantial form of something else. The first of these is that the form is, for the thing of which it is the form, the principle of existing substantially. By "principle" I do not mean a factive [principle], but a formal [principle], by which something exists, and is denominated "a being." Whence the other [requisite] follows, which is that form and matter coincide in one existence: which does not hold for an effective principle and that to which it gives existence. And this existence is [that] in which the composite substance—which is one according to existence, composed of form and matter—subsists.[29]

Whether or not a human soul, as described by Aquinas, could satisfy these conditions is unclear to me. A human soul, *qua* being the substantial form of a human body, looks as though it could "coincide in existence" with a human body. But whether or not the additional feature of its instantiating some properties which it has independently of the body (i.e., its capacities for cognition and volition) would be sufficient to prevent its in fact coinciding in existence with a human body seems to be debatable. Aquinas, for what it is worth, of course thinks that it does not.[30]

Anthony Kenny has raised the following objection to Aquinas's account of the human soul:

> The first two articles of question seventy-five [of the *Summa Theologiae*] in a manner cancel each other out. The first argues to the conclusion that the soul is incorporeal in the sense that it is abstract, not concrete: it is not a body but an actuality of a body. The second argues to the conclusion that the soul is incorporeal in the sense that it is a non-physical part of a human being: it is an agent with no bodily organ. But an agent cannot be an abstraction, and what is abstract cannot be a part of what is concrete.[31]

The problem with this objection is that Aquinas does not think that an existing substantial form is an abstract item. Just describing it as "an actuality of a body" is not sufficient to guarantee abstractness. All existing material forms—all "actualities of a body"—for Aquinas are in some sense individuals, and therefore in some sense *concrete* items.[32] And *ceteris paribus* there is no difficulty in ascribing agency to a concrete item.

IV

It is time to offer some fine-tuning to this account, and to try to see whether it can deal with the objections against P-substance-dualism, physicalism, and property-dualism mentioned above. Since, as I pointed out, Aquinas's account is closer to substance-dualism than it is to the other two positions, its ability to deal with the objection to P-substance-dualism will be crucial. But it will still be worth seeing whether it can offer convincing responses to the objections against the other two positions as well.

Aquinas clearly argues that the fact that a human soul is the substantial form of a human body *explains* the further properties—the capacities for cognition and volition—which a human soul instantiates. Thus, a human soul's essential property is in some sense a sufficient

condition for a human soul's instantiating its other necessary properties. But in what sense? There seem to me to be two different but related
questions here. First, the capacities for cognition and volition are very
different from the property of being the substantial form of a human
body. So, how might these capacities arise from, or be in some way
related to, the explanatorily basic property? And, second, in virtue of
which properties of the human body does such a body have capacities
for cognition and volition? The two questions are not quite the same.
The first relates to Aquinas's clear *anti-reductionism:* the cognitive and
appetitive capacities of the human soul are clearly not *reducible to* any
set of bodily properties. The second question relates more closely to
the possible *explanatory* role of the bodily properties in allowing the
irreducible capacities of the human soul to arise.

Aquinas argues that the whole human soul is created directly by
God. None of a human soul is the result of any *natural* causal process.
Thus, both the property of being the substantial form of a human body,
and the capacities for cognition and volition, are caused directly by
God.[33] For a reason which I will give in a moment, this account does
not look very plausible. But supposing that it is correct, it obviates the
necessity for answering the first question at all. The capacities for cognition and volition, though they are not reducible to any set of bodily
properties, do not "arise from" its being the substantial form of a human
body at all. They are directly created by God. Accepting Aquinas's
account here, however, would not render an answer to the second question otiose. God might have decided to endow the human soul with
certain capacities in virtue of its being the substantial form of a human
body. Aquinas does not give any hints here: but presumably possession
of a brain of a certain degree of complexity will be necessary (and part
of a set of jointly sufficient conditions) for God's creating the human
soul with its sorts of cognitive and appetitive capacities.[34] Nevertheless,
Aquinas's account does not take very seriously his own claim that
propria are *caused by* the "essential principles of a species"—viz., the
essence.

Aquinas's claim—that the human soul is created directly by God—
does not look to me to be very plausible. My reason is that the properties of a human body look much like the properties of other animate
bodies. But it seems fairly implausible to claim that none of the essential properties of a human body (barring materiality, which according
to Aquinas is not had by a body in virtue of its soul) are brought about

by natural causal processes. We can trace the origin and development of the properties of a human body from their earliest embryonic stages: and there seems to be no discernible jump from a state of being produced naturally to a state of being produced supernaturally. It is odd to claim that my body's properties are created directly by God, whereas those of Felix the cat are not: where both sets of properties seem in principle empirically traceable to natural causal origins. On the other hand, while Aquinas's claim looks to me to be implausible, I do not know of an argument to show that it is impossible.[35]

If Aquinas's account of the origin of a human soul is implausible, we will be faced with finding alternative stories. One would be the following. The human soul is essentially the form of a human body. As such, the soul could be produced naturally as a necessary part of the generation of a human body. God could then create directly in this individualized form the capacities for cognition and volition. On this story, we still do not need to give an answer to the first question: and the answer to the second question can be exactly the same as the answer which would be given on Aquinas's own account.

Another possible story would appeal to accounts of emergence or supervenience.[36] The story would be that, in virtue of the human soul's essential property of being the substantial form of a human body, certain higher-order capacities supervene on the human soul. It is important to get this account straight. The claim is not that certain higher-order properties supervene on the human *body*. The claim is that these higher-order properties supervene on the human *soul*. Making this claim, as we shall see, avoids some of the problems associated with property-dualism.

By far the simplest and most plausible of these three stories, in my view, is the second: viz., that God creates the capacities for cognition and volition directly in a naturally produced individual (i.e., the human soul). The third story relies on accounts of supervenience: and the whole concept of supervenience is not one which many philosophers are happy with, at least with regard to *mental* properties. (Physicalists, for example, will reject the applicability of the concept in this context.) On the other hand, the third story obviates the need to appeal to the special causal activity of God.

Whatever view we take of these stories—and I would emphasise that only the first is found in Aquinas—we need to see how well Aquinas's account can deal with the objections to physicalism, property-dualism, and P-substance-dualism given in the first section. The problem for a physicalist is in explaining how it is that some prima facie non-physical properties (i.e., mental properties) are in fact reducible to merely physical properties. This is not a problem for Aquinas's far more dualistic account: and indeed I do not know of any objections to physicalism which would constitute objections to Aquinas's account. The problem for a property-dualist lies in explaining how a merely physical substance can instantiate non-physical properties. This is not a problem for Aquinas's account, since Aquinas's account does not claim that a human being is a merely physical substance. Some property-dualists appeal to conceptions of supervenience or emergence, in a manner related to my third Thomistic story above. According to these property-dualists, a sufficiently complex physical substance might be such that non-physical properties could supervene on it. I do not now want to comment on whether or not this account is plausible. But I am sure that the third Thomistic story I told above is more plausible. Although it appeals to the controversial idea of emergence, it does not need to explain the further (and far more difficult) problem of how non-physical properties could supervene on a merely physical substance. The human soul, on Aquinas's account, just like any other substantial form, is not in itself at all a merely physical substance, or even a physical substance at all.

It is worth pausing to tighten this claim up a bit. In the relevant sense, a physical substance on this account will be one which *includes* matter. A physical property—such as the substantial form of a physical substance in Aquinas's account—will be one which *inheres in* matter. A non-physical property will be one which does *not* inhere in matter. The Thomist claim is that the human soul is a physical property which is the subject of non-physical properties. A subset of the set of non-physical properties in this sense will be *mental* properties. Now, thus construed, Aquinas's position will be immune to the objection against property-dualism just outlined. The reason is that, by the definitions just given, a property, whether physical or not, cannot *itself* be the subject of a physical property. Thus, the properties which a form has will be non-physical. And *ceteris paribus* there seems no reason why some of these non-physical properties might not be mental properties. In other words, it will be up to the *opponent* of Aquinas's position to demonstrate the impossibility of Aquinas's position.

More important is the ability of Aquinas's account to block the objection given above against P-substance-dualism: that the P-substance-dualist has difficulty explaining how soul and body can exercise any causal influence on each other. There may be ways for P-substance-dualists to block this objection. But it is important to see whether Aquinas's account can provide an answer to the objection, since although his account is not an instance of P-substance-dualism, it clearly exhibits some of the properties of a substance-dualist account. On any substance-dualist account, there will be a two-way linkage between body and soul. The body can in some sense act causally on the soul, and the soul can act causally on the body. Aquinas was well aware of both kinds of linkage. One of his arguments in favor of his own view against P-substance-dualism is that his view, unlike P-substance-dualism, can provide a satisfactory account of both of these linkages. Aquinas notes that it is empirically evident that brain states and other physical events affect mental states, at least insofar as the correct functioning of the physical organism is a necessary condition for the correct functioning of human cognitive and appetitive capacities.[37] On Aquinas's account, the individual subsistent (the human soul) which is the human mind, is also that in virtue of which a human body has the essential properties which it has. Being that in virtue of which a human body has the essential properties which it has is itself a property of the soul. And this is tantamount to a second claim: that the human soul in some sense includes (some of) the human body's essential properties as parts.

If Aquinas's account of the soul can be held to entail the claim that the human soul in some sense includes some of a human body's essential properties (or even if Aquinas's account is merely consistent with this claim in a way in which P-substance-dualism is not) then it seems that he will have no difficulty accounting for the causal activity of the human body on the human soul. On the proposed scenario part of the human soul is a part of the body: and the causal influence of the human body on the human soul can be explained by the soul's being causally affected by one of its own properties. This seems prima facie unproblematic. It therefore seems to me that we should prefer the claim that a substantial form in some sense includes, or is (partly) composed of, a body's properties to the claim that a substantial form is (in some sense) the source of a body's properties (such that it does not itself include as parts any of the body's properties). While it is easy to see how something which includes bodily properties can be part of a body, it is much harder to see how something which is merely the source of a body's properties (without itself including any of the body's properties) could be part of a body.

What about the second linkage: the causal influence of the soul on the body? Aquinas's proposed solution will again depend on the fact that the individual subsistent which is the human mind is also that in virtue of which a human body has those essential properties which it has. In explaining how his account differs from P-substance-dualism, Aquinas makes the following point:

> The soul does not move the body by its existence (in virtue of which it is united to the body as a form). Rather, [it moves the body] by its motive power, the action of which presupposes a body already made actual by the soul, so that thus the soul according to its motive power is the moving part, and the animated body is the moved part.[38]

As the substantial form of a human body, the human soul is, in the relevant sense, a part of the human body. And the causal influence of the soul on the body can be explained in terms of the body's being affected by one of its own parts. Equally, when moving the human body the soul also moves itself. (Again, this account seems to entail that there is a sense in which a human soul includes some of the body's essential properties.) I am not sure whether this account is sufficient: but it seems at least to be a step in the right direction.

V

Does Aquinas's account offer anything to us today? For it to do so, it will have to be coherent. As I have spelt out Aquinas's account, it will entail the claim that the human soul is essentially the substantial form of a human body. But Aquinas also claims that a human soul could survive the demise of the human body. I do not see how something which is essentially the substantial form of a human body could survive the demise of the body. To be coherent, then, Aquinas's account will have to abandon one of these two claims. I argue this case more fully elsewhere.[39] Equally, if Aquinas's account of the human soul is to have some purchase in the contemporary debate, it will clearly have to be detached from his untenable account of prime matter. (As Peter Geach has pointed out, "The application of such talk [of *the same matter* or *the same stuff*] to fundamental physics seems out of the question; the identification of parcels of matter seems here to lose its sense, and so indeed does the idea of a perfectly unleaky vessel.")[40] On the other hand, the notion of substantial form does not entail that of prime matter in Aquinas's sense. A substance could have an individualized organizational principle (such as Aquinas's substantial form) without having prime matter. What it would need would be some basic physical parts irreducible to any lower-order constituents, such that the complex arrangement of these various parts would be sufficient to form a substance of some kind. It would not matter what these physically basic units were—quarks, for example, would do—and it would not matter whether there were many different sorts of such basic constituents, just so long as they were irreducible to lower-order constituents. The notion of substantial form is not shifted in any philosophically significant way by these suggestions about matter. What is being proposed is that the principle organizing these basic physical constituents in the case of a human being is itself a (non-physical)[41] property-bearer, such that it could have certain properties which are not properties of its human body. I do not know whether this position is successful: but I would suggest that it is a recognizably, and distinctively, Thomistic position, and that it represents a significant contribution to the mind-body problem.[42]

Notes

1. I use the following editions of the works of Aquinas: *De Ente et Essentia* (= *DE*), edited by M.-D. Roland-Gosselin, Bibliothèque Thomiste 8 (Kain, Belgium: *Revue des Sciences Philosophiques et Théologiques*, 1926); *De Veritate* (= *DV*), in *Quaestiones Disputatae*, edited by R. M. Spiazzi and others, 2 vols. (Turin and Rome: Marietti, 1949); *Summa contra Gentiles* (= *SCG*), edited by Petrus Marc and others, 3 vols. (Turin and Rome: Marietti, 1961–67); *Summa Theologiae* (= *ST*), edited by Petrus Caramello, 3 vols. (Turin and Rome: Marietti, 1952–56); *De Anima* (= *DA*), edited by James H. Robb, Studies and Texts 14 (Toronto: Pontifical Institute of Mediaeval Studies, 1968); *Expositio super Librum De Causis* (= *IDC*), edited by H. D. Saffrey, *Textus Philosophici Friburgenses*, 4/5 (Fribourg: Société Philosophique; Louvain: Nauwelaerts, 1954).

2. *DA* 9 c. (p. 149).

3. *DV* 10.4 c. (1:198a); *ST* 1.84.1 c. (1:407a); *DA* 1 c. (p. 60).

4. *ST* 1.75.2 c. (1:352a): the claim here is that a mind which was *per impossibile* physical or bodily could not instantiate mental properties.

5. See for example *SCG* 2.43, nn. 1193–1200 (2:160b–161a); *ST* 1.45.8 (1:233b–234b); *ST* 1.66.1 (1:321b–323a).

6. *ST* 1.76.1 c. (1:358a).

7. *ST* 1.66.1 (1:321b–323a).

8. *ST* 1.110.2 c. (1:520b); see also *ST* 1.65.4 c. (1:320b–321a). The reference is to Aristotle, *Metaphysics* Z.8 (1033b17).

9. For substantial forms as individuals, see *DV* 10.5 c. (1:199); *SCG* 2.59, n. 1356 (2:187a); *SCG* 2.75, n. 1545 (2:217a–b); *ST* 1.50.2 c. (1:253b); *DA* 3, arg. 17 (p. 80); *IDC* 4 (p. 34). Aquinas clearly holds, analogously, that accidental forms are individualized items: see *ST* 3.77.1 ad 3 (3:465a). For a discussion of individualized forms in Aquinas, see Peter Geach's seminal paper, "Form and Existence," in *Aquinas. A Collection of Critical Essays*, edited by Anthony Kenny, Modern Studies in Philosophy (London and Melbourne: Macmillan, 1969), pp. 29–53 (pp. 35–41), and the comments in Christopher Hughes, *On a Complex Theory of a Simple God. An Investigation in Aquinas' Philosophical Theology*, Cornell Studies in the Philosophy of Religion (Ithaca and London: Cornell University Press, 1989), pp. 10–14; also Gyula Klima, "On Being and Essence in St Thomas Aquinas's Metaphysics and Philosophy of Science," in *Knowledge and the Sciences in Medieval Philosophy. Proceedings of the Eighth International Congress of Medieval Philosophy*, edited by Simo Knuuttila and others, 3 vols. (Helsinki: no pub., 1990), 2:210–11.

10. On individuation in Aquinas, see Joseph Owens, "Thomas Aquinas," in *Individuation in Scholasticism. The Later Middle Ages and the Counter-Reformation, 1150–1650*, edited by Jorge J. E. Gracia, SUNY Series in Philosophy (Albany: State University of New York Press, 1994), pp. 173–94, and the works cited there.

11. For the description of substantial form as a set of characteristics, see Eleonore Stump and Norman Kretzmann, "Being and Goodness," in *Divine and Human Action. Essays on the Metaphysics of Theism*, edited by Thomas V. Morris (Ithaca and London: Cornell University Press, 1988), pp. 281–312 (p. 285).

12. It seems clear that substantial form, thus construed, cannot do any *genuinely* explanatory work, and that in fact we might do better to think of a substantial form as in some sense a set of bodily properties. I will in any case argue below that for Aquinas's position to be successful against the objection to P-substance-dualism, he will have to argue that there is a sense in which a substantial form *includes* some of a body's properties. Thus, whether or not Aquinas would agree with Stump and Kretzmann that a substantial form is a set of characteristics, I think there is good reason to suppose that he *ought* to agree with them. Someone accepting the claim that a substantial form is a set of properties would not, of course, be thereby committed to the claim that a substantial form is merely an *aggregate* of such properties.

13. For an excellent account of some of the problems of *Metaphysics Z*, see Daniel W. Graham, *Aristotle's Two Systems* (Oxford: Clarendon Press, 1987), chapters 8 and 9.

14. *DE* 2 (pp. 10–12); *ST* 1.75.4 c. (1:353b).

15. Aquinas, in the texts cited in the previous note, makes it quite clear that we can talk of "common" matter, and that materiality belongs to an essence in virtue of its containing common matter.

16. *ST* 1.76.1 c. (1:358a); *DA* 1 (p. 59).

17. *ST* 1.75.2 (1:352a).

18. *SCG* 2.69, n. 1464 (2:204b); *ST* 1.76.1 ad 4 (1:359b).

19. *ST* 1.76.1 ad 4 (1:359b).

20. *ST* 1.29.2 ad 5 (1:56b); *ST* 1.75.2 ad 1 (1:352a).

21. *ST* 1.76.1 ad 4 (1:359b).

22. *ST* 1.3.3 c. (1:16a–b); *ST* 3.2.2 c. (3:12b–13a).

23. *ST* 1.77.1 ad 5 (1:370b).

24. *SCG* 2.69, n. 1464 (2:204b).

25. *ST* 1.75.2 (1:352a).

26. *ST* 1.77.5 (1:373a–b).

27. *ST* 1.76.4 ad 2 (1:364b): I will discuss this passage in detail below.

28. *ST* 1.75.2 ad 2 (1:352b).

29. *SCG* 2.68, n. 1450 (2:202b).

30. *SCG* 2.68, n. 1450 (2:202b).

31. Anthony Kenny, *Aquinas on Mind*, Topics in Medieval Philosophy (London and New York: Routledge, 1993), p. 136.

32. For a defense of the claim that many property instances are concrete, see William E. Mann, "Divine Simplicity," *Religious Studies* 18 (1982): 451–71 (pp. 466–67).

33. *SCG* 2.86–87, nn. 1706–21 (2:248a–250b).

34. Aquinas holds that a disembodied soul could exercise some cognitive and appetitive activities. But he makes it quite clear that a disembodied soul would exercise these activities in a very different way from the way in which it exercises them when united to a body: see *SCG* 2.81, nn. 1625–27 (2:235a–236a); *ST* 1.89.1 (1:436a–437b).

35. For a defense of Aquinas's claim that each human soul is created directly by God, see Victor B. Brezik, "The Descent of Man according to Thomas Aquinas," in *Thomistic Papers,* vol. 1, edited by Victor B. Brezik (Houston: Center for Thomistic Studies, 1984), pp. 83–108 (pp. 99–101).

36. For a useful summary of both the issues and the literature related to the concept of emergence in this sense, see Timothy O'Connor, "Emergent Properties," *American Philosophical Quarterly* 31 (1994): 91–104.

37. Aquinas does not, however, think that physical events can have any direct *causal* role in cognition: see *ST* 1.84.6 c. (1:413b).

38. *ST* 1.76.4 ad 2 (1:364b).

39. See my "Is Aquinas's Proof for the Indestructibility of the Soul Successful?" *British Journal for the History of Philosophy* 5 (1997): 1–20. Including some of a human body's essential properties (i.e., being the substantial form of the human body) is according to Aquinas an essential property of the soul: and Aquinas is quite clear that no substance can survive without any one of its essential properties: see *SCG* 2.25, n. 1021 (2:137a); *ST* 1.3.5 ad 1 (1:18b).

40. G. E. M. Anscombe and P. T. Geach, *Three Philosophers* (Oxford: Basil Blackwell, 1963), p. 72, cited in Kenny, *Aquinas,* p. 41.

41. "Non-physical" in the sense of not including matter.

42. I should like to thank James Sadowsky for kindly reading an earlier draft of this paper and making a number of helpful suggestions.

CHAPTER FOUR

The Breakdown of Contemporary Philosophy of Mind

John Haldane

I

Readers of Gilson's great work *The Unity of Philosophical Experience* may recognise in my title a partial echo of that of one of his chapters. Gilson begins chapter 11, "The Breakdown of Modern Philosophy," by remarking that when Spengler first published *The Decline of the West* many of his readers felt at odds with his conclusions but few doubted that the West was actually in decline.[1] I am not sure whether many analytical philosophers of mind would agree with the conclusions for which I shall be arguing and most would probably resist the very suggestion that the subject is breaking down. Part of the reason for this resistance may lie in the fact that, by and large, and in contrast, for example, to Thomists and to those in the Continental tradition, analytical thinkers (allowing for some notable exceptions) are not particularly interested in, or knowledgeable about, the history of philosophy, especially that of the pre-modern period. Accordingly they may be more prone to parochialism with respect to their assumptions and ways of thinking and less able to view them from more distant perspectives.

The very possibility of parochialism (to which we are all to some degree liable) tends to be obscured in periods when there is a dominant style or method, especially when this is associated with a common academic language; and obscured also by the progessivist conviction, implicit or otherwise, that what is latest is best because enquiry always moves forward. So it was in the immediate pre-modern period when the Latin philosophy of the West had become dominated by a set of scholastic assumptions in logic, epistemology, and metaphysics and was conducted with a degree of confidence (one might say arrogance) that contributed to its subsequent fall; and which certainly ill-equipped it for recovery from this precipitate decline. Indeed scholasticism in general and Thomism in particular have still to reestablish their place in the main international centres of academic thought.

Part of the historical problem was that the neo-Aristotelian tradition of philosophy as taxonomy had developed (or degenerated) to a point where it seemed sufficient for dealing with an issue to give a name to it, or more likely to give several names to its parts and aspects. The classification of species—natural, entitative, predicational, intentional, material, formal, sensible, intelligible, impressed, and expressed—is an example of this. Meanwhile beyond the 'schools', humanists, proto-empiricists, and reactionary neo-Platonists were operating free of the established orthodoxies. By the time the scholastics began to look beyond their own prejudices it was too late—for them. A few figures jumped ship, such as Francis Bacon, who rejected Cambridge Aristotelianism in favour of inductivist experimentalism, John Locke, who turned his back on Oxford scholasticism and proceeded to develop philosophical empiricism, Agostino Nifo, who turned to Christian-neo-Platonist syncretism, and later the likes of Arnold Geulincx, who converted from Louvain neo-Aristotelianism to Cartesianism. Meanwhile those who remained behind, within scholasticism, lived to see their intellectual world swept away.

It is uncomfortable to contemplate the circumstance, tragic from our perspective, of those such as the Coimbra and Louvain-educated scholastic John of St Thomas. As elsewhere in Europe, Descartes and others searched for a new method in philosophy freed of what they regarded as the adhesive errors of the past, in Alcalá John of St Thomas worked to produce the *Cursus Philosophicus Thomisticus*, classifying, dividing, composing, synthesising and otherwise respectfully cataloguing and applying the accumulated distinctions of Thomistic commentary.

One and the same year, 1637, saw the publication, in French, of Descartes' *Discours de la Méthod* [*of rightly conducting the Reason and seeking for Truth in the Sciences*], and in Latin of the first edition of John of St Thomas's *Cursus Theologicus* (Alcalá) and the first Roman edition of his *Cursus Philosophicus* (originally published in Alcalá in 1631). In the *Discourse* Descartes writes, "in my college days I discovered that nothing can be imagined which is too strange or incredible to have been said by some philosopher." He had in mind the scholasticised Aristotelianism taught him at La Flèche through the textbooks of Coimbran authors, the very *Cursus Conimbricensis* that also provided the basis of John of St Thomas's education. In 1641, a decade after the first appearance of the *Cursus Philosophicus*, Descartes published the *Meditationes de prima philosophia*, and in 1644, the year of John of St Thomas's death, the *Principia philosophiae*. A philosophical tradition was swept aside, if not into oblivion then at the very least away from the centre of Western thought.

So it may be in our own time also. Like late scholasticism, analytical philosophy (particularly in its epistemology and metaphysics) has tended to narrow the range of possible formulations of problems and their treatments. In earlier phases it gave near-to-exclusive place to semantic presentations of issues; now it commonly favours formulations in terms of (scientific) naturalism. The immediate point is not the narrow one that only naturalistically adequate or scientifically respectable accounts are deemed permissible (though this is widely held to be so), but rather that proposals are described and assessed in terms of a presumed contrast between the 'natural' and the 'non-natural' that begs several questions as to how the former (and hence the distinction) should properly be conceived.

This tendency to a presumptively scientistic conception of nature has been complained about by thoughtful authors within the analytical tradition, such as David Wiggins and John McDowell,[2] but although they have otherwise been influential their complaints in this regard have largely gone unheeded. It may be no accident, therefore, that these figures have also looked beyond the analytical fold towards phenomenology and hermeneutics and to the philosophies of earlier periods, in particular those of Aristotle and Kant. And as they have widened their horizons so they have loosened their attachment to earlier analytical conceptions of the range of intelligible possibilities. McDowell, for example, has recently written as follows:

I have described a philosophical project: to stand on the shoulders of the giant, Kant, and to see our way to the suppression of traditional philosophy that he almost managed, though not quite. The philosopher whose achievement that description best fits is someone we take almost no notice of, in the philosophical tradition I was brought up in, although I have mentioned him a couple of times before: namely, Hegel.[3]

II

These historical and metaphilosophical reflections are prompted by considering the state of things in recent and contemporary analytical philosophy of mind, particularly with regard to the ontology of the mental and the understanding of intentional relations between persons and their environment(s). While these issues have been the focus of a very great deal of intellectual effort over the last twenty years—far greater indeed than in any previous period—these decades have brought more frustration than relief. It seems that the intensification of certain research programmes—such as those of developing causal and / or representational theories of mind—has only succeeded in restricting the subject to a point where it has become almost impossible to accommodate the basic features of mindedness as these are revealed in experience and reflection, let alone to find space for non-representational forms of intentionality, such as that of the body as discussed by Merleau-Ponty, who writes of how

> Our bodily experience of movement is not a particular case of [intellectual or conceptual] knowledge; it provides us with a way of access to the world and the object, with a *'praktognosia'* [practical knowledge], which has to be recognised as original and perhaps as primary. . . .
> Habit expresses our power of dilating our being-in-the-world, or changing our existence by appropriating fresh instruments. . . . [To know how to type] is knowledge in the hands, which is forthcoming only when bodily effort is made, and cannot be formulated in detachment from that effort.[4]

The style of closely and acutely observed account provided in the *Phenomenology of Perception* is rarely to be found within English language philosophy, notwithstanding the former's plausible claim to capture familiar and compelling truths about what it is to be an embodied agent. It was not always so, however, as admirers of Wittgenstein's philosophical psychology well know. In the *Philosophical Investigations* and elsewhere Wittgenstein provides illuminating reminders of how we actually speak about ourselves and others, our thoughts, feelings, and actions. But the decline of interest in Wittgenstein's work, and in that of others influenced by him, is itself a mark of the naturalistic-cum-scientific turn.

Compare, for example, the previous passages with the following from Elizabeth Anscombe's *Intention* (a work of broadly Aristotelian philosophical psychology developed using the methodology of Wittgenstein):

> a man usually knows the position of his limbs without observation. It is without observation because nothing *shews* [sic] him the position of his limbs; it is not as if he were going by a tingle in his knee, which is the sign that it is bent and not straight. . . .
> . . . People sometimes say that one can get one's arm to move by an act of will but not a matchbox; but if they mean 'Will a matchbox to move and it won't', the answer is 'If I will my arm to move in that way, it won't', and if they mean 'I can move my arm but not the matchbox' the answer is that I can move the matchbox—nothing easier.[5]

What Merleau-Ponty and Anscombe in their different ways are pointing to is evidence for the claim that agency is not a matter of mental command and control of a mindless body. If they are right, there can be no understanding of action in Cartesian terms—whether the mind element in that two-part story is conceived of as an immaterial self or, as in materialist (brain-body) dualism, as an organ of thought. But in recent representational and cognitive theories of mind this is all swept aside with the claim that bodily activity can only result from (and be sustained by) internal monitoring, calculation, and behaviour implementation. Accordingly, knowledge of one's bodily movements must depend upon sub-conscious or, perhaps equivalently, sub-personal attention to kinaesthetic sensations. In other words practical or agent knowledge is secondary, being based on observation. This, of course, is what Merleau-Ponty and Anscombe are precisely concerned to deny, the latter when she writes "it may indeed be that it is because one has sensations that one knows this; but that does not mean one knows it by identifying the sensations one has."[6] Her point, I take it, is to distinguish the causal, or more broadly material conditions of knowledge and agency from the epistemic or intentional as such. We act and know we act in virtue of being agents, not by receiving and conveying messages to and fro across the nervous system. As Wittgenstein remarked: *nothing is hidden.*

Reflecting on the common-sense realism of Aquinas, Chesterton once wrote that "since the modern world began in the sixteenth century, nobody's system of philosophy has really corresponded to everybody's sense of reality."[7] Suitably adjusted in respect of time and subject matter this seems a particularly apt characterisation of contemporary analytical philosophy of mind. For Chesterton the solution to the broader problem was to move back to an earlier pre-modern tradition. That is a movement with which I and other contributors to this volume are sympathetic; and speaking for myself I am enthusiastic about the possibility of incorporating Merleau-Ponty's phenomenological and Wittgenstein's 'grammatical' insights within a broadly Aristotelian-Thomistic metaphysics.[8] In the present context, however, I am less concerned to prescribe a Thomistic alternative than I am to argue that the current situation within analytical philosophy is untenable, and that space needs to be found for a range of alternative approaches drawn from non-analytic sources, particularly historical ones. The best way of making that point, I think, is by looking at one area in which current orthodoxies seem to be breaking down and to be doing so without prospect of repair or, as yet, of replacement.

III

According to physicalism, mental states of a given perceptual type (in such and such a sensory modality—sight, say—and with such and such a content) either are states of a certain physical type, or else they are variably realised or tokened by states of one or another physical types.

In the latter case it is widely supposed that the perceptual properties of such states are dependent or supervene upon some or possibly all aspects of their physical realisers. Depending upon whether such states are individuated by narrow content, i.e. without regard to the environment (as is favoured by internalism), or are defined by broad content in some way that makes reference to it (as is advocated by externalism), the physical base may be restricted to part or all of the subject's body, or extended to an aggregate or mereological sum of body-plus-environment: call these alternatives 'individual' and 'aggregate' supervenience, respectively. In either event, the supposition is that perceptual content supervenes on an ontologically prior and determining material base.

What exactly such supervenience amounts to has been a matter of considerable debate.[9] However, following Donald Davidson's original characterisation of mental/physical supervenience[10] and not withstanding some dissent, a commonly held view would have it that states (or other entities) alike in their physical properties must be alike in their perceptual ones and that there cannot be perceptual change without an appropriate physical change. It is also clear enough why this supposition of determinative supervenience is made, for without the idea of systematic co-variation (qualified by some form of asymmetry) it is hard to make sense of the idea that the mental *depends upon* the physical; and without (asymmetrical) dependence the assertion of physicalism becomes nothing more than a prejudice. Admittedly the idea associated with some versions of externalism that the same type of bodily physical state may serve as a (partial) realiser of different types of intentional state may be taken to represent a weaker (because less restricted) form of aggregate dependency but it is not as such a rejection of the basic claim of supervenience.

However, in their concern to distance themselves from reductionism some physicalists have sought for a yet weaker form of relationship between the mental and the material domains. John Haugeland, for example, explicitly rejects both type and token identity theories and limits his materialism to the claim that nothing could have been other than as it is without something physical having been otherwise. As he puts it:

> The world could not have been different in any respect, without having been different in some strictly physical respect—that is, in some respect describable in a canonical language of physics.[11]

This explicitly avoids any claim about individual or even (sub-total) aggregate dependence and is formally consistent with denial of any form of mental-physical identity. But precisely for these reasons one has to wonder about the content and motivation for a position of this sort, *viz.* that of 'global supervenience'. One obvious thought is that it is unstable. There has been some debate as to whether it does not collapse back into a stronger form of supervenience.[12] However even if it does not, the question arises of how it differs from something that the non-supervenient dualist could countenance. After all, the content of the thesis is just the brute and limited one-way variation claim that for all worlds if they are physically indiscernible then they are non-physically indiscernible:

Indeed, unless it is strengthened or supplemented in the direction of Davidsonian supervenience it seems quite bizarre, allowing as it does that the mental and physical are so loosely related that a difference in the former, say in my entire psychology, is compatible with the only physical change being in some remote and causally insulated corner of the universe; and conversely, without further restriction, that *any* physical difference is compatible with the existence of the same mental state. Evidently what global supervenience, as characterised, fails to capture of the physicalist world view are (a) the presumed dependence of the mental upon the physical, and (b) the latter's determination of the former. But once systematic constraints are added and made salient by a scheme envisaging the co-ordination of psychological states or features with constitutively relevant physical aggregates or individuals, then the move to identity, or at least to reductionism, becomes hard if not impossible to resist.

If, however, strengthening and supplementation are rejected at the outset and it is insisted that nothing more is presumed than global variation then the obvious question to press is why one should believe that this is so; why in other words hold on to physicalism when it can yield nothing in the way of understanding the existence or character of the mental, or the mode(s) of its physical determination. One reply is that it corresponds to a basic intuition that thinkers and agents are material objects; but this proposition is neither clear in its meaning and implications, nor is it even a pre-theoretical intuition. It is instead a highly conditioned philosophical judgement. Indeed, if common opinions are to be brought into play they generally favour dualism, and probably substance dualism at that. After all, the very reason why some physicalists have retreated from type (and now from token) identity theories is in order to accommodate what they themselves identify as 'Cartesian intuitions'. More likely, then, the determination to hold fast to some residue of physicalism while having yielded everything else to the dualist or pluralist suggests a prejudice rather than an intuition.

IV

Setting aside for the present general issues about the motivation for physicalism, let us suppose that the following characterises, albeit crudely, the principal perceptual property of a given state: *being as of a hand in front of the viewer*. Let us further suppose with the non-reductive physicalists, that intentional perceptual content (whether widely or narrowly construed) is not reducible to a type, or to a closed disjunction of types, of purely physical properties. Setting aside cases of hallucination which no doubt have causes of their own, it is natural to suppose that the existence of perceptual states of the sort in question is standardly an effect of circumstances present to the subject and represented in his perception: he has an experience of a hand in front of him (in part) because there is a hand in front of him.

In their weaker versions, broad content theories claim no more than that for certain purposes we may choose to individuate states in such a manner as to make reference to relevant environmental causes, but that this involves only a contingent conjunction. As it is now generally understood, however, and as it is favoured, externalism about perceptual content holds that the relation between a perceptual state and its object is not contingent: either because that object is a constituent of the experience, or (perhaps more modestly) because the existence of the perceptual state is metaphysically dependent upon the existence of that object in a manner analogous to the necessity or essentiality of origin as that is conceived of by Kripke: "anything coming from a different origin would not be this object."[13]

The notion of a perceptual 'object' introduced in the previous paragraph is intended formally, i.e. without prejudice in regard to what the range of objects might be. In the late-scholastic and modern periods the favoured candidate has indeed been objects in the sense of basic spatio-temporal particulars; but in the twentieth century states of affairs have been included in the range, and in some accounts they have been made the primary, and occasionally the sole, objects of perception. Accordingly, if some or all perceptual states are propositional in content and their proper objects are the states of affairs specified in the propositions, then externalism holds either that perceptual states are state-of-affairs-involving, or that they are state-of-affairs-dependent. In his highly regarded book *Mind and World* (and in earlier writings) John McDowell appears to subscribe to the first of these when he writes:

> That things are thus and so is the conceptual content of an experience, but if the subject of the experience is not misled, that very same thing, that things are thus and so, is also a perceptible fact, an aspect of the perceptible world.[14]

V

Is the conjunction of the various claims introduced in the preceding section (in brief, a dominant form of non-reductive physicalism plus perceptual externalism) coherent? Many would suppose so. McDowell, for example, in addition to advancing externalism, advocates a form of non-reductive materialism broadly in line with Davidson's anomalous monism. He writes:

> one can refuse to accept that all the events there are can be described in 'physical' terms, without thereby committing oneself to non-physical stuff, or compromising the thesis that persons are composed of nothing but matter.[15]

I say 'broadly in line' since, as this passage shows, whereas Davidson is monistic about *events* and allows a duality of characteristics, McDowell sees no reason to insist on the universal physicality of events but relocates monism at the level of *substances*. Elsewhere he writes (considering the conflicting views of Bernard Williams and of Thomas Nagel):

> Nagel's point [that facts about how it is phenomenally for a subject are only intelligible from a standpoint of sufficiently similar phenomenological character] is not at all met, as Williams seems to imply, by the thought that the totality of objectively graspable facts may *determine* the facts about consciousness. That thought—which is indeed highly plausible—is quite compatible with the falsity of any physicalism strong enough to rule out attribute dualism. . . .[16]

For my own part, however, I suspect that the combination of ideas
described above is not in fact a coherent one and my doubts are encouraged by seeing in this issue a counterpart to the more familiar and now
widely discussed difficulty of reconciling physicalism with genuine
mental causation. The coherence of the combination is threatened by
two problems, both of which are traceable to the core assumptions of
physicalism. First, according to the favoured view experiential/percep-
tual events and physical events and/or attributes are related as follows:

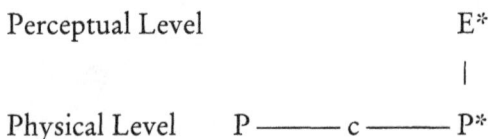

Perceptual Level   E*

                                              |

Physical Level   P ——— c ——— P*

That is to say, at its simplest, some physical state of the environment
(P) causes a physical state in the subject (P*) which determines the subject's experiential/perceptual state (E*).

There are two relations involved here. The first is one of efficient
causation; the second is one of 'determination'. What is the nature of
the latter? It cannot be logical or else reductionism would immediately
result by way of the implication that reference to the experiential state
is just a re-description of all or part of the physical state of the subject.
On the other hand it is not clear that it can be causal in the sense of the
first (environment-subject) relation. One reason is that if it were causal
then there would be two distinct states or events—a physical one and
a perceptual one—and that would imply a real dualism of particulars,
be it of a non-strictly Cartesian sort. (Whether that possibility is otherwise excluded is not an issue I am concerned with here; the point is only
that it is incompatible with the physicalist assumptions I am examin-
ing.) A second reason is that such a relation would presumably be contingent (or at least, again *ad hominem,* that is the standard physicalist
view), and that threatens the idea that sameness at the physical level
entails sameness at the mental level. Though as noted above, this assumption may be modified in respect of the extent of the supervenient
base, I have argued that it cannot altogether be abandoned without
thereby removing any significant sense to the claim that the mental is
dependent upon the physical. Besides, for these and other reasons it
seems appropriate to think in terms of a non-logical, non-causal relation of metaphysical necessitation between the physical and perceptual

levels. And that, indeed, is the conclusion of most advocates of this view of the determination of perceptual content.

What we have on this view, then, is that x's seeing o (or that p) is a result of a combination of the effect of an object (or of a state of affairs) on x's physiology plus the necessitation by that neurophysiological state of a perceptual one. Clearly, therefore, X's perception is indirectly related to its object. This may run counter to the phenomenology of perception since such content seems directly *of* the scene, varying with it not consequentially but unmediatedly. That fact might seem to challenge both elements of the assumed combination of causality and upward determination. Though in response it might well be observed that given what we already know about the physics of perception, sight, say, is mediated via reflected light and retinal activation. Hence, if the presumed phenomenological directness of visual perception must, after all, be compatible with such mediation why should it not also be in harmony with the general form of mediation introduced in the physicalist's account.

Admittedly the weight of the phenomenological consideration is uncertain. What is not in doubt, however, is that this account of the generation of perceptual states is at odds with the assumptions of strong and even weak externalism. According to both, one could not be in a given (veridical) perceptual state without the environment being in an appropriate state. This necessity is incompatible with the first stage of perception generation, and possibly with the second if it too is thought of as a case of efficient causation. For on the standard accounts of efficient physical causation one could be in a given perceptual state though the world was quite otherwise. It might be replied that this confuses the causal origins of a perceptual state with the intentional relation between it and its object.

That is an interesting suggestion to which I shall return, but the important point to note now is that this is not a distinction to which the physicalist can usefully appeal given that on his or her account any intentional relation will either reduce to a causal relation or supervene on one, and a necessary relation cannot supervene upon a contingent one. This latter fact is central to the immediate objection, but it is of wider, and unappreciated, importance in the general case against attempts to reconstruct traditional epistemological and metaphysical ideas (such as those of the a priori and the necessary) on a physicalistic or 'naturalistic' basis.

The second problem concerns causation more generally. In the now familiar problem of mental causation the difficulty is to show how non-reducible mentality could have a role in the production of action given that physical causes are sufficient for the (physical) states upon which mentality supervenes. Suppose we wish to say (a) that the mental super-venes upon the physical, (b) that the physical properties in a sequence are causally related (P causes P*, etc.), and (c) that the mental proper-ties of the events in sequence are also causally related, then we have the following familiar picture.

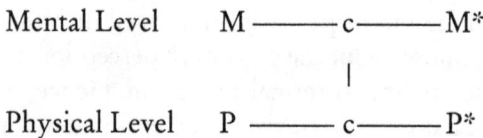

$$\text{Mental Level} \quad \text{M} \overline{\quad\quad} c \overline{\quad\quad} \text{M}^*$$

$$|$$

$$\text{Physical Level} \quad \text{P} \overline{\quad\quad} c \overline{\quad\quad} \text{P}^*$$

Since, by hypothesis, P is metaphysically sufficient for M and P* is likewise sufficient for M*, and moreover P causes P*, it appears as if the attempt to find a role for M in relation to M* faces the dilemma of overdetermination or epiphenomenalism. How can M make a contri-bution since the occurrence of M* is already provided for from below? Adopting the emergentist suggestion of downward causation, one might suggest that M brings about M* not directly but by causing P*. That, however, involves denying the causal sufficiency of P for P* and violates the causal closure of the physical: every physical event that has a cause has a wholly physical cause (not a principle to which I am myself committed but which, as with others previously mentioned, I assume for the purposes of testing the physicalist position).

The counterpart of this problem in the case of perception is that of *mental affection*. The immediate issue is not the threat of ephiphe-nomenalism, though that appears quickly enough given the ordinary assumption that perceptual states (qua perceptual) play a role in the production of action—and, indeed, of non-intentional behaviour (start-ing with fright at the sight of an attacker, for example). Rather the issue concerns the possibility of perception being caused by physical states of the environment.

Jaegwon Kim has pressed the case against antireductionist (*sic*) physicalism (and emergentism) by invoking the problem of the causal exclusion of the mental by the physical, itself a consequence of the causal closure of the physical.[17] Since his concern has been with the production of physical events (bodily movements), he has concentrated on the idea that in explaining the occurrence of such an event one need never go outside the physical domain: physical events have all and only physical causes. But the governing idea behind this implies symmetry between cause and effect. Kim writes: "If x is a physical event and y is a cause or effect of x, then y too, must be a physical event."[18] So if perceptual content is not physically reducible it is not caused. At most one may say that it is brought about by its substanding base being caused, and by that base determining its existence. But now what is to be made of this relation of determination? Ex hypothesi it is not logical, and now we see that it cannot be causal either.

Writing of the relationship between a sensation and a conception, Thomas Reid remarked that the latter arose by being "conjured up, as it were, by a natural kind of magic."[19] That is the sort of thing that contemporary philosophers are quick to ridicule but I cannot see that the very widely favoured combination of ideas with which I began has any better account to offer. In fact it is evidently worse, for Reid was a dualist and did not pretend that these matters could be accounted for physicalistically (or, to avoid anachronism, materialistically). He was right in this regard. More ironically, the idea of a non-logical, non-causal relation of determination between neurophysiology and psychology is just the sort of thing that the dualist requires.

VI

Reductive physicalism is untenable and non-reductive physicalism is in something of a mess. In itself this should be enough to lift the ontological prejudice in favour of the physical. And if it were not enough then recall that there is good reason to believe that physicalism together with its favoured account of causation excludes the possibility of perceptual (or indeed any other form of intentional) externalism. In the face of these difficulties some may be driven to eliminativism, but that is only further evidence of a determination to adhere to physicalism whatever the cost—in Fodor's witty phrase, persisting in "a cure for which there is no adequate disease." St Paul advised the Thessalonians to 'test everything and hold fast to that which is good'; I cannot see what the good in physicalism might be that would encourage such an act of faith, particularly given the test results identified above.

So as not to be wholly negative let me outline a way forward. We need to do, at least, three things. First, to take seriously, as do Aristotle and St. Thomas, a notion of psychophysical substantiality that does not reduce to substance monism plus attribute dualism. Second, to reintroduce a notion of formal causation that does not reduce to efficient causation. This is to say, bring back into play the historical Aristotelian-Thomistic notion that how things are composed and disposed is directly, and non-reducibly, relevant to what they are and to what they do, but that such an organising principle is not a material force acting upon things. And third, we need to distinguish between (a) the relation of efficient physical causation holding between the extra-cranial environment and a subject's neurophysiology, and (b) the non-physical relation of formal identity holding between the content of a subject's perceptual state and the perceptible and intelligible structure that is its object. Then, indeed, we might be in a better position to provide a metaphysics adequate to the reality of mindedness and to the possibility of perceptual realism; but that metaphysics would certainly exclude physicalism and thereby raise wider and yet more profound questions about the nature and origins of reality.[20]

Consider just the first element, psychophysical substantiality. In "Functionalism and Anomalous Monism" (see note 15), McDowell writes of rejecting event-physicalism without "compromising the thesis that persons are composed of nothing but matter"; but this leaves unaddressed such questions as how two radically different kinds of events come to be systematically related in one and the same substance, of how they combine and interact (if indeed they do), and of how the non-physical can be real and genuinely distinct while nonetheless being necessarily inherent in an exhaustively material substance. In another context he remarks of supervenience that it

> requires only that one be able to find differences expressible in terms of the level supervened upon whenever one wants to make different judgements in terms of the supervening level. It does not follow from the satisfaction of this requirement that the set of items to which a supervening term is correctly applied need constitute a kind recognisable as such at the level supervened upon.[21]

This minimal doctrine of no supervenient difference without a substanding one is reminiscent of Haugeland's position and more generally seems to be an expression of global supervenience. Such claims represent a significant departure from the philosophical context in which Davidson introduced the idea of non-reductive determination in order to rescue physicalism from the criticisms directed against type-identity theory. If my reading of McDowell's general orientation, and of the trend of his later work, is correct, then I suspect that by now he might not even want to insist that the mental supervenes upon the physical in any sense relevant to the maintenance of physicalism. But since he also rejects substance dualism it seems that he and others dissatisfied with orthodox analytical philosophy of mind would do better to recognise that the original alliance between physicalism and non-reductive intentionalism has broken down, give up the project, and start afresh free of the inherited assumptions.

VII

If that course is not pursued, but instead philosophers go on working within the established paradigm, the danger is that rather than make progress they will be reduced, like the late scholastics, to introducing refinements in a terminology inadequate to the philosophical task. Perhaps the comparison to jumping ship is not altogether apt, but I feel that the analogy of being swept away by a tide of change is relevant to the prospect facing analytical philosophy of mind in the coming years. Thomistic readers may not need much persuasion of this danger, though they too might like to contemplate the historical parallel, one side of which constitutes a caution against neo-scholastic self-assurance. More positively, they can certainly assist their analytical cousins by helping, as others in this volume have done, to express the insights of Aristotelian-Thomistic philosophy in forms less scholastic and more accessible to those not already familiar with them. That exercise would also be self-benefiting as it freed important ideas from some of the historical accretions acquired in extended periods of introversion. It would also be assisted by greater knowledge of some of the main achievements of analytical thought.

Earlier (at the end of section III) I noted that many physicalists have retreated from the position once occupied by traditional identity theories because they have been persuaded that, given the plausibility of certain intuitions, it is difficult if not impossible to take seriously type-type identity between mental and physical characteristics. I described these intuitions as 'Cartesian'. Certainly they are in keeping with the spirit of the *Meditations* and in some cases run parallel to arguments of Descartes; but in the forms in which they have found favour they actually originate with some of the most gifted of contemporary analytical authors. In broad terms the ideas in question fall into two categories: intuitions concerning phenomenal states ('qualia') and intuitions concerning mental subjectivity. The most notable presentations of these ideas are found in the writings of Saul Kripke and Thomas Nagel, respectively.

In *Naming and Necessity*, Kripke argues that from the necessity of identity together with the fact that certain expressions 'rigidly designate' their referents, it follows that identity statements flanked by such designators are metaphysically necessary, notwithstanding any appearance to the contrary.[22] Accordingly, and assuming that "pain" and "C-fiber stimulation" are both rigid (an assumption for which Kripke provides powerful argument), the statement "pain is C-fiber stimulation" expresses a necessary—though neither analytic nor a priori—truth. Since, however, it is conceivable that pain not be (or 'not have been') C-fiber stimulation, it is not, after all, the case that they are necessarily identical. In context, however, it follows from their not being 'necessarily' identical that they cannot be identical at all. From the conceivability of one in the absence of the other it follows that they are distinct.

In a footnote to his discussion of the application of semantical considerations to the metaphysics of mind (n. 73, p. 144), Kripke observes that some philosophers have denied the possibility of identities between mental and physical *types* (or properties) but have argued that this is nonetheless compatible with maintaining the identity of particular sensations and brain processes. Kripke insists that his own style of argument is equally applicable to token identity theories, and that it tells against the views of certain philosophers, namely, Thomas Nagel and Donald Davidson. Whatever the correctness of this claim about token-identity theory, it is important to bear in mind that both Nagel and Davidson have been concerned to argue against type identity.

Davidson's argument turns on the rational holism of the intentional: the idea that the very having of beliefs and desires is only intelligible under conditions of general psychological coherence or rationality.[23] This, he argues, has no counterpart in physical theory;

accordingly, there is no way to hold the mental and the physical together at the level of types. Nagel's argument, by contrast, is quite different.[24] He believes that the old standard objections to physicalism,
including those relating to intentionality, can be dealt with, but that
there remains a feature of mentality that resists physical explanation
and physical description. This is the fact that there is something it is
'like' to have sensitivities and sensibilities both in respect of the kind of
being one is and in respect of one's individual identity. While every
other fact about the universe may be characterised by an objective
description, facts about what it is like to have experiences or to wonder at the wonder of it all are ineliminably subjective or, in an extended
sense, 'phenomonological'.

Interesting as these various arguments are, it is worth observing
that those of Kripke and of Nagel are less likely to commend themselves to philosophers in the Aristotelian-Thomistic tradition than the
argument of Davidson. The reason is not hard to find. According to
Aristotle and Aquinas, what is distinctive about human persons and
what separates them from the rest of animate nature (so far as we know
it) is not their sentience but their capacity for reason. Thomas is quite
happy to attribute to non-human animals what we would now describe
as phenomenal states; he would hardly be persuaded that their being
subject to such states provides any ground to regard them as possessed
of non-material attributes. Yet he argues for the immateriality of the
power of the human intellect (and from that argues further to the existence of a subsistent rational soul) precisely on the ground that human
conceptual intentionality is a non-material power.

It is ironic that the most widely favoured contemporary styles of
anti-physicalist argument, the neo-Cartesian ones of Kripke and of
Nagel, should meet with opposition from a tradition viewed by contemporary analytical philosophers as being given to unwarranted anti-
materialism. Seen from the other perspective, it is equally ironic that
so many contemporaries should be willing to concede intentionality to
physicalism when, if the Thomists are correct, this alone is the key to
proving the falsity of materialism. Clearly there is scope for exchange
of ideas between the two groupings. For that to be effective, however,
the arguments of each need to be made fully perspicuous. I have given
a brief characterisation of those of Kripke, Nagel, and Davidson, a task
made relatively easy by the clarity with which they have been presented
by those authors. When one turns to Thomism, however, my own

assessment is that the arguments are often poorly expressed and that they need reformulation free of the standard scholastic vocabulary and outdated analogies.

A number of 'proofs' of the immateriality of mind are presented in the *Summa Theologiae* and elsewhere in the main corpus of Aquinas's own writings. Three of these predominate and are, I think, overdue for serious and concentrated attention within as well as without the Neo-Thomist community. The first argument is from the capacity of the intellect to know the natures of all things, not omnisciently but distributively: there is no nature of which the mind cannot think.[25] The second argument is from the fact that intellection has as its object not empirical particulars but abstract universals: not this or that horse but equinicity per se.[26] The third argument arises from the self-reflexivity of thought: the fact that in thinking of something I may be aware of my so doing—not as a second-order act directed upon the first-order cognition but as an aspect of the original cognition. That is to say, in thinking that St Andrews is by the sea I may, ipso facto, be aware of thinking this.[27]

Now is not the occasion to explore these arguments, though I should say that I do not believe that they are equally compelling or that exploration of them is likely to be equally fruitful. The first is problematic even in Aquinas's own terms. It relies on the idea that in order to know a thing one has to take on its nature and that one cannot do so if one already has that nature. Accordingly, if there is no nature that the intellect cannot think then there is no nature that it itself has; and since every material thing (or characteristic) has a nature it follows that intellect cannot be a material thing (or feature). The problem with this argument is that in order to make sense of the idea that thinking involves taking on the form of the object, Aquinas has to distinguish different modes of instantiation (so as to avoid the absurdity that in thinking of a horse I become one). That being so, however, one cannot then easily argue that the capacity to think of an F entails that one cannot have F nature, for one could take it on in one mode (intentionally [*in esse intentionale*]) even if one already possessed it in another (naturally [*in esse naturale*] or materially).

The second and third arguments by contrast seem much more promising but I believe they also need a good deal of examination before we can really assess their cogency and indeed their meaning.[28] This is a task for which the tools of analytical philosophy are particularly well suited, just as the insights of the Thomist as to the real locus of immateriality may help the contemporary philosopher of mind relocate his efforts away from neo-Cartesianism. Each side has something to learn from the other: one, the benefits of analytical acuity, logical rigour, and dialectical power; the other, the merits of a genuinely non-reductive and non-egocentric metaphysics. Happily the dialogue has already begun, and is continued by this and other essays in this collection. Let it continue to grow and bear fruit.[29]

Notes

1. Etienne Gilson, *The Unity of Philosophical Experience* (London: Sheed and Ward, 1938).
2. See David Wiggins, "Cognitivism, Naturalism and Cognitivity," in John Haldane and Crispin Wright, eds., *Reality, Representation and Projection* (Oxford: Oxford University Press, 1993), pp. 301–13; and John McDowell "Two Sorts of Naturalism," in Rosalind Hursthouse et al., eds., *Virtues and Reasons* (Oxford: Clarendon Press, 1996); reprinted in John McDowell, *Mind, Value and Reality* (Cambridge, Mass.: Harvard University Press, 1998).
3. John McDowell, *Mind and World* (Cambridge, Mass.: Harvard University Press, 1994), p. 111.
4. Maurice Merleau-Ponty, trans., Colin Smith, *Phenomenology of Perception* (London: Routledge, 1989), pp. 141–44.
5. G. E. M. Anscombe, *Intention* (Oxford: Blackwell, 1958), pp. 13, 52.
6. Ibid., p. 49.
7. G. K. Chesterton, *St. Thomas Aquinas* (London: Hodder & Stoughton, 1933), p. 172.
8. John Haldane, "Analytical Philosophy and the Nature of Mind: Time for Another Rebirth," in Richard Warner and Tadeusz Szubka, eds., *The Mind-Body Problem: A Guide to the Current Debate* (Oxford: Blackwell, 1994).
9. See the contributions to Elias Savellos and Ümit Yalçin, eds., *Supervenience: New Essays* (Cambridge: Cambridge University Press, 1995).
10. Donald Davidson, "Mental Events," in Lawrence Foster and J. W. Swanson, eds., *Experience and Theory* (Amherst: University of Massachusetts Press, 1970); reprinted in Donald Davidson, *Essays on Actions and Events* (Oxford: Clarendon Press, 1982), p. 214.
11. John Haugeland, "Ontological Supervenience," *Southern Journal of Philosophy*, 22 Supplement, 1984, reprinted in John Haugeland, *Having Thought: Essays in the Philosophy of Mind* (Cambridge, Mass.: Harvard University Press, 1998), p. 110.

12. See the essays by J. Klagge and B. McLaughlin in Savellos and Yalçin, eds., *Supervenience: New Essays.*

13. Saul Kripke, *Naming and Necessity* (Oxford: Blackwell, 1980), p. 113.

14. McDowell, *Mind and World,* p. 26.

15. John McDowell, "Functionalism and Anomalous Monism," in Ernest LePore and Brian McLaughlin, eds., *Actions and Events: Perspectives on the Philosophy of Donald Davidson* (Oxford: Blackwell, 1985); reprinted in McDowell, *Mind, Value and Reality,* p. 339.

16. John McDowell, "Aesthetic Value, Objectivity and the Fabric of the World," in Eva Schaper, ed., *Pleasure, Preference and Value* (Cambridge: Cambridge University Press, 1983); reprinted in John McDowell, *Mind, Value and Reality,* p. 125.

17. Jaegwon Kim, *Philosophy of Mind.* (Boulder, Colo.: Westview, 1996), pp. 147–48, 232–33; and Kim, *Mind in a Physical World* (Cambridge, Mass.: MIT Press, 1998), pp. 37–38.

18. Kim, *Philosophy of Mind,* p. 147.

19. Thomas Reid, *An Inquiry into the Human Mind on the Principles of Common Sense* (1764), ch. 5, sec. III, in Ronald Beanblossom and Keith Lehrer, eds., *Thomas Reid's Inquiry and Essays* (Indianapolis, Ind.: Hackett, 1983), pp. 43–44.

20. See John Haldane, "The Mystery of Emergence," *Proceedings of the Aristotelian Society,* 96. 1996; "Forms of Thought," in L. Hahn, ed., *The Philosophy of Roderick Chisholm* (Chicago: Open Court, 1997); and "A Return to Form in the Philosophy of Mind," in D. Oderberg, ed., *Form and Matter* (Oxford: Blackwell, 1999).

21. John McDowell, "Non-Cognitivism and Rule-Following," in Stephen Holtzman and Christopher Leich, eds., *Wittgenstein: To Follow a Rule* (London: Routledge & Kegan Paul, 1981); reprinted in McDowell, *Mind, Value and Reality,* p. 202.

22. See Kripke, *Naming and Necessity,* pp. 144–55.

23. See Davidson, "Mental Events."

24. The first presentations of the following line of argument occur, I believe, in Thomas Nagel, "Physicalism," *Philosophical Review,* vol. 74 (1965), pp. 339–56, and in "The Boundaries of Inner Space," *Journal of Philosophy,* vol. 66 (1969), pp. 452–58. Over the years Nagel has developed and modified his argument. The canonical formulation is probably that presented in *The View from Nowhere* (New York: Oxford University Press, 1986). Recent writings suggest, however, that he may now be inclined to make less, metaphysically, of subjectivity: see Thomas Nagel, "Conceiving the Impossible and the Mind-Body Problem," *Philosophy,* vol. 73 (1998), pp. 337–52, and "The Psychophysical Nexus," in Paul Boghossian and Christopher Peacocke, eds., *New Essays on the A Priori* (New York : Oxford University Press, 2000).

25. Thomas Aquinas, *Summa Theologiae*, Ia, q. 75, a. 7.

26. Thomas Aquinas, *Summa Theologiae*, Ia, q. 75, a. 5.

27. Thomas Aquinas, *Summa Contra Gentiles*, II, c. 50.

28. For arguments in this general area, which though they are indebted to Aquinas are not offered as renditions of his own proofs, see J. Haldane, "Psychoanalysis, Cognitive Psychology and Self-Consciousness," in P. Clark and C. Wright, eds., *Mind, Psychoanalysis and Science* (Oxford: Blackwell, 1988), pp. 113–39, and "Naturalism and the Problem of Intentionality," *Inquiry*, vol. 32 (1989), pp. 305–22.

29. Sections II–VI of the present essay also appear as "The State and Fate of Contemporary Philosophy of Mind," *American Philosophical Quarterly*, vol. 37 (2000), pp. 301–11.

CHAPTER FIVE

Voluntary Action and Non-Voluntary Causality

C. F. J. Martin

This essay aims at a discussion of the difference between voluntary and non-voluntary causality, as a possible preamble to a discussion of the difference between free human action and non-rational causality. Free human action I take to be a species of voluntary action, and throughout this essay I shall be taking examples of free human action as examples of the voluntary. To what extent these considerations are applicable to non-human animals will need to be teased out in later work. This I take to be a Thomistic project, in that St Thomas places his discussion of the will (at *Summa Theologiae* I q.80 a.1, for example) in a context of non-human voluntariness, and that again in a context of non-sensitive tendency or *appetitus*. But I shall not be making a direct exposition of the text of Aquinas: rather I hope to use some contemporary or near-contemporary discussions of practical reasoning as devices to clarify to ourselves the Thomistic situation of the problem. I take it for granted, following St Thomas, that voluntary action is a mode of causality: that it is a way in which certain bodies initiate changes in other bodies. The very word *agent,* which we still use in such contexts, is evidence for this (see also *Quaestio disputata de malo* q.6 c., which begins with the Aristotelian tag of "origin in itself"). I shall concentrate, as I said, on the voluntary causality of rational bodies. The question I want to answer is, how does this mode of causality differ from non-voluntary causality?

There has been over forty years a great deal of detailed discussion in the English-speaking philosophical world on voluntary causality and related topics, most of which I shall ignore. Most of the discussion has turned on whether or not beliefs and desires are causes of actions. On this question I am agnostic. It is the causality of the agent I am interested in, not in the causality of beliefs and desires. Clearly, voluntary agents cause changes in the world about them in some sense *because of* their beliefs or desires, but I do not want to discuss what this "because of" means: whether it reflects an efficient, a formal, or a final cause, or none of these. My strategy is to try as hard as I can to assimilate non-voluntary and voluntary causality, in the hope that there will be some element in voluntary causality that resists assimilation. I shall do this by assimilating non-voluntary causality to voluntary causality rather than vice-versa. Again, I think this is a Thomistic element. The point is disputable, but it is at least often alleged that St Thomas, like other Aristotelians, went too far in assimilating non-voluntary causality to voluntary causality, particularly in his use of the notion of final cause.

Let us take a feature involved in free voluntary action that has seemed to some to mark the difference between free action and non-voluntary causality: that of the defeasibility of practical reasoning. It was Kenny, himself frequently and profoundly influenced by Aquinas, who first fully developed an account of this feature, and as recently as 1989 claimed that it was the crucial difference between free action and non-rational causality. In *The Metaphysics of Mind* he writes: "Because rules of practical inference are defeasible, while causal laws are not, reasons cannot be regarded as causes."[1]

The answer to this is: only on certain conceptions of causal laws are they undefeasible. It is for the moment irrelevant whether causal laws are taken to be real features of the world, e.g. certain necessities that hold between properties or objects, or are taken to be some sort of linguistic items that describe or express certain necessities that hold between properties or objects: my complaint is with the notion of necessity involved. I want to maintain that non-voluntary causality should be described in terms of "laws" that express or describe tendencies. This point is similar to the point generally made nowadays about what are called "ceteris paribus" laws: a causal law does not tell you what will happen, or necessarily happens, but only what will happen, other things being equal. I would maintain that (at least) a large majority of causal laws are *ceteris paribus* laws, and that we should concentrate our attention on them, and find a way of expressing them that does not seek to assimilate them, inadequately, to necessary causal laws, if there are any such. In order to assimilate non-voluntary causality as far as possible to voluntary causality, I shall offer a sketch of an alternative framework of description according to which descriptions of causal setups display defeasibility: a description not in terms of laws but of tendencies.

Perhaps the notion of "defeasibility" may be unfamiliar. It is carried across by Kenny and others into philosophy from the English law: unfortunately it is apparently not a concept that is much used in systems of law that are more closely related to Roman law. The idea is that some entitlement, say, may be defeasible: it stands unless challenged. In a similar way, a prediction based on a causal law, or the causal law itself, will tell us what will happen unless there are other relevant considerations to be made; as, in fact, there nearly always are. What this notion means in Kenny's account of practical reasoning is this: it seems to mark a spectacular difference between theoretical reasoning and practical reasoning. In theoretical reasoning, if a conclusion S follows from a set of premisses P,Q, then it also follows from the set P,Q,R. In theoretical reasoning you cannot defeat, annul, or invalidate a conclusion merely by adding additional premisses. E.g: If $2+2=4$, then $4-2=2$; but $2+2=4$, so $4-2=2$. No premiss which can be added can defeat or invalidate this conclusion.

Kenny points out that this is not the case with practical reasoning. From a set of premisses P,Q, a conclusion S may follow: but from the set of premisses P,Q,R, the conclusion ~S may follow. To use Kenny's own example: I am to be in London by 4.15. The 2.15 train will get me to London by 4.15. So I'll take the 2.15 train. This is clearly valid practical reasoning. But suppose we add another premiss, such as, for example, the considerations that it would be good to work on the train, and the 2.15 train is always so crowded as to make this difficult. The conclusion no longer follows. Adding premisses to a piece of practical reasoning may defeat the conclusion: practical reasoning is defeasible.[2]

The problem with Kenny's remarks is that reasoning about non-voluntary causal processes is also defeasible: and it becomes more clearly so if we express our premisses in terms that are more explicitly descriptions of tendencies. To give an illustration: instead of the mathematical example I gave above, I first thought of an equally lame physical example. If it's raining, the pavement in the patio will be wet; but it is raining: so the pavement in the patio will be wet. Clearly this conclusion need not follow: if we add in the premiss that there is a powerful current of hot air being blown continuously across the pavement of the patio, it does not follow.

To this it will be objected that I have not invalidated, annulled, or defeated the reasoning: I have merely shown that the first premiss was not true. All premisses such as this one, one might say, which purport to state causal connections, involve a tacit extra "ceteris paribus" premiss such as "and no other considerations are relevant" or "provided that there is no interference" or "other things being equal."

The first answer to this is that it is sufficient that we *can* describe non-voluntary causal processes in ways that makes the conclusion defeasible. My aim is to assimilate accounts of non-voluntary causal processes to accounts of practical reasoning, in order to discover whether or not there is any unassimilable residue. Hence the *possibility* of descriptions of causal processes that display defeasibility is sufficient: I do not have to maintain that such descriptions are the only or the best descriptions available. That they are possible should cause no surprise. It has been familiar since (probably) long before the time of Aristotle that we can describe Nature, or natural agents, as if they were rational agents, with certain goals and purposes. (Whether it is a good idea to do so is another question.) If this is so, then causal processes can be described in a way that makes the reasoning that we carry out in describing them parallel in respect of defeasibility to the reasoning we carry out in deciding what to do.

Second, the move of objecting that the example of causal reasoning I gave is incomplete can be made in practical reasoning as well. We can always insist that the first premiss of a piece of practical reasoning should likewise contain a clause that removes the defeasibility. (One sometimes finds people wanting to make just this move when discussing practical reasoning.) If the first premiss of the getting-to-London example had been "I'm to be in London by 4.15, and no other considerations are relevant," or "I'm to be in London by 4.15 and that's all I'm interested in," then the conclusion would have been indefeasible. But this would be a thoroughly misleading account of the way we usually do perform practical reasoning: we could reason that way, but we usually don't. We have no reason to. Do we have any reason, except prejudice, to try this trick in the case of natural causality?

(It may be worth pointing out that while the notion of defeasibility is alien to St Thomas's thought—doubtless because he was not fortunate enough to be familiar with recondite notions of English law—there is at least a parallel between Kenny's use of the notion and Aquinas's thought. Compare what he has to say about the intellectual grounds for the freedom of the will—the universality of the intellect, and the universal, and thus indeterminate, application of the notion of goodness—in *Summa Theologiae* I q.83 and *Quaestio disputata de malo* q.6.)

To include the extra premiss in our natural causal reasoning would turn it into a kind of causal reasoning that we very seldom perform. We very seldom perform it, because it would usually be useless. Other things very seldom are equal; other considerations will often be relevant; there is almost always some interference. It needs an enormous amount of planning to pull off a decent scientific experiment—i.e. to produce a setup where no other considerations are really relevant—and even in a scientific experiment the trick is partly done by refusing to count as a result of the experiment any outcome in which other considerations are relevant. For example, if someone throws a boot and upsets the apparatus—thus introducing another relevant consideration—this is not counted as a result of that experiment (an example drawn from Anscombe in her paper "Causality and Determination").[3] Also, in a scientific experiment the field is already carefully delimited, so that chemical considerations can be considered irrelevant in an experiment in the physics lab. They say that the alleged discovery of cold fusion a few years back was brought about by the experimenters treating chemistry as so irrelevant that they could only look for a physical explanation, such as fusion, of their result, which was probably due to a chemical reaction. This, if true, shows the dangers of ignoring the possibility of interference.

Let me offer, then, an alternative sketch of a framework within which both practical reasoning and causal reasoning will fit, allowing them to display defeasibility. (This sketch follows ideas derived from a paper given by P. T. Geach, "Teleology and Laws of Nature," at a conference on Finality and Intentionality at the Université Catholique de Louvain in 1990. I have been unable to establish whether this paper has been subsequently published. He was developing ideas he had used in Anscombe and Geach, *Three Philosophers*).[4] Causal setups are to be described as stating tendencies. These tendencies are specified in terms of their end, of that to which they are tendencies. Substances A and B, when mixed, have a tendency to produce an explosion. Given the additional premiss that substances A and B have been mixed, we very happily conclude that there will be (or has been) an explosion. But suppose that we add in extra premisses, as for example that substances A and B have been mixed in a medium of substance C: and that substance C has a tendency to interfere with the operations of these tendencies of substances A and B. We conclude that there will be no explosion. This reasoning is as defeasible as practical reasoning is.

If causal premisses are taken to express tendencies, which can be interfered with, and if this interference may invalidate any conclusion that may be drawn from the premisses, the parallels between causal reasoning and practical reasoning seem to be clear. That which may defeat the conclusion of the causal reasoning is interference, that is, the action of other causal tendencies not mentioned in the original premisses. Meanwhile, that which may defeat the conclusion of practical reasoning is the addition of other goal-expressing premisses.

This parallel can be developed. The relevant premisses in practical reasoning are premisses which express goals; in causal reasoning, premisses which express or describe tendencies. The premisses in both cases involve an unavoidable reference to an end. This is clear in the case of practical reasoning: but it should be no less clear in the case of causal reasoning. A tendency is specified in terms of what it is a tendency towards: the notion of an end is thus unavoidably involved.[5] (This paragraph exhausts my recollection and notes of Geach's paper: what follows is my reflection on it. It may be that this reflection has been guided by unconscious memories of other points Geach made.)

So far we have managed to assimilate the two modes of causality. Is there any ineliminable difference? Another suggestion of Kenny's may seem to offer a lead. In *Will, Freedom, and Power* he alleges that when non-voluntary causal tendencies are interfered with, they are not fulfilled: when rational causal tendencies are affected by the addition of extra goal-expressing premisses, they may be fulfilled.[6] In the example of practical reasoning given above, the tendency expressed in the first premiss "I am to be in London by 4.15" is fulfilled equally by the conclusion "So I'll take the 2.15" and by the conclusion "So I'll take the 1.15." But the tendencies of substance A and substance B, when mixed, to produce an explosion are fulfilled by the conclusion "So there will be an explosion," but not by the conclusion "So there won't be an explosion," which describes what comes about as a result of these two tendencies having been interfered with by the tendency of substance C.

Kenny regards this as good reason to reject the idea of giving an account of practical reasoning in which additional premises are to count as "interfering tendencies": and if his account of non-voluntary tendencies is correct then he will be right. Nevertheless, as we have seen, and as Kenny's argument admits, there is good reason to see an analogy between additional practical premises and interfering tendencies. Can we continue to observe this analogy, instead of rejecting it as Kenny does, and try to find another way of expressing the difference between the two elements in the two modes of reasoning?

It seems that Kenny's description of the difference is inaccurate. There is clearly a difficulty with it: he tells us that causal tendencies may not be fulfilled. But if causal tendencies are not fulfilled, it is hard to see how anything happens in the world at all: surely every event that is the result of a causal process is *eo ipso* in some sense the fulfilment of a tendency. We postulated tendencies in order to account for causality: tendencies produce effects by being fulfilled. Are we now to kick away the ladder we are standing on by saying that very few causal tendencies are in fact fulfilled, because most are interfered with?

It is true that an explosion is not produced, in the imagined case: and to that extent the tendencies of substances A and B to produce an explosion are not fulfilled. But though these tendencies, under that description, are not fulfilled, there are surely other descriptions of the same causal tendencies of substances A and B under which the tendencies are fulfilled. We have to tell some such story as that, while substance A has a tendency to combine with substance B in such a way as to produce an explosion it also has a tendency to combine with substance C to produce some compound which does not have a tendency to produce an explosion when combined with substance B. Both these tendencies could perhaps be redescribed in general terms of, e.g. valency, etc., in such a way that both tendencies can be seen as species of one and the same generic tendency, just as both effects—the combination with B to produce an explosion, and the combination with C to prevent an explosion—can be seen as different fulfilments of the same tendency. We are not to think of tendencies becoming wholly inoperative when interfered with. A mixture of A and B in a medium of C is something with quite different causal tendencies from those of the same quantity of C alone, though both are equally unlikely to explode. The tendencies of A and B continue to exist and to have some fulfilment. The same tendencies, we want to say, under certain descriptions may be fulfilled, and under other descriptions may not be fulfilled.

A question may arise of what right I have to speak of "the same tendencies under different descriptions." If a tendency is specified by its end, as it surely must be, then a tendency with a different end is a different tendency. I believe this problem can be circumvented. Every tendency has an end: but this end will be variously describable. Quite a lot of what one is first taught in science classes, I would say, consists in establishing alternative (and more general) descriptions of given tendencies. For example, in basic dynamics: attaching such-and-such a weight to this rope, running over a pulley, has a tendency to lift such-and-such other weight attached to the other end. An alternative description of this tendency, in terms of force, and alternative descriptions of the weights in terms of mass, are made available. It is clearly the same tendencies which are differently described here; the proof being that these tendencies are described differently in terms of their relationship to one and the same outcome, result, or end, itself differently described.

This may give the clue to an answer. We should not say that a tendency that is "frustrated" by interference is not fulfilled: we should rather use some such expression as that it is fulfilled in a non-paradigmatic way. Each tendency will be specified in terms of an end: the end will be an event, and hence the tendency will be specified by a description of an event. A tendency is a tendency to produce an explosion, for example. The paradigmatic fulfilment of the tendency will be the occurrence of an event that falls under the description that was used in specifying the tendency: in this case, an explosion. There may well be no such occurrence, no explosion, in which case there will be no paradigmatic fulfilment of the tendency. But there will be some fulfilment of the tendency: a non-paradigmatic one. That is, there will be some description of the explosion (which does not occur) which turns out also to be true of whatever does occur. We redescribe the tendency to produce an explosion in such a way that the failure of the mixture to explode is also a fulfilment of the tendency: e.g. by redescribing it as a tendency to combine with other substances in such-and-such ways. But a fulfilment of a tendency will be paradigmatic or non-paradigmatic relative to a certain description of the tendency: for every fulfilment of a tendency that is non-paradigmatic under a certain description, there will be another description of the tendency such that the fulfilment is paradigmatic under that description. ("Another description," I say: I am inclined to think that the scientific enterprise demands that we should expect that there should be indefinitely many other descriptions. If not, how could we hope, as we do, to relate any given causal tendency to indefinitely many other causal tendencies with which it might interact?) The combination of substance A with substance C, and the failure of substance A to produce an explosion despite the presence of substance B, will both be paradigmatic fulfilments of the same tendency of A under different descriptions; or, better, we can describe the tendency in A to produce an explosion in the presence of B as being also a tendency to the paradigmatic effect of failing to explode in the presence of B and C.

This will need tightening up. A first objection to this would seem to be that since any event can be described as "something happening" this doctrine is wholly without content. "If there is a tendency for something to happen, something will happen" does not look helpful. (We may notice, though, that even this example is not wholly vacuous: it has enough content to be false. If the conflicting or interfering tendencies are equally balanced, then nothing will happen.) But the point is well made. We will need some kind of stipulations about levels of generality of descriptions of ends to be used in specifying tendencies. A first shot would be to stipulate something like the following: when we are dealing with conflicting or interfering tendencies, we are to seek for alternative, more general, descriptions of these tendencies such that both tendencies are fulfilled paradigmatically. That is, the tendencies are to be specified in such a way that both are fulfilled paradigmatically. If we then stipulate that the least general such description is to be taken, we shall avoid the uninformativeness of attributing tendencies to bring it about that things happen.

That is, we don't want to have laws of chemistry that say something like "When substances A and B are put together, something happens." But neither do we want laws that say "When substances A and B are put together, an explosion occurs," which would be false. We want a description of the tendencies of A and B such that the event described by "an explosion occurred" and the event described by "an explosion did not occur" are equally paradigmatic fulfilments of the tendencies.

We may want to add here a suggestion that the scientific project is one of determining appropriate levels of generality of description. The least general level is the place to start, but this, in our example, may get us no further than saying that A has a tendency to combine with B to produce an explosion and to combine with C to avoid an explosion. This is not yet a scientific explanation: but it seems to be the place at which to start a scientific investigation, to see what further more general and more explanatory, and hence more appropriate, descriptions of this tendency in A we can produce. Appropriateness here is a difficult notion to specify, but it is one which it is necessary to use. What we want is a level general enough for us to be able to say that the tendencies are fulfilled paradigmatically, but not so general as to be uninformative: and not so particular, meanwhile, as to be useless for explanation.

The notion of explanatoriness seems to be making an entrance here. Explanatoriness is a mysterious concept, but there are features which it is known to have which can be seen to be relevant here. The giving of an explanation creates a non-extensional context: to use Anscombe's example, to say "There was an international crisis because the President of the French Republic made a speech" is explanatory, while "There was an international crisis because the man with the biggest nose in France made a speech" is not explanatory, even if the President of the French Republic is the man with the biggest nose in France.[7] That is, explanation is in some sense relative to a description: it should occasion no surprise, then, that causal reasoning in terms of tendencies, which is supposed to be explanatory, should turn out to have description-relativity built into it. This is yet another parallel to practical reasoning: actions are said to be intentional only under a description, and here we have it that effects are attributable to a tendency only under a description.

This account clarifies a number of difficulties about non-voluntary causality and allows us to make clear the difference between voluntary and non-voluntary causality. Non-voluntary causality needs to be described in terms of tendencies, tendencies to some paradigmatic effect. These tendencies may often not be fulfilled paradigmatically, because of interference. That is, there may well be no possible description of the effect which is also a description of the paradigmatic fulfilment. However, the tendencies will always be fulfilled, if only non-paradigmatically: there will always be some description of the tendency, in terms of some paradigmatic fulfilment, such that the tendency, so described, is fulfilled paradigmatically. The apparent vacuousness of this is limited by the fact that if the paradigmatic fulfilment does not occur, there will always be some interference: and the actual outcome will also be a non-paradigmatic fulfilment of the interfering tendency. Once we are committed to taking the least general descriptions of the two tendencies, the account we give will be the starting place, at least, for the search for an appropriate explanation: it will describe the outcome as the paradigmatic fulfilment of the conflicting tendencies. There will always be such a description available, barring the case of miracles.

That said, we seem to have gone a long way towards assimilating reasoning about causal processes to practical reasoning, to assimilating voluntary and non-voluntary causality. Both kinds of reasoning are defeasible; both involve reference to an end; both involve relativeness to a description. What remains as an uneliminable difference? We have, that is, rejected the two suggestions Kenny makes about how to establish the difference. But some of the conceptual tools that we have developed in the process of this rejection enable us to see what the difference really is.

One important difference is that there is nothing in voluntary causality analogous to the distinction we made, in non-voluntary causality, between paradigmatic and non-paradigmatic effects. It is this which makes the analogy between additional goal-expressing premisses and interference of other tendencies break down. The description of the outcome given in an end-specifying premiss does not give a paradigmatic description of the fulfilment of the voluntary tendency of the agent: it just gives a description of its fulfilment. The voluntary tendency cannot be fulfilled non-paradigmatically: it is either fulfilled or not. In the case imagined, it is fulfilled, equally, by the action of taking the 2.15 or by the action of taking the 1.15: and should other considerations arise which lead one to abandon the whole project, the tendency is not fulfilled at all. Perhaps the analogy and the difference can best be brought out by saying that non-voluntary tendencies are always fulfilled, except in the case of miracles, sometimes paradigmatically, but almost always non-paradigmatically. Voluntary tendencies, on the other hand, may fail of their fulfilment: but if they are fulfilled at all they are fulfilled paradigmatically, in that if they are fulfilled then what results from them is describable by the same description that specifies their end. Aquinas's comments in *Summa Theologiae* I–II q.1 a.2 on how all agents act for an end, but only human beings act for an end grasped as an end, may be relevant here.

Thus in non-voluntary causality there is no parallel to having inconsistent ends. Interfering non-voluntary tendencies are not inconsistent, though their paradigmatic fulfilments may be. That is, one might wish to say that the tendencies have different descriptions under which their fulfilments are incompatible: but that does not make the tendencies incompatible, as they also have other descriptions under which they are compatible. And since conflicting tendencies both exist, and both are fulfilled, it is clear that the tendencies themselves are compatible. Meanwhile, in voluntary causality, there is no parallel to interference, strictly speaking: there is nothing that is analogous to the composition of forces. Conflicting or inconsistent goals give rise to tendencies not all of which are fulfilled. Conflicting goals are not compounded but either all achieved or not all achieved.

It may be objected that a conflicting goal, even if given up, may surface in the form of regret. This is true, but I want to insist that regret is not a conflicting tendency that modifies the outcome. If I have the conflicting goal of staying at home and not going to London at all, I may regret going to London all the time that I am on the train, or I may stay in bed and regret not having gone to London: but the outcome, whether going to London or staying in bed, is not modified. In the case of interference of other tendencies in non-voluntary causality, the outcome is always modified: the tendencies involved are always fulfilled, even if non-paradigmatically. (The explosion or the non-explosion are paradigmatic or non-paradigmatic fulfilments, relative to different descriptions, of the tendencies of the substances involved.) My going to London, however, is not any kind of fulfilment of the tendency that arises from my end of staying in bed, and my staying in bed is not any kind of fulfilment of the tendency that arises from my end of going to London. My regret, one might want to say, is some kind of a non-paradigmatic fulfilment of the tendency that arises from my end of doing the other thing: but regret is precisely not a case of voluntary causality. Feeling regretful is not something I do, voluntarily.

Non-voluntary causal tendencies are in some sense physical things and enter into physical relations: or, if this is too strong, we can tell some story about their having physical vehicles.[8] Only the descriptions of non-voluntary tendencies enter into logical relations. The goal-expressing premisses of voluntary tendencies in themselves enter into logical relations, such as inconsistency. The descriptions of the paradigmatic effects of non-voluntary tendencies may be inconsistent: indeed, I suppose, in a case of interference, always are. The content of goal-expressing premisses need not be.

Clearly both interference in non-voluntary causality, and adding additional goals in practical reasoning, can be described as having the effect of "changing the conclusion": but the way they change it is different. Interference makes the effect non-paradigmatic. It means that the description used in the specification of the end of the tendency is not a description of the outcome. Adding other goals does nothing of the sort. If the practical reasoning is successful, if the goals are not incompatible, and an action follows, the description of the goal will also be a description of the outcome. The action, the practical conclusion, will not be any the less of an achievement of the goal, a fulfilment of the tendency. But if the reasoning is unsuccessful, or the goals are incompatible, then at least one of the goals will be *wholly* unachieved.

All this seems to point to the big and so far undiscussed difference: that in causal reasoning we are describing what happens, in practical reasoning we are making things happen. In non-voluntary causal reasoning we are giving descriptions in terms of ends, or paradigmatic fulfilments, but the ends do not yet exist, and, indeed, may never exist. Thus they cannot enter into efficient causality. In voluntary causality the ends are in some sense already existent, at least intentionally, and thus have some possibility of exercising efficient causality through the agent in whose intentionality they exist. In some sense, in voluntary causality, the propositional content of the goal-expressing premiss is itself causally effective: but in non-voluntary causality what is causally effective is the existing tendencies, which can be described in one way or another. It would be absurd to think of the propositional content of these descriptions being causally effective.

There is a question of onus of match here. When we are describing causal processes we are describing what happens: it is up to our descriptions to match the world. More in detail, we are altering the description of the tendency to fit the outcome, by altering the description of the paradigmatic fulfilment or end of the tendency to fit the actual outcome. In practical reasoning the onus of match is the other way round. By our action we seek to fit the world to the description: we have to bring about the outcome in such a way that it fits the description of the goal given in our goal-expressing premiss. (All this fits with the account given by Aquinas between the relationship between our mind and the world we contemplate, on the one hand, and between God's mind and the world he makes, or between our mind and our own productions and actions, on the other: see *Quaestio disputata de veritate* q.1 a.2.)

All this is slightly paradoxical. The usual account of the difference between voluntary and non-voluntary causality is that voluntary causality admits interference whereas non-voluntary causality doesn't. If my considerations are well-founded, this turns out to be precisely wrong.

Notes

1. Anthony Kenny, *The Metaphysics of Mind* (Oxford: Oxford University Press, 1989), p. 145.

2. See Anthony Kenny, *Will, Freedom, and Power* (Oxford: Blackwell, 1975), p. 70.

3. G.E.M. Anscombe, *Collected Philosophical Papers of G.E.M. Anscombe*, vol. 2: *Metaphysics and the Philosophy of Mind* (Oxford: Blackwell, 1981), p. 142.

4. G. E. M. Anscombe and P. T. Geach, *Three Philosophers* (Oxford: Blackwell, 1991), pp. 101–9.

5. See P. T. Geach in *Three Philosophers*, p.104.

6. Kenny, *Will, Freedom, and Power*, p. 117.

7. The example is drawn from "Causality and Extensionality," in Anscombe, *Collected Papers*, vol. 2, p. 175.

8. See, for example, Anscombe, *Collected Papers*, vol. 2, pp. 71–73.

CHAPTER SIX

Thomistic Agent-Causalism

Stefaan E. Cuypers

Sometimes, perhaps usually, I act out of habit and am determined by my dispositions. But sometimes, perhaps not often, I act robustly and determine myself. How, one could ask, is such robust action and self-determination possible?

In order to account for this possibility, some sensible philosophers have appealed to causation by the agent himself. When I act robustly and self-determined, I myself cause my actions. Agent-causation is, however, widely regarded with suspicion in contemporary philosophy of action and free will. In light of current naturalism and compatibilism, such a type of causation is deemed utterly obscure and mysterious. The underlying scientific image of much present-day thinking in analytical philosophy only allows event-causation in the constitution of action and free will. A type of causation over and above causation by events is considered totally unfit for the modern mind.

Against the mainstream, I claim that agent-causation cannot be eliminated or reduced. My argument for the plausibility and credibility of primitive agent-causation is structured as follows. Firstly, I reject mechanistic event-causalism, because it is fatally infected with the problem of activity. Secondly, although standard Reidian agent-causalism in a way solves this problem, I cannot wholeheartedly endorse this version of agent-causalism, because it runs into the problem of infinite regress and there is a para-mechanistic flavour about it. Thirdly, in view of the difficulties with event-causalism as well as standard Reidian agent-causalism, I draw on Aquinas's theory of action and free will to construct a *teleological* model of agent-causation. Accordingly, I make a distinction between para-mechanistic and teleological agent-causalism, and try to show the fruitfulness of a Thomistic view on primitive agent-causation for contemporary philosophy of action and free will.

I

In his presidential APA address of 1981 Alan Donagan contends that there is no better example of progress in contemporary philosophy than the postwar study of human action.[1] Especially the recently developed causal theory of action is looked upon as an improvement as well as a completion of the classical Aristotelian-Thomistic tradition in the philosophical study of human action. Some unorthodox non-causal analyses left aside,[2] all analyses of human action in contemporary analytical philosophy are causal. However, this ubiquitous causalism is not so much conditioned by a pious respect for the Aristotelian-Thomistic tradition as it is conditioned by a scrupulous acknowledgement of the demands of reductive naturalism and thus physicalism. Contemporary causal theories of action are constrained by an explanatory framework in which only explanations in terms of events and event-causation are legitimate.

In this perspective, contemporary causalism and classical causalism are, *pace* Donagan, not at all continuous but strongly conflict with each other. The primitive concept of agent-causation as well as the concepts of formal and final cause, which were all of the utmost importance to the Aristotelian-Thomistic tradition, are banned from the explanatory framework of contemporary causal theories of action as illegitimate. These classical elements should be eliminated altogether, or at least reduced. Hence, orthodox causalism in contemporary analytic philosophy amounts to mechanistic event-causalism in which actions are construed as events *efficiently* caused by other events.

All contemporary event-causal theories of action in some form or other hold that an event must have a specific causal history in order to be an action.[3] To simplify matters, I concentrate on the best-known version of this event-causalism, which states that an observable bodily movement is an intentional action if and only if the movement is caused by desires and beliefs (reasons or propositional attitudes). One of the most vigorous proponents of this desire-belief causalism is Donald Davidson:

> We end up, then, with this incomplete and unsatisfactory account of acting with an intention: an action is performed with a certain intention if it is caused in the right way by attitudes and beliefs that rationalize it.[4]

In order to exclude the possibility of deviant or wayward causal chains from the causal definition of action, Davidson adds the requirement that the bodily movement must be caused 'in the right or normal way' by the desire-belief pair. Because of the complications with the attempt to characterize 'the right way' in non-circular terms,[5] I leave out this requirement. My interest here is confined to the basic conceptual issue about agency, namely the question about how to distinguish what an agent does from what merely happens to or in him. To this question about the *nature* of action the (simplified) event-causal theory of action answers that actions are caused by desires and beliefs, while mere happenings are not so caused. Highly technical problems with desire-belief causalism have been raised and addressed,[6] but not so often discussed is the central problem of the *disappearance of the active agent*, or for short, the problem of activity. The problem is this.

Agency tautologically signifies taking action, i.e. taking an active part in the occurrence of events. The agent evidently plays an active role in the occurrence of an action such as intentional arm-raising, while he plays a passive role in the occurrence of a mere bodily movement such as spastic arm-rising. According to the event-causal theory of action, this active role of the agent in his actions has to be analyzed in terms of the causal history of the bodily movements which constitute his actions. However, what turns a bodily movement into an action only depends upon its causal history *before* the occurrence of the movement itself. At the time of the occurrent movement no additional requirements have to be met for making it into an action. Since the prior causal history of an event is not a part of the event itself, there is, accordingly, not any inherent difference between 'the fact that I raise my arm' and 'the fact that my arm goes up'. Now because the difference between an action and a mere bodily movement is purely extrinsic, both events at the time of their occurrence have the same status with regard to the active role of the agent. Consequently, the role of the agent in the occurrence of an action at the time of its occurrence is just as passive as the role of the agent in the occurrence of a bodily movement at the time of its occurrence. Accordingly, the agent does not play an active role in the occurrence of an action at the time of its occurrence.[7]

The problem of activity jeopardizes desire-belief causalism not only with regard to the action at the time of its occurrence, but also with regard to the prior causal history itself. Even during the complete history of the antecedent events that bring about the subsequent event which supposedly consummates an action, there is no agential involvement or participation. According to the event-causal theory of action, desires and beliefs as such cause bodily movements. But, if desires and beliefs in themselves cause bodily movements, then nobody—*no person*—does anything. The person does not play an active role in the causal history but just figures as the vehicle of the causing attitudes. Surely, the person implicitly could be construed either as the body which moves or as the bundle of mental states and events among which lie the causing attitudes. But this construal would not cast the agent in its active role, since the activity of the moving body is precisely what has to be accounted for, while the sheer combination of whatever mental events in and of themselves never amounts to agential participation. Consequently, the role of the agent during the causal history which supposedly leads to his action remains entirely passive—the agent is simply uninvolved.[8]

The event-causal theory of action does not require anything of the agent, nothing at the time of acting and nothing before the time of acting. Hence, it just leaves the active agent out of the picture. To be sure, desire-belief causalism explicates *some kind of* activity in agency. The antecedents of action are after all not just natural events which cause change in the world, but intentional events which cause action. The attitudes do not cause the bodily movements of the agent like the stormy wind causes the bowing and bending of the branches of a tree. However, what is lacking in the event-causal theory of action is an account of *robust* activity in agency. What is missing, in other words, is an account of agency in which the agent plays his proper role by participating and being engaged in the occurrence of events. Accordingly, the problem of activity in desire-belief causalism reveals the absence in its analysis of agency of what is characteristic for real human action.

Human agency typically exhibits activity in the strong sense which implies freedom of and moral responsibility for action.[9] And the analysis of activity in the weak sense in desire-belief causalism—which focuses only on what might be called 'quasi-activity'—appears to be utterly insufficient to take these essential features of human action into account. Perhaps the event-causal analysis of agency can be sufficient to account for animal movement and behaviour, but what seems to be necessary for an adequate analysis of human action is an account of robust activity.

II

I claim that we cannot account for robust activity—free activity which carries moral responsibility—in the phenomenon of human agency unless we rely on causation by *the agent himself*. Agent-causation won't be reduced and won't go away. An appeal to the agent-causal theory, which traditionally posits a *sui generis* type of causation by the agent, seems to be inevitable. After Roderick Chisholm inaugurated the agent-causal theory in the post-war study of human action in the 1960s,[10] it went out of fashion in the '70s and '80s under the growing influence of reductive naturalism upon contemporary philosophy of mind and action. However, some kind of rehabilitation project started about ten years ago, with such philosophers as William Rowe, Timothy O'Connor, and Randolph Clarke trying to make a case for a credible and viable agent-causal theory.[11]

The agent-causal theory can be held not only with regard to physical movement (bodily actions) but also with regard to psychical movement (mental acts). Drawing upon Aquinas's distinction between commanded acts (*actus imperati*) and elicited acts (*actus eliciti*),[12] I shall in what follows discuss the agent-causal theory in connection to the latter: acts or determinations of the will (volitions) such as decisions and choices. Now, the agent-causal theory of mental action can readily be combined with the volitional theory of bodily action. Accordingly, a bodily movement is turned into an action, if and only if, the movement is caused by a volition, which in its turn is directly caused by the agent. Since the common denominator of the contemporary rehabilitation project still remains Reidian agent-causalism, I confine myself here to Reid's classical model of primitive agent-causation.

Agent-causation does not so much account for this or that particular (free) action, as it explains how robust activity and freedom are possible at all. In his *Essays on the Active Powers of the Human Mind* (1788) Reid apprehended the phenomenon of freedom and robust activity in terms of the employment of active powers which only persons enjoy. According to him, the necessary and sufficient conditions for person S to be the agent-cause of volition v are the following:[13]

(1) S is a *person* that has *power* to bring about v.
(2) S *exerts* its power to bring about v.
(3) S has the power *to refrain* from bringing about v.

When these conditions are fulfilled, the agent-cause S brings about the effect v.[14]

Conditon (1) says that active power is a quality possessed by a person or a substance. According to Reid, only beings that have will and understanding—persons—possess active powers and, consequently, only persons can be efficient causes in the original, strict, and proper sense. Condition (2) states that the exercising of active power by the person constitutes action or activity. Power and its exertion are necessarily connected, since power that cannot be exerted is no power. So, if a person has the power to produce volition v, then he necessarily can exert that power. Condition (3) establishes that the concept of active power includes the contingency of activity. If a person really has power to bring about volition v, then he also has power not to bring it about. The bringing about of v is a contingent existence, because it is 'up to the person' whether or not to exert his active powers.

Condition (3) is vital to the robustness of activity. If a person could not refrain from bringing about volition v, he would have been subject to necessity, lacking all power. Consequently, the person himself would not have played any active role in the occurrence of v. Moreover, (3) secures the impossibility of caused agent-causing. If a person were caused to agent-cause volition v, then he could not have refrained from agent-causing v. Because the necessary existence of v would violate the requirement of contingent activity, caused agent-causing is impossible. Hence, since no event or other person can cause a person to agent-cause a volition, he is the *uncaused cause* of that volition. Correspondingly, robustly active persons are 'unmoved movers' or 'uncontrolled controllers'. That persons themselves are real originators of their volitions and actions is the one and most important principle of the agent-causal theory. As a consequence, Reidian agent-causalism clearly solves the problem of activity. The agent robustly participates in the occurrence of events by the exertion of his active powers. The agent-causal theory appears, however, to generate an infinite regress. The problem is this.

Reid's second condition for agent-causation establishes the core element of robust activity in the production of human action. S's exertion of his causal power—S's own activity—in the production of volition v is identical with *the event of agent-causing:* the further separate event of S's *causing v*, henceforward abbreviated as event e. However, if S's exertion of his active power constitutes an additional event e separated from the produced event v, then either e has no cause, or e has an agent-cause in its turn. Of course, e cannot have an event-cause, because it is impossible that an event of agent-causing was caused by another event (or person).

The 'no cause' alternative is not really an option because it contradicts the common-sense principle that every event (change) must have a cause.[15] But the 'agent-cause' option straightforwardly leads to an infinite regress. If event e (S's *causing v*), just like event v, is agent-caused, then S has also to exercise his active power to produce e; this extra activity of S is identical with the event of agent-causing an agent-causing: the still further separate event e^* (S's *causing e*). And if this event e^*, just like event e and event v, is agent-caused in its turn, then . . . ; and so on *ad infinitum*.

Confronted with this problem, the agent-causalist can, however, suggest that S's exertion of his active power in the production of volition v just is not an event. Accordingly, although it is not a nothing, S's *causing v* is not the sort of thing which requires a cause. Consequently, since the question of prior causes simply does not arise, there is no need to be worried about the threatening regress. But, it will be objected, what else could S's *causing v* be, if it is not an event? Are you not bordering upon ontological incoherence, if you suggest that agent-causings are not events? The suggestion that S's exertion of his active power is not an event is not wholly absurd.[16] If events just are changes things undergo, then S's *causing v* is not an event, because it is not a change S undergoes. Exertions of power, unlike mental occurrences—such as volitions, thoughts, and appetites—and unlike bodily movements, are not changes a substance undergoes. Exertions of power are things a substance *does*. They constitute a substance's own original activity, its own original exercise of active power. Accordingly, *S's causing v* is not an event, but a pure original *act* (action, doing) of a substance.

The price this suggestion has to pay is the admission of a special ontological category besides those of a substance and changes a substance undergoes (events, states), namely the *primitive* category of a substance's pure original activity. The acceptance of this additional ontological category just amounts to the acknowledgement of what primitive agent-causation, in contradistinction to event-causation, really is. However, although I do not think, in the end, that this ontological price is too high, the primitiveness of Reidian agent-causation remains empty and unembedded. In other words, agent-causation is too much a brute fact in a Newtonian universe. Let me explain.

Although Reid rejects David Hume's empiricist epistemology, he as well as Hume accepts Newtonian mechanism with regard to the natural world. Hume also 'attempts to introduce the experimental method of reasoning into moral subjects', whereas Reid on the contrary holds on to 'the principles of common sense' with regard to the moral world, i.e. the world of human actions. In light of his basic asymmetry between fictional event-causation—causation in the 'lax and popular meaning'—and real agent-causation—causation in the 'strict or philosophical meaning'—Reid sets the passive, natural world of necessity against the active, moral world of contingency.[17] Now I cannot wholeheartedly endorse Reidian agent-causalism, because there is, to my mind, a *para-mechanistic* flavour about it.[18] Since event-causation is insufficient to explain how robust activity and freedom are possible at all, a special type of causation—by the agent himself—is postulated to do the explanation. The mechanistic notion of a necessary cause is hereby turned into the para-mechanistic notion of a contingent cause. The transfer from ordinary causes in the natural world to special causes in the moral world stays within the mechanistic framework of cause and effect. In light of this common framework, represented by Newtonian ontology and reductive naturalism, the worn-out criticism that agent-causation is a metaphysical miracle is understandable and even to the point.

I venture the hypothesis that the emptiness and the brutish character of Reidian agent-causalism stems from this Reidian para-mechanism. The mechanistic framework of cause and effect still determines Reid's model of agent-causation. According to Reid, agent-causation is efficient causation by a substance and the only type of causation there is. Consequently, the Aristotelian-Thomistic format of the four causes—efficient, final, formal, and material—is, in Reid's opinion, not a matter of fact but one of words and meanings.[19] However, if the four causes—especially the final causes—are not interpreted linguistically but ontologically, and if agent-causation is embedded within this ontological format, then primitive agent-causation will, in my opinion, lose the status of being a brute fact and gain substantial content. For this substitution of the ontology of mechanism by the ontology of teleology with regard to agent-causation, I turn to Aquinas's theory of action and free will.

III

The contemporary expressions 'event-causation' and 'agent-causation' were not used by Reid, nor by Aquinas.[20] However, in light of the content of the current concept of agent-causation, I offer the hypothesis that not only for Reid but for Aquinas as well, an instance of agent-causation is *a contingent exertion of a person's will-power by which an effect is brought about*. But whereas Reid situates such robust activity and self-determination within the ontology of (para-)mechanism, Aquinas embeds them in the ontology of teleology. To substantiate this claim, I sketch the outlines of Aquinas's view on agent-causation by drawing on, firstly, his theory of voluntary action and, secondly, his theory of 'free will' and of the relationship between will and intellect.[21] I start with some basic aspects of Aquinas's theory of action.

Drawing upon a familiar distinction Aquinas made,[22] we can say that human actions (*actus humani*) are robustly active bodily movements, while acts of men (*actus hominis*) are bodily movements in which the agent does not (fully) participate. This last category is a mixed bag of not only completely involuntary and unintentional bodily movements such as eye-winking and spasms, but also nearly involuntary and unintentional bodily movements bordering mechanical movements such as absent-minded nose-scratching and nervous finger-tapping. Now only the full-blooded human actions are under a person's control and, according to Aquinas, a person is master of what he robustly does through his intellect and will.[23] Accordingly, human actions proceed from deliberate will, i.e. reasoned deliberation and volition. In sum, robustly active bodily movements are 'deliberate' and 'voluntary' actions.

Aquinas's theory of action is an intellectual version of voluntarism. The principles of human action are partly cognitive, partly conative or appetitive. These principles may not, however, be confounded with the desire-belief principles in contemporary event-causal theory of action, because volitions are distinct from just having desires and practical reasoning involves more than just having beliefs. Now Aquinas's intellectual voluntarism must be interpreted in the light of his general ontological teleology and eudaimonism. Accordingly, voluntary action is purposive action towards the good and happiness. Let me clarify this.

The internal moving principles of voluntary action are intellect (knowledge) and will.[24] Now the will has its place in a metaphysical hierarchy of tendencies towards ends. The will is a species of appetite, and appetite, in turn, is a species of inclination. Natural appetite or animal desire (e.g., hunger and sex) is distinguished from natural inclination (e.g., a stone falling towards the earth) by the fact that the first follows concrete sensory cognition. The will—rational appetite—is, then, distinguished from natural appetite by the fact that the first follows abstract intellective cognition.[25] Hence, will is rational appetite directed towards an end. Which end?

According to Aquinas, absolutely every substantial form—of inanimated things, like fire and stones, as well as of animated beings, like plants, brutes, and humans—has an essential inclination or tendency.[26] Correspondingly, every substantial form is associated with a naturally necessitated end. Now the will is a rational appetite which is, Aquinas says, by nature necessarily directed towards goodness and happiness.[27] Hence, will by its own nature necessarily tends to its proper object, the good-as-the-ultimate-end. This constitutes Aquinas's doctrine of the teleological and eudaimonistic necessitation of the will. One important consequence of such a picture of the will is that the will is not a neutral instrument of implementation (as it is for example in contemporary rational choice-theory), but a psychic organ with a definite character and finality of its own.

Will is not natural inclination or animal appetite, but rational appetite. Since the will is in the intellect,[28] the will is essentially related to the intellect (reason). Accordingly, the operation of the will is not 'blind' or instinctual, like natural inclination or animal appetite, but depends upon the intake of intelligible forms. Consequently, the will does not function purely autonomously: it depends on something else for the objects of its volitions. Although the will is an appetite for goodness, it does not itself determine what is good. This determination of what is good requires knowledge of the ends and the goods. Apprehending and judging objects insofar as they are good is an intellective function. The will is presented by the intellect with goods-as-apprehended and because the will is an appetite for goodness it follows these intelligible forms. Accordingly, voluntary action proceeds, via the will with its own bent towards goodness, from the intellect's apprehension of the ends, deliberation about the means, and judgement on the goods.

It is important to note here the distinction between the universal good (*bonum universale*) and the particular good (*bonum particulare*), between good without restriction and good under some description, or between goodness in general and specific goods. The will is by its own essence necessarily directed to the universal good, whereas the intellect presents the will only with a particular good—*this* or *that* good. Moreover, the intellect presents the will with particular goods-*as-apprehended*. One consequence of this is that the object to which the will, as informed by the intellect, tends is not necessarily a true good. The will just tends to whatever is apprehended as good and, therefore, the object of will can be only apparently good (*bonum apparens*).[29]

With the ontology of teleology in place, I claim that Thomistic agent-causalism amounts to the thesis that an instance of agent-causation is *a contingent exertion of a person's will-power in a teleological context*. I explore this thesis by following the lead of Reidian agent-causalism which consists of substance, activity, and contingency. In Thomism, however, the 'efficient' engine of agent-causation in addition depends upon the 'final' engine of teleology. My exploration of Thomistic agent-causalism mainly draws upon Aquinas's view on the causal interaction between will and intellect, and his theory of free decision (*liberum arbitrium*).

Agent-causation is causation by the agent himself (substance) and not by a part of him. Now the locus of agent-causation in Aquinas, according to my thesis, is the will. However, the will is not a *homunculus*, but it *is*, in a way, the agent or person. Why can the will be equated with the person? As explained below, the will is the person's central power, because the will not only sets itself and the intellect in operation, but also all the other psychic powers (except the vegetative powers). And since the will is directed towards goodness and happiness in general, it is concerned for the perfection of the whole. The will, therefore, represents the person himself. The will takes care of the totality of the person, like a good king who takes care of the entire society.[30]

Agent-causation secures self-mastery and self-determination (contingent activity). Agent-caused control guarantees self-control and precludes control by something else. Hence, if an instance of agent-causation is in Aquinas, as I claim, an actualization of will-power, then the question of agent-causation comes down to the question of the will's autonomy. Accordingly, the question whether persons are 'uncaused causes' or 'unmoved movers' amounts to the question whether the will is self-determining and not necessarily determined by something else.

The Thomistic answer to this central question is quite complex. The answer depends, firstly, upon whether the will (volition) is considered *qua object* or *qua exertion*. The object of the will necessitates volition only in one case (that of unrestricted goodness), whereas the exertion of the will is never compelled. And the answer depends, secondly, upon the frame of reference under consideration. Within the frame of *proximate* causes, the will qua exertion is an uncaused cause, while within the frame of *distal* (ultimate first) causes, the will is not its own cause. Let me try to unpack this complex answer.

Firstly, every psychic power can be considered qua exertion or qua object. A psychic power (potency) is, of course, not always exerted (actualized). In order to set a psychic power in operation two principles are required: one from the side of the subject and the other from the side of the object. Consequently, any psychic power can be affected subjectively and objectively.[31] The first kind of affection relates to *exercising* an action—performing an activity—while the second to *what kind of* action—the species of activity—it is. The specific character of an action is determined by its object, which shapes the form of that action. In sum, the subject is an activity-starter, whereas the object is an activity-former. For example, applied to the power of sight qua exertion and qua object, we have (1) that you either see or not (your eyes are open or closed) and (2) that you either see a cat or a cow. Correspondingly, applied to will-power qua exertion and qua object we get (1) that you either are willing or not (you have a volition or not) and (2) that you either will an ice-cream or a bar of chocolate (your volition has this or that specific character).

Qua object the will is determined by the intellect. The intellect does not subjectively but only objectively influence the will. As said, although the will is an appetite for goodness, it is the function of the intellect to determine the objects of will—the goods-as-apprehended. However, Aquinas's theory of the dependence of will on intellect is *not* a version of rational necessitation which says that will necessarily has to follow what reason dictates. On the contrary, freedom of decision and choice—acts of the will (volitions)[32]—precisely depends upon the openness of reason to opposites or alternative possibilities. Why is reason open to opposites? The openness to alternatives belongs to the very nature of reason, especially its universality. Universal reason transcends whatever particular option is presented. Therefore, it is not necessarily fixed upon one option. By his faculty of reason, a person can consider this option or that alternative one, and he can weigh the pros and cons of either option. Hence, because of reason's openness to opposites, reason can supply the foundation for the freedom of the rational appetite which is the will. According to Aquinas, then, practical rationality grounds liberty.[33] Since free judgement on alternatives underpins free decision and choice, the practical role of reason is essential to the constitution of free will.

It follows that although the intellect objectively determines the will, the former does not thereby violently compel or coerce the latter. When the intellect determines the will qua object, the intellect does not necessitate the will to will the object. Put in the format of the four causes, the intellect is the formal cause as well as the final cause but not the efficient cause of the will.[34]

When the intellect presents the will with an object, the will does not necessarily have to accept that object. The object is a good-as-apprehended and, therefore, a form held in knowledge. Now if the will accepts the object, that is to say, if will-power is exerted with regard to the object, then the specific character of the volition depends upon the intelligible form. For example, if I will an ice-cream, then my willing is the willing of an ice-cream and not of a bar of chocolate because of the intellective apprehension of an ice-cream as good. The object as an intelligible form determines *what* is willed and, thus, specifies the intentional content of the volition. Hence, intellect is will's formal cause.

Moreover, if the will accepts the object, then the volition and the ensuing bodily movements occur for the sake of getting the good-as-apprehended which the intentional content specifies. For example, if I will an ice-cream, then my willing and my subsequently taking an ice-cream occur in order to get an ice-cream which is apprehended as good by the intellect. A final cause is present in a person's intention as a formal cause.[35] So, what is willed specifies, at the same time, the *end* of the willing. The will wills in order to get what it wills. The acts of will which are directed towards the universal good-as-the-ultimate-end depend upon the intellective apprehension of the particular goods-as-the-specific-ends. Hence, intellect is will's final cause.

By furnishing the specific object and concrete goal, the intellect certainly moves the will, but the former does not set the latter in action of necessity.[36] This general rule has one notorious exception. Given the doctrine of teleological necessitation, if the will is presented with an universally good object—i.e., absolute goodness and total happiness—then the will *necessarily* wills this object.[37] But apart from this exceptional case, there is no necessitation of the will whatsoever from the side of the object. When an object is only good under some description (and not good under another), the will retains its capacity to refuse the object or to consider its opposite. So, although the will necessarily wills the universal good, it only contingently and thus freely wills the particular goods—this or that specific good. Consequently, the autonomy of the will can almost always be secured on the side of the object; only in one exceptional case—that of unrestricted goodness—the will loses its autonomy.

Qua exertion, the will determines itself. In order to exercise its power—perform its activity—the will does not depend upon something else; within the frame of proximate causes it is a *causa sui*. Now the will subjectively influences—determines qua exertion—besides itself all other psychic powers, including the intellect. Accordingly, the exertion of whatever power (except vegetative ones) depends upon the exertion of will-power. This centrality of the will in the operation of a person's faculties was the reason why I equated, earlier on, an instance of agent-causation with an exertion of will-power.

The way in which the will determines the other faculties differs from the way in which it determines itself. Put in the causal format, the will is the efficient cause of the intellect and all other psychic powers (as well as all bodily movement which constitutes human action), whereas it is not the efficient but the final cause of itself. The will does not compel itself, but it does compel—i.e., efficiently cause—the other faculties to operate when it wills.[38] In this way, the will can actively interfere in the operation of the intellect and all other psychic powers. In particular, the will can secure its independence from the intellect by efficiently causing the intellect to consider the opposite of a presented object or, more radically, to stop deliberating.

Since the will determines itself qua exertion, the will's autonomy is guaranteed on the side of the subject. The self-determination of the will qua exertion implies that the will's activity is not necessitated but contingent and thus free. Aquinas says:

> As to its own proper act [elicited act], however, the will cannot be exposed to violence.[39]

> ... the will is master of its own activity, and whether to will or not to will lies within its own power.[40]

This freedom of the will qua exertion, together with the centrality of the will in the operation of a person's other faculties, makes it possible for the will to play the role of agent-causation. This constitutes the rationale of my thesis that an instance of agent-causation in Aquinas comes to the same thing as a contingent exertion of a person's will-power which guarantees robust activity and freedom. In conclusion, I highlight the theoretical advantage of the teleological context of Thomistic agent-causalism.

The will qua exertion is an 'unmoved mover' or a self-mover. Accordingly, the will initiates itself or sets itself in operation. Aquinas explains the self-movement of the will in terms of *volitions causing other volitions*.[41] As said, the will is not an efficient cause but a final cause of itself. More specifically, the will moves itself via the final (or formal) causation of the intellect (deliberation). Now this explanation of will's self-movement presupposes a first exertion of will-power as given and employs the means-to-end scheme. Accordingly, a first act of willing an end causes a second act of willing the means via a process of deliberation about the appropriate means to the given end. The chain of causes is constituted thus: willing an end (as well as willing deliberation about the means) efficiently causes deliberation about the means-to-end relationship by the intellect which, in its turn, finally causes willing the means. Hence, the coming about of the second exertion (volition about the means) is explained by the first exertion (volition about the end). By willing one thing—for example, health as an end—the will moves itself to willing another thing—taking exercise outdoors as the means.

Second, although within the frame of proximate causes the will determines itself qua exertion, within the frame of distal causes it does not. This becomes apparent when we ask what causes the first exertion of will-power—the willing of an end. As just said, the will sets itself in operation by willing an end. However, given that the will is not always actually willing, it has to start willing an end at some particular moment. But what then explains the initiation of this first exertion of will-power? What then causes the will to start willing an end? Is it the will itself or another external agency?[42]

If the will itself initiates the first act of willing an end, then a *regressus ad infinitum* follows. As shown, the self-motion of the will depends upon a process of intellective deliberation which results from willing deliberation (as well as an end). So, if the will itself initiates the first act of willing an end (v), then this volition results from some deliberation which itself results from willing that deliberation (v^*). But, of course, the will has not always actually been willing that deliberation either. Therefore, this other volition must, in its turn, also be the result from some other deliberation which itself again results from willing that other deliberation (v^{**}); and so on *ad infinitum*. Now, according to Aristotle and Aquinas,[43] there can neither be an indefinitely prolonged series of efficient causes, nor of final causes.

Consequently, in order to block the infinite regress, Aquinas posits an external principle to explain the initiation of the first exertion of will-power.[44] Which principle? The external moving principle of the will is not a principle of astronomy (the heavenly bodies) but of teleology and theology. Aquinas says:

None other than God can be the cause of man's willing.[45]

God moves a person to act, not only by presenting an object of desire to his senses or by effecting an organic change in his body, but also by setting in motion the will itself. Every activity, of both nature and will, comes from him as first mover.[46]

God is will's cause. Aquinas explains this by the *exitus-reditus* scheme. God is the first cause and the ultimate end of the will. When God created man, He efficiently caused man's will-power. And God is the final cause of the will, because the will is an appetite which is by nature directed to the absolute goodness and total happiness—i.e., to God.

Within the framework of distal causes, the will is, therefore, not a *causa sui*. However, the theistic determination of the will does *not* damage the autonomy of the will. This is why. Within the framework of psychical (proximate) causes, will and intellect are still the autonomous internal moving principles of voluntary action, although, within the framework of metaphysical (distal) causes, they themselves are determined by another external moving principle.[47] Furthermore, will's autonomy does not require that the will is its own first cause, just as being a cause of something does not require being its first cause.[48] And most importantly, theistic determinism is not the same as theistic necessitation. God does not violently coerce the will. On the contrary, God determines the will according to *its own nature*.[49] And it belongs to the nature of the will to be the source of contingent activity—to be autonomous. Even when the absolute goodness and total happiness necessitates the will to will the object, the will does not diverge from its own nature. Hence, the necessitating *telos* of the will cannot conflict with the autonomy of the will. On the contrary, the teleological necessitation of the will guarantees the authenticity of the will.

Thomistic agent-causalism contains, in my opinion, the elements for a credible and viable agent-causal theory. Of course, the metaphysical presuppositions of this Thomistic account of robust activity—teleology, intentionalism, and theism—stand in need of further clarification and justification. But although Thomism bears a heavy metaphysical load in the eyes of contemporary reductive naturalism and mechanistic physicalism, the metaphysical doctrines of Thomism are not without defence, even within contemporary analytical philosophy.[50]

Notes

I am grateful to Jos Decortet, Inge Janssens, and Carlos Steel for helpful comments on an earlier draft of this paper. I am especially indebted to John Haldane for his stimulating discussions and inspiring writings.

1. A. Donagan, "Philosophical Progress and the Theory of Action" (1981), in J. E. Malpas, ed., *The Philosophical Papers of Alan Donagan*, vol. 2: *Action, Reason, and Value* (Chicago: University of Chicago Press, 1994), 1–24.

2. For example, C. Ginet, *On Action* (Cambridge: Cambridge University Press, 1990).

3. For a critical review of such theories, see M. J. Costa, "Causal Theories of Action," *Canadian Journal of Philosophy* 17 (1987), 831–54.

4. D. Davidson, *Essays on Actions and Events* (Oxford: Clarendon Press, 1980), 87.

5. Cf. J. Bishop, *Natural Agency: An Essay on the Causal Theory of Action* (Cambridge: Cambridge University Press, 1989), 125–75.

6. D. Davidson, "Problems in the Explanation of Action," in P. Pettit, R. Sylvan, and J. Jorman, eds., *Metaphysics and Morality. Essays in Honour of J. J. C. Smart* (Oxford: Basil Blackwell, 1987), 35–49.

7. For this problem of activity at the time of the action, see H. G. Frankfurt, "The Problem of Action" (1978), in his *The Importance of What We Care About* (Cambridge: Cambridge University Press, 1988), 69–79.

8. For this problem of activity before the action, see D. Velleman, "What Happens When Someone Acts?" (1992), in J. M. Fischer and M. Ravizza, eds., *Perspectives on Moral Responsibility* (Ithaca, N.Y.: Cornell University Press, 1993), 188–210.

9. Cf. St. Thomas Aquinas, *Summa Theologiæ (ST)* I–II q.1 a.3.

10. R. M. Chisholm, "Human Freedom and the Self" (1964), in G. Watson, ed., *Free Will* (Oxford: Oxford University Press, 1982), 24–35.

11. W. L. Rowe, "Two Concepts of Freedom" (1987), T. O'Connor, "Agent Causation," and R. Clarke, "Toward a Credible Agent-Causal Account of Free Will" [1993], all three in T. O'Connor, ed., *Agents, Causes, and Events: Essays on Indeterminism and Free Will* (Oxford: Oxford University Press, 1995), 151–215. See also O'Connor, *Persons and Causes* (Oxford: Oxford University Press, 2000).

12. *ST* I–II q.1 a.1 ad 2.

13. Cf. W. L. Rowe, "Responsibility, Agent-Causation, and Freedom: An Eighteenth-Century View" (1991), in J. M. Fischer and M. Ravizza, eds., *Moral Responsibility*, 263–85.

14. Cf. *The Works of Thomas Reid, D.D.*, 8th ed. (1895), by Sir William Hamilton (reprint by Georg Olms Verlag, 1983), 266; 268; 514–15; 523; 603; 609.

15. "And everything that undergoes any change, must have some cause of that change." T. Reid, *Works*, 603.

16. Cf. W. L. Rowe, *Thomas Reid on Freedom and Morality*, (Ithaca, N.Y.: Cornell University Press, 1991), 273.

17. Cf. T. Reid, *Works*, 74; 522–27; 603–8.

18. I borrow the term 'para-mechanical' from Gilbert Ryle, *The Concept of Mind* (1949) (Harmondsworth: Penguin Books, 1963), 20–21.

19. Cf. T. Reid, *Works*, 75; 526.

20. Reid uses the term 'agent,' in the strict and philosophical sense, only for personal efficient agency, whereas Aquinas uses it (*agens, agentia*) indifferently for personal, animal, and even unanimated efficient agency.

21. For my reconstruction of Aquinas's view on agent-causation (with regard to elicited acts), I found helpful the following material: A. Kenny, *Aquinas on Mind* (London: Routledge, 1993); N. Kretzmann, "Philosophy of

Mind," in N. Kretzmann and E. Stump, eds., *The Cambridge Companion to Aquinas* (Cambridge: Cambridge University Press, 1933), 129–59; E. Stump, "Sanctification, Hardening of the Heart, and Frankfurt's Concept of Free Will" (1988), and "Intellect, Will, and the Principle of Alternate Possibilities" (1990), both in J. M. Fischer and M. Ravizza, eds., *Moral Responsibility*, 211–62; R. McInerny, *Aquinas on Human Action: A Theory of Practice* (Washington, D.C.: Catholic University of America Press, 1992).

22. *ST* I–II q.1 a.1.

23. Ibid.

24. *ST* I–II q.6 a.1.

25. *ST* I q.80 a.1, a.2.

26. Ibid.

27. *ST* I q.82 a.1; I–II q.8 a.1, q.10 a.1.

28. *ST* I q.82 a.1 obj.2.

29. *ST* I–II q.8 a.1.

30. *ST* I q.82 a.4. See also *ST* I–II q.10 a.1.

31. *ST* I–II q.9 a.1; St. Thomas Aquinas, *Quæstiones Disputatæ de Malo* (*QDM*), 6.

32. The problem of 'free will' in Aquinas is the problem of free decision (*liberum arbitrium*) and choice (*electio*). An act of choice—opting for one alternative and rejecting another—constitutes an exertion of *the power of free decision*. Since free decision is, like will, also a rational appetitive power, free decision and will are not two powers but one. See *ST* I q.83 a.3, a.4. In this light, I shall treat choices and, less accurately, also decisions as *acts of the will or volitions* (elicited acts).

33. *ST* I q.83 a.1.

34. *ST* I q.82 a.4; I–II q.9 a.1.

35. *ST* I–II q.1 a.1 ad 1.

36. *ST* I–II q.9 a.1 ad 1.

37. *ST* I q.82 a.1, a.2; I–II, q.10 a.2.

38. *ST* I–II q.9 a.1.

39. *ST* I–II q.6 a.4.

40. *ST* I–II q.9 a.3.

41. Ibid.; *QDM*, 6.

42. *ST* I–II q.9 a.4; *QDM*, 6.

43. *ST* I–II q.1 a.4.

44. *ST* I–II q.9 a.4.

45. *ST* I–II q.9 a.6.

46. *ST* I–II q.6 a.1 ad 3.

47. *ST* I–II q.6 a.1 ad 1.

48. *ST* I q.83 a.1 ad 3.

49. *ST* I–II q.10 a.4.

50. See, for example, Haldane's contribution to J. J. C. Smart and J. J. Haldane, *Atheism and Theism* (Oxford: Blackwell, 1996).

CHAPTER SEVEN

Habits, Cognition, and Realism

Jonathan Jacobs

One of the central problems of analytic philosophy is how the normativity of concept-use is to be accounted for. This problem has two key
dimensions. One dimension is metaphysical; what underwrites the
applicability of general concepts to particulars? The other dimension
focuses more on philosophy of mind and epistemological concerns;
what is it, on the side of the mind, that makes for the correct use of a
concept, that makes for going on to apply it in the right way? These
dimensions are the two sides of the coin which is the currency of
thought. Philosophers have long been exercised by this dual problem
of what are the right concepts to apply to the world and what is
involved in going on to use them in the right way, and if we look at
recent analytic philosophy we find formulations of these issues that
are strikingly clear and which are emblematic of the strategies of analytic philosophy.

Quine's formulation of the issue of translation, Goodman's grue
paradox, and Kripke's plus-quus paradox are paradigms of analytical
depth and clarity, each using key illustrations to make points that are
at the same time wide in scope and fundamental in importance.[1] Each
has its own focus (and has generated its own literature in response), and
each can be considered on its own. But there is something crucial that

they have in common, something symptomatic of a shared philosophical concern. Each is either motivated by or motivates skepticism concerning realism about the normativity of concept-use. Each raises basic doubts about there being features of reality that can be registered or represented in cognition and that ground the generality and rightness of our use of concepts. Quine's questions about the use of *rabbit* rather than *rabbit-stage,* Goodman's questions about why *green* and *blue* and not *grue,* Kripke's questions about what makes it a *plus-*function rather than a *quus-*function are all questions about whether and how it is possible to have in mind and use in thought whatever it takes to get right something general (even if it concerns mathematics and not, say, natural objects and their properties). Quine focuses on meaning, Goodman on induction, and Kripke on rule-following (another approach to meaning); but all three give reasons to doubt that there could be a realist basis for concept-use.

We could, without being anachronistic, go back to Hume and his reflections about necessary connection and to his skeptical solution of the doubts about it for the modern source of this constellation of problems. We would find in Hume's work a formulation of skepticism concerning a realist basis for concept-use that any analytic philosopher could recognize without strain. (Quine for example says, "The Humean predicament is the human predicament.")[2] Here we will go back much further and find in the Aristotelian-Thomistic (A/T) tradition resources for a non-skeptical solution of the sorts of doubts that drive Hume's philosophy and its analytic descendants. My suggestion is not to ignore those sorts of doubts, doubts about the mind-world relation, and about the realist interpretation of concept-use. Such doubts are symptomatic of the healthy rigor of analytic philosophy. What I will focus on is how the Aristotelian-Thomistic philosophy can be articulated to account for how it is that we can have concepts that realistically apply.

The main concern is not primarily epistemological, if that means providing conditions for warrant or the justification of beliefs. It is a more bedrock concern about cognition, viz., in order to have beliefs and make judgments we need concepts, and we need an account of how it is possible for human beings to have a conceptual grasp of features of reality external to mind.[3] According to antirealist theories, the project is to explicate how mind constitutes the world, to domesticate the world to mind. In that way the issue of how to get from thought to object is demystified and we can substitute for it the issue of what are the conditions of objectivity or warranted assertibility or justification given the way we think and speak. Norms of concept-use are not world-guided, they are world-constituting, because we print the currency of thought. After all, the reasoning goes, there is no question of comparing the world to what is thought or asserted; there is no standpoint from which realist reference could be secured; and any notion of what there is and what it is like is already inescapably and pervasively textured by our conceptions and descriptions. Taking these together, there seems to be no leverage for upholding realism. Antirealists do not regard their positions as settling for something less than what thought and language properly aspire to. They claim to give us all the objectivity and reality there could be: the alternative is realist-motivated-skepticism.[4]

The peculiar strength of the Aristotelian-Thomistic principles is in how they enable us to provide an integrated account of object and concept, and without recourse to transcendental idealism, verificationism, or any other strategy that requires us to interpret what there is in terms of its being conditioned by how we think or what statements we will accept. The basic Aristotelian-Thomistic principle of cognition is that to have a concept is for mind to be informed in the same manner as the reality the concept applies to.[5] Formal causation is what realistically connects concept and object. Mind is a potentiality for cognition, and it is actualized by the form of its object.

There are some fundamental objections to this which merit serious consideration. First, it is widely held that the notion of form is not explanatory and cannot plausibly figure in contemporary theorizing. Second, the mind-world identity thesis that the notion of form supports is implausible because it seems to involve the view that mind can grasp essences. Third, even if we relaxed our philosophical scruples and let in the notion of form, what work would it do with respect to the problem of the normativity of concept-use? The remainder of the discussion will be, for the most part, a response to these objections. Taking them in order will be a way to make clear the main notions to be used, show how they are to be used, and finally exhibit the special sort of success achievable by using them.

Forms are not the pre-scientific exotica they are often caricatured as. Indeed, they are remarkably familiar. When we identify or describe a substance as elastic, or as red, or as aluminum, or as cheddar, we are identifying and describing form. When we discover that it is nucleic acids and not amino acids that transmit genetic information we make a discovery about form; and so too when we ascertain that the symptoms of a disease are caused by a bacterium and not by a virus. Forms are not occult entities inaccessible to empirical investigation and the methods of science. To speak of form is just to generalize over what is intelligible. Common sense and science articulate and comprehend form. One can recognize Fs, and have some understanding of what Fs are and do, on account of one's mind, one's cognitive potentiality, being actualized by features of Fs. If I can pick out dogs, reliably discriminate them from other things, and exhibit competence in the use of the term "dog" it is because I possess a concept, have a cognitive ability. To have this ability is for my mind to be informed in some determinate way, *by what dogs are* (even if a good deal of my comprehension is via description rather than by direct encounter). Concepts can be concepts of what they purport to apply to because mind and object are alike in form. This implies or presupposes nothing about fixity of species, or about intuiting natures without empirical inquiry, or about non-empirical things-in-themselves somehow "behind" or "underlying" material objects. Whatever particular scientific claims (say, about elements, or reproduction, or what natural kinds there are) were accepted by Aristotle or Aquinas, the general philosophical point about form is not dependent upon them, and in fact is congenial to contemporary science. To speak of (natural) form is to speak of the determinate, intelligible ways in which matter is organized and the ways in which it behaves.[6] To the extent that things in the world are intelligible it is because there can be a cognitive actualization of form, i.e., conceptualization of them. When we are thinking about objects and their features we are thinking about them and not about mental contents. (See, e.g., *ST,* I.85.2) We are able to do this because the object of thought is somehow present to mind, and it is present to mind by informing it.

The Aristotelian-Thomistic principles provide the explanatory resources for an account of what many antirealist and idealist theories are often silent about, viz., how it is that we come to have concepts at all.[7] On this view coming to have a concept is a change that takes place in a living being of a certain kind, and the cause of this change is (broadly) interaction with the environment. What explanation in terms of form accounts for is how cognition is not a matter of conceptualization constituting objects; rather, what is being thought about is present to mind by its intelligible features being conceptually actualized.

The formal identity of mind and world might seem less strange in the artifactual context. Defense officials give the engineers performance requirements for a long-range military air transport, and the engineers produce a design, a form. That form is then realized in the blueprints for the aircraft, and finally actualized in the aircraft. There are here three different realizations of form. It may be objected that this is so different from the situation of natural form being intellectually actualized that it is not an appropriate analogy. And it is not enough to say that the latter is like the former, just the other way round. But there is an analogy here, and we can see that there is when we consider what is involved in acticulating the content of a concept. When we do that we are describing features of what the concept is a concept *of*. Suppose I did not design the aircraft, but I'm learning about it. To say what is in my concept of a C-5 is to say that a C-5 is 246 feet long, with a wingspan of 222 feet; it is 65 feet high with four engines, clamshell rear cargo doors, etc. Here the informing is in the direction of object to mind, the opposite of artifactual production. But to the extent that my concept is a concept of the C-5 (or of whatever) it is by virtue of my mind being actualized by formal features of it. Concepts are realistic in that the reality they apply to can be present to mind by informing it.

This may make it sound as though formal causation is a mysterious process of intelligible species being transmitted from object to mind. But there is no occultism involved. Mind is a capacity for abstraction of the intelligible, and on the basis of perceptual experience it makes concepts.[8] Its doing this involves and depends upon, but is not equivalent to, immensely complex physical and physiological processes. The product of abstractive cognition is not a stripped-down sensory idea somehow having a general representational function. (That would *still* be form, but sensible form). The making of concepts is the immaterial actualization of what is intelligible, and as immaterially realized it is universal.

Aristotle says of the various kinds of knowledge including science, craft, and metaphysics:

> From experience again—i.e., from the universal now stabilized in its entirety within the soul, the one beside the many which is a single identity within them all—originate the skill of the craftsman and the knowledge of the man of science, skill in the sphere of coming to be and science in the sphere of being.
> We conclude that these states of knowledge are neither innate in a determinate form, nor developed from other higher states of knowledge, but from sense-perception. . . . The soul is so constituted as to be capable of this process. (*P.A.*, 100a 7–14)

To have an intellectual soul is to be capable of abstractively producing concepts, but this activity, while it is a making by the intellect,
cannot be wholly independent of sense experience. (See, e.g., *ST,* I.84.7
and I.85.1) It is not the constituting of the object; it is the intentional
actualization of the formal features of the object. If it is asked why it
should be that the abstractive cognitions made by the mind are such
as to realistically apply, the answer concerns causality. There is nothing
for mind to be except as it is informed by features of reality through the
interaction of perception. (Of course much of our thinking goes on in
the absence of experiential encounter with its objects, and a great deal
of our comprehension is via description. But for there to be original
acquisition of concepts and cognitive activity, perceptual encounter is
necessary. Once mind is actualized there is a great deal of cognitive
activity independent of perceptual encounter.) The antirealist and idealist domestication of world to mind does not supply a solution to the
problem of universals by taking objects to depend upon conceptualization. It just internalizes the difficulty, without offering an account of
abstractive cognition that solves a problem that realism allegedly cannot solve. According to Aristotelian-Thomistic realism the making of
concepts is an activity occurring in natural beings and on account of
their relations to and interactions with things in the world. An intelligible species is not a strange, intuited object, it is the concept, the
familiar product of intellectual abstractive activity. The notion of form
is indeed explanatory. It is the notion in terms of which it is possible
to explain how the world can be an object of cognition, how thought
can be thought of an order independent of it, but in being made intelligible by mind, present to it.

In intellectually actualizing form, does the making of concepts "get
things right"? That is, one might grant a great deal of what has been
said, but still object that even if concepts are what the A/T principles
say they are, there is no reason for thinking that mind abstracts *real*
forms, as against abstracting forms which though they serve as concepts, do not conform to the real order of things. Worse yet, it might
seem that according to the A/T view, not only is it claimed that the
intellect abstracts real forms, it is held to be reliably veracious in com-
prehending essence. In responding to this second main objection I'll
proceed by addressing the second part of it first, and work back to the
first part of it.

Neither Aristotle nor Aquinas held that we easily or typically
achieve complete comprehension of essences. In the contemporary

idiom, the view would be that we can refer to real kinds even without knowledge of their essences, and that we may never fully comprehend essences. Our imprecise and incomplete comprehension of dogs is a referential tether to a real kind, and it is what enables us to go on investigating that kind and achieve a deeper, more detailed comprehension of it. But one might well have a concept *dog*, before being able to discriminate breeds, and before having any explanatory comprehension of canine nature. Aristotle in *De Anima* writes:

> the knowledge of the essential nature of a substance is largely promoted by an acquaintance with its properties: for, when we are able to give an account conformable to experience of all or most of the properties of a substance, we shall be in the most favorable position to say something worth saying about the essential nature of the subject. (402b 22–25)

We should not confuse the A/T characterization of perfect demonstrative science with the type of understanding people generally have; it is not a confusion either Aristotle or Aquinas is guilty of. There are many degrees of comprehension that fall short of scientia, and these can be steps in the direction of it. Just as a person can act well without having perfect virtue, an individual can have comprehension without having scientia. It is certainly not the case that one has no understanding in the absence of scientia. Aquinas says:

> So likewise principles of definition are known before the thing defined is known; otherwise the thing defined would not be known at all. But as parts of the definition they are known after. For we know man vaguely as man before we know how to distinguish all that belongs to human nature. (*ST,* I.85.3)

We can refer to a kind, and have in mind some cognitive actualization of its form even if it is imprecise and imperfect. This partial comprehension is not less than cognition; it is a knowing comprehension, but an incomplete one.

In his explication of Aquinas's view, John Jenkins writes:

> we can see that our initial grasp of quiddities may fall far short of full understanding—one may only apprehend part of the essence and remain ignorant of many or most essential properties. When

this occurs, one's understanding may be expressed in a sort of nominal definition in which proper accidents stand in place of essential differences, as signifying the essence that is their cause.[9]

He attributes to Aquinas what he calls *"an externalism for concepts,* the view, current in philosophical literature, that the individuation of at least some of our concepts depends not only on what is 'in our mind' (as we have access to this through introspection), but also depends on the environment."[10] The present view attributes concept-externalism to Aquinas, and also endorses it. It helps explain what is (by way of concepts) in the mind, and it helps explain what is involved in persons having different degrees of comprehension of the same realities. This holds with respect to the natures of kinds (as in the dog example) and also with respect to causal relations. To illustrate the latter, imagine that one person observes an aircraft lose speed, begin to descend, and then plummet to the ground, while another (looking at the same phenomena) observes the aircraft to slow below its stall speed, lose adequate lift for flight on account of boundary-layer separation, and go into a dive too steep to climb out of even if the engine can be restarted. One individual has a more articulate, detailed comprehension through being more completely informed, through fuller cognitive actualization of form.

There may be confusion in one's comprehension, as when one cannot discriminate between aluminum, steel, and platinum. But what is in mind is *some* actualization of form, enough perhaps to know that metals are very different in kind from plants and animals and paper and cheese. Thus informed, one has the basis for a cognitive habit that can be developed. (See, e.g., *ST,* I.79.6 and 84.7.) There is an analogy here to the ethical context. There it is habits of desire and response in conformity with what reason understands to be good that are crucial to developing good character and practical reasoning. Values are transmitted, as it were, by desire being informed by habituation and later by understanding. Early on, one might be able to recognize that an injustice has been done, and even have a sound sense of what to do about it, but not have a very articulate understanding of justice or be capable of sound, confident judgment in complicated or difficult cases. With maturity, discriminations and deliberations can be more fine-grained, more subtle and articulate. Compare this to the acquisition and use of concepts of natural objects and features. One's concept of trees is very likely acquired by having some pointed out, but without discrimination between deciduous and coniferous, the many different types, their geographical distributions, their biological relations, and so forth. Our kind concepts are progressively elaborated, detailed, corrected . . . they are progressively informed. A child may think all cats are roughly the size of typical domesticated cats, until he or she goes to the zoo, or looks in an encyclopedia or sees a movie with lions or tigers in it. (There is a vast amount of comprehension one can have which is still a long way off from knowledge of essence.)

The mind's abstracting concepts is the activity of cognitive potentiality being brought into conformity with reality. This is not a matter of essences somehow being stamped onto mind. Close looking and hard thinking are needed, just as they are in the ethical context. In each context, potentiality is actualized in determinate ways by the acquisition of habits. And just as one can act justly without having much comprehension of justice or human good, one can employ concepts in judgment and reasoning without full (or even very much) comprehension of the referents of those concepts. The principle that mind in cognition is informed in the same way as its object is not the thesis that our comprehensions *in fact* actualize *all* of the intelligible features of objects.

We turn now to the issue of whether mind, in actualizing intelligible form, does this realistically. That is, what is it in the Aristotelian-Thomistic view that explains how we abstractively make the right concepts, and are able to go on applying them in the right way?

Aquinas writes:

Now the proper object of the intellect is the *quiddity* of a material thing; and hence, properly speaking, the intellect is not at fault concerning this quiddity; whereas it may be astray as regards the surroundings of the thing in its essence or quiddity, in referring one thing to another, as regards composition or division, or also in the process of reasoning. (*ST,* I.85.6)

He is following what he takes to be Aristotle's view in Book III of *De Anima.* In his commentary on it he writes:

So he [Aristotle] adds that just so far as the mind bears on an essence, i.e. understands *what* anything is, it is always true; but not just insofar as it relates one thing to another.

The reason for this is that, as he says, essence is what the intellect first knows; hence, just as sight is infallible with respect to its proper object, so is the intellect with respect to essence. It cannot, for instance, be mistaken when it simply knows *what* man is; on the other hand, just as sight can be deceived in respect of what is joined with its proper object, e.g. in discerning that some white object is a man, so too the intellect sometimes goes astray in relating one object to another.[11]

This sort of confidence that the intellect carves the world at its joints often elicits either skepticism, contempt, or condescending amazement.

A way to interpret this sort of view would be to say not that our understanding is perfect, but that what the mind abstracts are the forms encountered in reality; that is, this is a way of articulating part of a version of concept-externalism. What could make for the rightness of the abstraction of form? For one thing, the initial abstraction is just that; it is the activity of mind making a concept, generated abstractively from experiential encounter. It is not a matter of making judgments, asserting propositions in the way that is the main concern of so much recent epistemological theorizing. So, it is not a matter of thinking or asserting something true or false, but of mind making concepts which can then be used in making judgments. Also, this level of cognition is the first operation of intellect in the sense that we have already emphasized, viz. there is nothing for mind to be (initially) except as it is informed by objects and features of reality. It is only in such a way that (a) there could be a relation of reference to an order other than mental contents; it is only in such a way that thought could be world-intending, and (b) it is only in such a way that our cognitive capacities can be progressively developed in such a way that the development constitutes an increasingly articulate comprehension of mind-independent reality.

Even apart from Aquinas's theological commitments that are meant to ground the reliability of our intellectual faculties, the A/T principle supplies a broadly natural basis for it. Mind is active in making concepts, but this activity is work that it does consequent to being acted on by things in the world. Abstraction is not antirealist domestication, it is mind being brought into conformity with its object; "And this enables us to see how intellect in act *is* what it understands; the form of the mind in act."[12] Aquinas uses the idiom of "assimilation of the knower to thing known,"[13] as a way of indicating the externalist feature of concept-making, and the basis of the reliability of this process is that the kind of causality involved is formal. Efficient causality on its own could cause some mental state or process or activity, but there would be no reason to think it to involve or have as a product a mental content conforming to its cause. Formal causation is not hobbled by that skepticism-inducing limitation.[14]

Of course we not only have imperfect comprehension, we also get many things just plain wrong. The A/T principle is not a universal solvent for error; it is a foundation for realist veracity. Our concepts are employed in judgment, inquiry, and criticism, and on the basis of these we make revisions in them. Some are vindicated, developed, and figure in explanatory understandings; others aren't and don't. At the commonsense level, and certainly from the culinary perspective, there are important differences between broccoli, cauliflower, and cabbage. These are, though, members of the same biological species, and with respect to taxonomy their differences are only morphological. This doesn't show that common sense is mistaken or that all classification is interest-relative. There *are* real morphological differences, even if it turns out that they are not explanatorily significant. Common sense and science can comprehend form in different ways—in all of the ways in which it is intelligible.[15] But we can still aspire to and achieve world-guided explanatory comprehension. For example, there just is no phlogiston . . . thinking there was, was a false theoretical interpretation of a quiddity. In that way the phlogiston case differs from both the botany case and from, say, the case of Frosty the Snowman. The song claims that when a hat was put on Frosty he began to dance around. There are no dancing snowmen, while there are physical phenomena of heat that phlogiston theory got wrong.[16]

With respect to those concepts that are right, that do realistically apply, how are we to explain what it is to *go on* using them in the right way? How do we join prescriptivity to conformity? The Quine, Goodman, and Kripke cases mentioned at the outset are each in their own way strategies for raising this issue. Quine's strategy focuses on the matter of evidential underdetermination.[17] Goodman focuses on what underwrites projectibility and inductive practice. Kripke focuses on what it is that could account for going on in using a concept with the same meaning, what it is to follow a rule. In this discussion we won't be taking up each strategy in turn. Together, they raise our main issue; viz., what is the basis of concept-legitimation and the rightness of continued use?

Aristotle and Aquinas do not address these questions in the idiom of contemporary analytic philosophy, but their theorizing is directly relevant to it. The combination of concept-externalism and interpreting mind as potentiality to be cognitively informed supplies the wherewithal to engage in the contemporary debate. There is a realist ground for concept-use in the realism of form. Mind is a potentiality for truth-apt world-guided conceptualization. It is only furnished with concepts through encounter with objects, and the encounter is a process of abstracting intelligible form. So, what is in the mind as a realized cognitive capacity is a concept as habit, a way of mind's potentiality being disposed in conformity (to some extent) with a feature of reality.

One thing all can agree on with respect to concepts such as rabbit-stage, grue, and quus is that they are contrived. This is not because they are evidentially underdetermined. And anyway, as Kim remarks in reference to Quine making so much of the fact that theory cannot be logically deduced from observation,

> Most of us are inclined, I think, to view the situation Quine describes with no great alarm, and I rather doubt that these conclusions of Quine's came as news to most epistemologists when "Epistemology Naturalized" was first published.[18]

An evidential approach to this issue, or one that seeks to resolve it by locating prescriptivity in some particular mental item is bound to play into the hands of the skeptic. But it is not just an historical accident that the contrived concepts are the contrived ones, and it is not a mystery either. If one objects that this isn't a problem with a realist solution, that it is just a matter of "how our minds work," this is half right. It *is* a matter of how our minds work, because of the realism of form. The cognitive actualization of form is the formation of a cognitive habit, an ordering of thought, enabling the individual to identify, judge, and reason. The prescriptivity of concepts is determined by the realism of form that specifies the habit.

Prescriptivity is not just a matter of what our linquistic practices are; the norms of concept-use are a *basis* for practice. Practice is activity and the activity of concept-use is the exercise of cognitive capacity; it is a habit in act. In this case, habit is not to be interpreted merely as "something done regularly" but as a specific capacity determined by intelligible form.[19] As abstracted, form is universal. A concept shares form with what it applies to but is not itself this or that enmattered particular. Knowing how to go on in the use of a concept is not a matter of having figured out what to do with a mental item. The prescriptivity of concept-use is world-guided through the likeness of form in different particulars. What makes practice a rule-following activity is its conformity to multiply exemplified intelligible form.

There are concepts such as grue or man-or-mouse or white-birch-next-to-single-family-dwelling that are as evidentially supportable as non-contrived concepts and which can be coherently applied. Why are they contrived; why are they any worse off than iron, sea-turtle, or American elm?

Hume held that many of our beliefs were, in effect, irresistible, in the sense that while they lacked rational justification and could not be proved to conform to reality, we naturally acquire certain habits of mind that are not a matter of choice, are not optional. Wittgenstein also held that while there is no question of comparing our concepts to their objects, there are criteria for correct use, criteria found in our linguistic practice, in habits of use. These are different interpretations of habit from the one appropriate to the A/T view. Hume *contrasts* habit with having rational justification.[20] Wittgenstein focuses on practice, the activity of language-use, as where we should look, rather than to the mind-world or concept-object relation. The latter, according to the (later) Wittgensteinian view, presupposes irresolvable metaphysical issues that in their very formulation misdirect us away from genuinely explanatory phenomena. For both Hume and Wittgenstein there is authority to what in fact we think and say that is not dependent upon the authority of metaphysically or epistemologically antecedent proof or criteria. There is no special fact of agreeing with reality to mark the rightness of concepts; there is no special fact grounding the rightness of how we go on in using a concept. The sorts of metaphysical and mental facts a realist account of these seems to need are just nowhere to be found.

Hume and Wittgenstein, in effect, agree that an explanation in terms of habit or practice is an *alternative* to an explanation in terms of realist conformity.[21] But these do not exclude each other, as is shown by the A/T principles. They enable us to articulate a realist interpretation of cognitive habit. In part, the strategy of the Humean and Wittgensteinian positions is to note that *of course* we take ourselves to be referring to an extra-mental order of things, and to be identifying and judging of things in it truly . . . but there is no realist underwriting of this.

An explanation in terms of habit is realist if we interpret possession of a concept as a manner of being cognitively informed. The formal cause of the cognitive capacity is the same in form as the objects or features it applies to. The normativity of concept-use is not ungrounded. A cognitive habit is a way of being disposed, determined by a formal cause. In this sense, mind is conditioned by objects rather than the other way round. In concept-use, what is going on in the mind bears affinity to the reality that is cognized; there is likeness of form. This is a realism that is not dependent upon a global a priori proof of the possibility of conformity of mind to world. It does not start with mind skeptically alienated from the world and then attempt, by argument, to bring the world into position to be an object for mind. What sustains the mind-world relation is causality. The presence of object to mind through formal causality is what initiates and sustains cognitive activity. So, the intelligibility of the cognitive activity is not distinct from and is not constitutive of the features of the world it refers to. When we articulate how we use a concept, when we specify its content, we are saying things about how we take the world to be. It is not a lucky coincidence that we are able to make concepts that conform to the world, since our making them at all is explicable in terms of what are the intelligible features of things in the world.[22]

Notes

1. See W. Quine, *Word and Object* (Cambridge: MIT Press, 1960). Also, Nelson Goodman, *Fact, Fiction, and Forecast* (New York: Bobbs-Merrill, 1965); and Saul Kripke, *Wittgenstein on Rules and Private Language* (Cambridge: Harvard University Press, 1982).

2. W. Quine, "Epistemology Naturalized," in *Ontological Relativity and Other Essays* (New York: Columbia University Press, 1969), p. 72.

3. Some will object that the acquisition of concepts occurs through coming to have beliefs and through learning the use of language, especially sentences. Without entering into that debate, I think we can safely acknowledge its significance and at the same time sustain a focus on the issue of what it is to have realist concepts.

4. Philosophers strongly influenced by Kant (such as Putnam) and also philosophers strongly influenced by Hume (such as Blackburn) agree, in spite of their many differences, that their antirealist or internal realist interpretations don't leave out or require us to forgo any of the legitimate objects or aspirations of thought and language. I do not at all feel that these assurances are convincing.

5. See, in particular, Book III of *De Anima*, chs. 4–8, and *Summa Theologica*, Pt. I, q. 79, art. 4; and Aquinas's *Commentary on De Anima* (New Haven: Yale University Press, 1951).

6. Form is not incompatible with explanations in terms of laws and events. Our options are not confined to (a) intuition of form and (b) nomological explanation, as exhaustive, exclusive alternatives. To the extent that lawlike explanation renders phenomena intelligible, it does so by specifying formal features of constitution, activity, interaction, development, and so forth.

7. Antirealists generally take *thought* to be unproblematic; only the "world" side of the mind-world relation is problematic, and this can be resolved by abandoning realism. The A/T principles have the virtue of explaining cognitive activity too, and in a way that is unified with the metaphysics of the objects of cognition.

8. See *ST*, I.79.5. "The active intellect is the cause of the universal by abstracting it from matter."

9. John Jenkins, "Aquinas on the Veracity of the Intellect," *The Journal of Philosophy* (1991), pp. 631–32.

10. Ibid., p. 631.

11. Aquinas, *Commentary on De Anima*, III, vi. 761–62.

12. Ibid. III, viii. 789.

13. See *ST*, 1.76.2.

14. Locke, for example, held that it was evident that in sense perception our simple ideas were caused by objects external to the mind. (See, for example, *An Essay Concerning Human Understanding*, Bk. IV, ch. xi.) But a theory such as his, which has no place for formal causation, leaves unaccounted-for how the product of a process of efficient causation could have the semantic and epistemological features that he attributed to ideas.

15. The botany example concerned common sense distinctions that do not figure centrally in scientific explanation. There are, of course, countless examples of science making distinctions that common sense does not. For example, it is held by many biologists that there are two kingdoms of bacteria: archaebacteria and eubacteria. To common sense, a bacterium is a bacterium; a "tiny little thing"; and so is an amoeba a tiny little thing. But to a biologist, to someone with a high degree of comprehension, the difference between a bacterium and an amoeba is, as one physiologist put it to me, "huge; *all* of the difference." In any case common sense and science do not have different objects; they are different degrees of comprehension of the one reality, and that reality has many intelligible features. Thus, there is no special problem about realism requiring "one true theory" or a single level of description.

16. Not only are there abstractive cognitions that do not realistically apply, there are also some that apply but are not explanatory. For example, a group of clouds may be arrayed to look like a bear. It may then look like the "bear" is lying down, for example. That the array looks like a bear is a

consequential feature of the clouds, not a constitutive one, and it does not have explanatory significance.

17. The issue of underdetermination is a theme throughout much of Quine's work, and it is quite right to recognize its philosophical significance. One merit of the A/T interpretation of cognition is that it indicates a direction for giving an account of cognition that is not hobbled by the shackle of underdetermination. The notion of form is not constrained by the evidentialist considerations that underdetermination emphasizes.

18. J. Kim, "What Is 'Naturalized Epistemology'?" reprinted in *Philosophical Perspectives: Epistemology* (Atascadero, Calif.: Ridgeview Publishing Company, 1988), p. 386.

19. See again *ST,* 1.79.6.

Now, the passive intellect is said to be each thing, inasmuch as it receives the intelligible species of each thing. To the fact, therefore, that it receives the species of intelligible things it owes its being able to operate when it wills, but not so that it be always operating: for even then it is in potentiality in a certain sense, though otherwise than before the act of understanding—namely, in the sense that whoever has habitual knowledge is in potentiality to actual understanding.

20. See, for example, the things Hume says about habit and custom in *A Treatise of Human Nature,* Bk. I, Part IV, Sec. 2, and *An Enquiry Concerning Human Understanding,* Sec. V, Part I, and Sec. VII, Part II.

21. Kripke attributes to Wittgenstein what (following Hume) he calls a "sceptical solution." See *Wittgenstein on Rules and Private Language,* ch. 3.

22. Several papers by John Haldane have been significant helps. In particular his "Mind-World Identity Theory and the Anti-Realist Challenge," in J. Haldane and C. Wright, eds., *Reality, Representation and Projection* (New York: Oxford University Press, 1993), pp. 15–37, helped orient and focus my own thinking.

CHAPTER EIGHT

Hylomorphism and Individuation

David S. Oderberg

1. Introduction

Nothing in philosophy approaches, in precision, refinement, and fecundity, the philosophy of the School. Philosophy would do well to return to it. Apart, however, from some small glimmers of awakened interest in a few quarters, it shows no sign of doing so. In Anglo-American thought the philosophy of the School has suffered a dual fate: on the one hand it has become the ossified material of an essentially tedious historical analysis; on the other, its substance has been strained and filtered through centuries of empiricism, reductionism, and materialism so that the remains have ended up as the stuff of what is now called analytical philosophy. And while the revivified interest of a small number of able analytical philosophers in what the schoolmen have to say is admirable, their output has been almost always critical, seeking to expose the many fallacies and falsehoods of which the schoolmen, in particular St Thomas Aquinas, are supposedly guilty. It is my conviction that philosophers would do better to defend the School, not to bury it; but also that the only way of doing so is, *pace* the opinion of some,[1] through the medium of analytical philosophy, which is the School's only legitimate heir. It is in this spirit that I want to examine that most vexed of scholastic questions, concerning the principle of individuation.

2. What the Principle of Individuation of Material Substances Is Not

The doctrine of the School is that matter is the principle of individuation. We must note, however: (a) the doctrine applies only to complete material substances, or else compounds of incomplete substances of which one is material (in the case of man); and (b) the precise doctrine is that *designated* matter (*materia signata*) is the principle of individuation (let us call it PDM). I do not propose to enter into exegetical questions concerning which schools held which views; it is well known that not every schoolman held PDM,[2] but it is still by far the dominant view, and is the Thomistic one, all schoolmen being obliged to hold the Thomistic opinion on all matters of philosophy as their default position. Let us briefly survey the reasons why no other principle of individuation (*p/i*) will do, since we will then have arrived at PDM by a process of elimination, on the assumption that there are no other plausible candidates. (I will not take it as evident that there are no others; there is no room to canvass all alternatives, only the most likely.) A caveat must be entered, however: the defence of PDM to be offered will still be in apparent tension with some of the objections to be raised in the general survey. I will have something to say about how this tension might be resolved but do not pretend to have disposed of it.

To begin with, prime matter is not the *p/i*. (1) It is common, i.e. multiply instantiable (wherever there is actuation by a substantial form), and it is a hallmark of individuality, including that of material substances, that it is, to use the scholastic term, incommunicable.[3] In analytic terminology, we can say (following E. J. Lowe): *x* is an individual if and only if *x* is an instance of something *y* (other than itself) and *x* itself can have no instances (other than itself).[4] (2) Prime matter is indivisible, being mere potentiality, so it cannot serve as the basis of the division of a species or nature into individuals. We cannot say, 'Here is some prime matter, and there is some more', but we can say, 'Here is Socrates, and there is Callias', or in other words 'Here is prime matter informed by Socrateity, and there is prime matter informed by Calliaeity'.

Second, the p/i cannot be matter as possessing such-and-such determinate quantity, i.e. size, shape, volume, location ('quantity' should be taken broadly to include location, since as we will see it is really *dimensionality* which the schoolmen understand by quantity in this context). (1) Determinate quantity is accidental (a contingent property in analytical parlance, though this is not a happy term), and accidents presuppose the existence (and hence individuation) of the individual substance in which they inhere, so the individuation of substance by accident would be circular. (I give only qualified endorsement to this standard objection, for reasons to be suggested later.) (2) A change in a substance's determinate quantity would change the individual, which is absurd.

Third, the p/i cannot be matter as disposed for the possession of such-and-such determinate quantity. Now such a disposition may not be accidental but essential to a thing's nature, but it still will not do. (1) Few if any substances have matter disposed to a determinate quantity (perhaps some micro-physical particles or micro-organisms do), only to a range of quantities. (2) A disposition to quantity *follows* from the possession by matter of substantial form: it is *because* Socrates is human that he is disposed (speaking now of ranges) to a height greater than six inches—Socrates would not be so disposed if he were an ant. Hence, as will be explained, even if a disposition to quantity were the p/i, form would have to play a role in individuation by giving otherwise indifferent prime matter whatever it is that enables matter to individuate.

Fourth, the substantial form, though it is in a sense the primary factor in individuation, is not the p/i itself. It is the primary factor in individuation because of what is now called the sortal-dependency of identity.[5] The p/i has to be formulated in terms of substances of the same species: two substances of the same species are identical[6] if and only if . . . ; or, taking F to be a substantial kind, we can say that object a is the same F as b if and only if. . . . What sortal-dependency amounts to, speaking in the ontic rather than the linguistic mode, is that information by a specific form is what lays the ground, as it were, for numerical identity and diversity. Since the individual substance is brought into being by the union of prime matter and substantial form, it is not surprising that substantial form plays a role in individuation, and indeed a far more complicated one than is often thought. As for the basic point being made here, we can quote Aristotle in support:[7]

We assert, then, that substance is one of the categories of being; and that this substance is partly what is called matter, which by itself is not this individual; and partly form and specific difference, by which a thing is at once denominated individual; and, lastly, the composite of both.

And commenting with approval on this passage, St Thomas says:[8]

Form is that by which a 'particular thing' actually exists.

Since the question 'Is *a* the same as *b*?', in order to be answerable, must be expandable in terms of some kind *F*—'Is the *a* the same *F* [dog, man, lump of wood] as *b*?'—we know that specific information makes individuation possible in the first place, and is in that sense primary, even if not the principle of individuation itself. Two reasons suffice to show that form cannot be the *p/i* itself: (1) form is common, whereas individuality is not (i.e. it is incommunicable to many, as was said above); (2) matter is an essential part of the material substance, which is a composite of matter and form; but individuality must take account of the individual's essential parts; so form alone cannot confer individuality.

Fifth, the existence of the material substance cannot be the *p/i*. (1) We can conceive of individuals which do not exist, such as fictional objects, the next president of the United States, and so on. One might object to this by saying that fictional objects, for example, have existence within their domain of quantification (Hamlet exists *in* the play, but not *in real life*). The reply is that existence is only the presupposition of an object's behaviour or actions, or more broadly of its role within a certain frame of discourse. We cannot conceive of Hamlet's being indecisive without conceiving of him as existing within the play; and we cannot conceive of the next president of the United States making an inarticulate speech without conceiving of him as existing. But we can, otherwise, conceive of a wholly non-existent individual, say a big brown bear, or a man who wins the presidency, without embedding the conception within any identifiable frame of discourse, and so without presupposing the thing's existence in any sense. Such a thing conceived of is no more or less than an individual essence, and it contracts its species just as a species contracts its genus whether or not the species has any actual members. (Think of the genus *polygon;* now think of the species *chiliagon;* now think of some chiliagon.) Similarly, a sculptor's ideal prototype of a Greek muse already has individuality before he brings it into existence. Hence individuality must be contained in the individual essence of a thing, not in its existence. (2) If existence is the actualization of an individual essence, it presupposes the individuation of that essence, i.e. it presupposes an individual potentiality. (3) What individuates existence? That is, what distinguishes the existence of *a* from the existence of *b*? If existence is self-individuating, then why not say the same of essence, which is prior to existence 'in the order of nature and of perfection', as the Thomist would say?

3. The Principle of Individuation of Material Substances

There are three elements to this, but only one which we should in general speak of as *the* principle of individuation. First, it is submitted that we cannot ignore the work of Suarez on this,[9] and must therefore say: Every material substance is the principle of its individuation by its own proper entity. It is the very union of prime matter to substantial form which constitutes the individual substance, as surely as the coming together of cogs and wheels (or chips and plastic) constitutes an individual watch. Individuality follows necessarily from substantial being, and if this is how we should take the Quinean slogan 'no entity without identity', that slogan expresses an important truth.

Second, to add to what was said above about the primacy of form, we must say that form holds a higher place than matter in the haecceity of the complete composite substance. Matter as such is inchoative, and *of itself* no more inchoative of this rather than that substance; whereas form perfects and determines the substance, turning what is wholly indifferent into something determined and singular.[10] It is a lack of regard for this point which seems to be at the root of worries had by some philosophers about whether the matter that individuates is 'thick' or 'thin', an issue to which I will return.

Third, it is matter which is the principle of individuation, in this sense: it is the *chief intrinsic principle* by which the entire substantial composite is individuated.[11] It is matter which divides common form, i.e. which turns the communicable into the incommunicable, which in union with form results in that which is "indistinct in itself and distinct from others."[12] The three claims are, then, to be reconciled in this way:

it is the initial or logically prior influence of common form on otherwise indifferent matter which gives to matter the character by which
it individuates the substance which, as a whole composite, is constituted
as an individual entity. So when we say that the substance is the principle of its individuation by its own entity, we pay regard to the fact
that every material substance, being a this-such, is ipso facto individual;
but we do not exclude the further fact that every material substance has
a component, namely its matter, by virtue of which it is a this-such.
Individuals can self-individuate without that self-individuation being
primitive or incapable of further analysis, just as pianists can by definition play the piano without their pianism being incapable of further
analysis.

But what kind of matter is it that is the chief intrinsic principle of
individuation? The well-known formula (PDM) is that the p/i is 'designated matter' (*materia signata*), more exactly matter designated by
quantity, even more precisely matter designated by *indeterminate*
quantity.[13] The unpacking of this concept is tricky, and here Thomists
of good will differ. The quantity is generally recognized as having to
be indeterminate because of the simple fact that substances vary in their
material quantity over time without losing their individuality. (I say
individuality rather than identity—although it is also true that they can
vary in material quantity without losing their identity—because of a
crucial difference between individuality and identity which will be
mentioned later.) What, however, is the term-of-art 'designation' supposed to mean? The most likely meaning is 'possession', so by saying
that matter designated by indeterminate quantity is the p/i, Thomists
mean that matter in possession of indeterminate quantity is the p/i.

But to speak of matter possessing quantity seems like just another
way of speaking of matter informed by quantity, and the objection goes
that matter cannot be informed by (really possess) indeterminate quantity, any more than it can have an indeterminate shape.[14] The principle
of individuation, however, must be real (as opposed to ideal or mind-
dependent) if substances, as is assumed, are really individuated. It is
important to be clear about what this objection is saying. It is not being
denied that real information by a specific form ipso facto entails information by every generic or higher-order form which that specific form
restricts. Analytically, this is expressed in terms of the hierarchical relation between sortals which successively restrict one another (where
restriction is transitive).[15] Hence a circle really is both a circle and a shape,

but it is not really an *indeterminate* shape. An indeterminate shape is a conceptual object, not a real, in the sense of mind-independent, one. (Compare the instructions: 'Think of an indeterminate shape', and 'Look in this book for an indeterminate shape'. *Pace* Berkeley, the former task is performable in a way the latter is not.) In addition, it is not being denied by the objector that there is at least a serious question about whether some substances (clouds? slime moulds?) have indeterminate boundaries. I take it that the world contains objects that are really circular, even if being really circular involves approximation, within a range, to a certain (perhaps ideal) limit. Further, many objects' boundaries are in constant flux, even those of relatively solid and stable objects such as lumps of inert matter. But this does not mean that if we choose a suitable non-arbitrary range and level of exactness, we cannot place every material object within some category or other in terms of real shape. However, goes the objection, the claim that information by indeterminate quantity could be the *p/i* goes further, by implying that what individuates is the real possession of quantity such that it is in principle impossible even to place any substance with such quantity, whether precisely, or approximately, or even plausibly, within one quantitative category rather than another. No material object, let alone substance, could have such inherent vagueness in reality, and so be really individuated by it.

It is this sort of objection which led to the modification by John of St Thomas of St Thomas Aquinas's formula: for John of St Thomas, it is 'matter *radically* designated by indeterminate quantity' which is the *p/i*, meaning that it is not actual information by/possession of indeterminate quantity which individuates, but a *disposition* to indeterminate quantity.[16] Further, it seems there is a need to speak of disposition because of the problem of the individuation of accidents, mentioned above in connection with the possession by matter of determinate quantity as a possible *p/i*. Of course, we might depart from the Thomistic position and hold, with Suarez, that accidents individuate themselves, and we will have no obvious circularity problem in declaring the possession of quantity, determinate or indeterminate, as the individuator of substances. But let us see if we can hold to the traditional position that accidents are individuated by their subjects (in this case the substances possessing them), whilst still allowing quantity to individuate, albeit via a disposition thereto. The picture, then, might be something like this. In every world in which a substance S exists at a time, its matter has a certain definite quantity at that time. But since that quantity will not be the same in every world, there is something indeterminate about it. But in no world does S's matter *have* indeterminate quantity; so we must say that it is the *disposition* of S's matter for different quantities in different worlds which gives rise to indeterminacy. In other words, S as such has, in every world in which it exists, matter disposed to indeterminate quantity even though the matter in each world is quantitatively determinate. Now, what individuates S in each world cannot itself be accidental, because S can lose its accidents and keep its individuality, and also because its accidents are themselves individuated by it. So we must say that S's disposition to indeterminate quantity, which is *essential* to S, is what individuates it in each world.

Perhaps this just will not do. Perhaps we cannot make sense of the idea that a disposition can individuate. After all, every substance of kind K will have the same disposition to indeterminate quantity if, as has been suggested, the disposition is itself a product of the 'exigency of form' (to use Joseph Owens's expression). So we would need somehow to combine the disposition of a substance S to indeterminate quantity with the quantity it (via its matter) actually possesses in order to have a genuine *p/i*, that is, an individuator that is indeed not shareable. But then, it seems, we would need to speak of something like *quantity-as-produced-by-the-disposition-of-matter*, or more precisely, given the Thomistic formula, *matter-insofar-as-through-its-dispositon-to-indeterminate-quantity-it-possesses-actual-quantity*, as the *p/i*. Now, leaving aside the fact that this is something of a mouthful, the formulation of the principle is beginning to look very complicated, which is, if not a reason for abandoning the task, at least a reason for pause.

What I propose, then, is that in our current limited state of understanding of the question of individuation, we should step back from the position of John of St Thomas (and Thomas Harper), thus leaving aside at present the role of dispositions in individuation, and return instead to the pure formula of St Thomas himself, namely that the *p/i* is matter designated by—which I interpret as *possessing*—indeterminate quantity. What this means, unfortunately, is putting on hold the vexed question of whether this inevitably involves a circularity in the individuation of substance and accident. Naturally one hopes that it does not, but the fact is that no one knows. Still we can, it is submitted, make headway with this formula alone, though we need to do some work. As a preliminary step, we simply must abandon the idea that quantity means, as it seems traditionally to have done, only spatial quantity. Hence the term *dimensions*, which the schoolmen often use, is far more suitable, because it allows *time* to play a role in individuation, time being just another dimension. For this I offer the following quotations of St Thomas in support:

> ... that which receives [the form] is matter, not understood anyhow, or in its generic signification ... but as bearing the nature of first subject; whereas its *determination* consists in its existing under fixed dimensions, which cause it to be demonstrable to sense in space *and time*.[17]

> There is something else, by which the nature of the individual is verified according to human cognition, viz. its determination to certain portions *of time* and space; because it is its property to be substantially existing here *and now*.

> ... For this reason, determined quantity *is said to be* the principle of individuation. Not that it in any way causes its subject, which is first substance; but it is the inseparable concomitant of the latter, and determines it in space *and time*.[18]

Quite clearly St Thomas is speaking in these passages of the epistemological questions concerning individuation, and it is well to remember that the question under discussion in this paper is not an epistemological but an ontological one.[19] Nevertheless, his readiness to admit time as a dimension or quantity along with space gives support to the idea that time can play a role in individuation. And the proposal to be outlined has it as one of the dimensive properties of matter by which matter individuates.[20]

4. How to Think of the Principle of Individuation by Designated Matter; and the Solution of Several Problems

My proposal is that we adopt as the principle of individuation—rather, as the proper formulation of that principle already enunciated by St Thomas—a proposal made but rejected by Kit Fine in his work on Aristotle's theory of individuation.[21] It is well known that Aristotle did not go so far as to formulate the idea of *designated* matter, but only of matter as such as individuating substance. This leaves it open whether he meant thin (prime) matter or thick (proximate) matter, and if the latter in what *way*, or by means of what *characteristics*, it individuated. And critics (often posing as supporters of Aristotle who sadly find the great man in a spot of bother) have had an enjoyable time poking holes in virtually everything the Philosopher says about individuation (and everything else). Fine, in particular, is impressed by the puzzle of Socrates and Callias: "Suppose that Socrates has at one time the same matter as Callias has at another time. Then their matter is the same; their form is the same; and since each of them is a compound of matter and form, they themselves are the same."[22]

I do not intend to enter into a detailed examination of Fine's ingenious thought about the supposed puzzle; suffice it to say that he canvasses, perhaps exhaustively, various options and appears to dispose of them all, making genuinely insightful points along the way. But what he has not successfully disposed of, I submit, is the solution he calls *Relative Composition*, whereby the time at which a substance is enmattered can individuate it. 'Can', because one needn't always appeal to the temporal dimension: if Socrates and Callias are in different places, then this property of their respective matters individuates them; if they are different sizes, then that also individuates them. But if, as we are encouraged by Fine to suppose, Callias undergoes an imaginary process whereby he slowly sheds his matter while eating Socrates for breakfast, taking on the matter of Socrates at exactly the same rate as he loses his own, and ending up consisting of all of Socrates' matter, as well as being exactly the same size as Socrates once was, and placing himself in exactly the same portion of space as Socrates once occupied—if this is all imagined, then what prevents Socrates from ever having been identical to Callias is that they never shared the same matter *at the same time*. Elsewhere I have argued that two substances of the same kind cannot be in the same place at the same time;[23] and the reason is precisely that it would be impossible in principle to say, on such a hypothesis, which matter belonged to which substance, and they would then not be individuated. Form is 'parcelled out' by matter in space and time, so if matter is shared (and by shared is of course meant *wholly* shared— substances can overlap) it makes no sense to speak of distinct parcels, i.e. individuals. Socrates and Callias might share their matter, and they might even do so in the same place; but it will not be at the same time.

Note that the reverse is not a possibility: they cannot share their matter at the same time but in different places; rather, they simply cannot share their matter at the same time. This follows from the asymmetry between time and space, but does not in the least make a difference to my claim that Relative Composition solves Fine's puzzle of Socrates and Callias.

Fine's objection to Relative Composition is that it makes the unifying role of form mysterious: "It cannot be that time is one of the elements that is unified. . . . Nor can it be that unification is relative to a time; for how can a time, as such, affect the manner whereby the form makes some given matter into one thing rather than another?"[24] Fine is correct on both counts. In particular, time does not affect the way form unifies. Rather, the way form unifies affects the temporal characteristics of a substance. As has already been suggested, it is through the exigency of form that matter receives the disposition to indeterminate quantity, where it can now be stated that we should understand indeterminate quantity as *whatever range of definite quantities, prescribed by the form itself, a substance happens to have.* Form unifies; matter receives; part of what it receives is a propensity to have the range of dimensions prescribed by the form, whether it be the range of dimensions appropriate to human beings, or snails, or lumps of marble. Further, *contra* Fine, there is nothing unduly 'selective' about Relative Composition: it is not as though the temporal index of a compound gives a certain portion of matter a privileged position as, say, the matter of Socrates. Why is Socrates made of this stuff rather than that? Because he is. That his stuff exists at one time rather than another is simply a by-product of the fact that he exists at all, and there is no objection I can see to regarding a thing's by-products as the way in which that thing is individuated, as long as the by-products flow *essentially* from the nature of the thing, as indeterminate temporal dimensions certainly do. There simply can be no substantial union of matter and form without matter in dimension.

Another case Fine proposes is that of an amoeba A_1 which divides[25] and whose descendants then fuse to form a distinct amoeba A_2 with the same matter and form as A_1. Now it might be tempting to say that this is a case of intermittent existence, so that $A_1 = A_2$ but where the amoeba did not exist during the interval in which the two fission products existed. Whether or not this is correct (and it would be a logically adequate response to Fine) the fact is that St Thomas does not appear to countenance the possibility of intermittent existence in the course of nature.[26] So again we can appeal to Relative Composition, and say that what numerically distinguishes A_1 from A_2 is that they do not have the same matter at the same time.

Again, Fine suggests the possibility of a Ship of Theseus scenario for amoebae: A_1 with matter M splits into a large and a small amoeba, surviving (let us suppose, plausibly) as the large one. It then fuses with a small amoeba, surviving as the fusion; and so on until the resulting amoeba A_2 possesses none of the original matter M, having shed a number of small amoebae which then fuse into an amoeba A_3 with all and only the matter M. Is $A_1 = A_2$ or is $A_1 = A_3$? Common matter and form suggests the latter, but a certain continuity of history suggests the former. As with the original Ship of Theseus puzzle, my response is that the original amoeba (or ship) goes out of existence at some time (though exactly when is another, and difficult, question) and that the descendants A_2 and A_3 are both numerically distinct from it. What about the fact that A_1 and A_3 share the same matter and form? Again, they do not do so at the same time.

But now we run up against an important problem for Relative Composition, which Fine recognizes. For does not Socrates himself have the same matter at different times? So how can the relativization of matter to time of existence be the principle of individuation? And again, can he not have different matter at different times (by variation)? So how can matter designated (inter alia) by temporal dimension be the p/i? It is at this point that we must return to the distinction between identity and individuality which I mentioned earlier. At the end of their discussion of John of St Thomas, Gracia and Kronen consider the objection to the thesis that matter possessing determinate quantity can be the p/i, an objection raised by St Thomas, Scotus, Suarez, and John of St Thomas himself, that it would entail the loss of a thing's individuality were it to vary in the determinate dimensions of its matter, as virtually every substance does. Gracia and Kronen reply that the objection is ineffective because it "confuses individuality with identity, failing to understand that the principle of one need not be the principle of the other, and therefore that, even if dimensions change, a different principle could ensure the continuity [i.e. diachronic identity] of the individual."[27] This point is, I submit, correct, though it must be qualified by saying that it does not follow that the p/i should indeed be determinately quantified matter after all; on that St Thomas is right. For the indeterminacy of dimensions, under the exigency of form, applies both modally, i.e. across possible worlds, and temporally. The point is that if Socrates, for instance, can be six feet tall in the actual world and six feet two inches in some possible world, what individuates him in any arbitrary world, i.e. what individuates him *simpliciter*, is whatever dimensions his matter happens to have in a given world, i.e. his matter under *indeterminate* dimensions. Since, as has been argued, it is temporal dimensionality which matters chiefly in individuation, given the shareability of spatial dimensions, what individuates Socrates (in any world) is whatever temporal index his matter happens to have (in that world).

The indeterminacy of dimensions also applies temporally, as was said. Within a given world, substances change their dimensions, their size, shape, and so on, and also the time at which their matter exists. Further, they can even (at least conceivably) change their entire matter without ceasing to exist. Why should so many schoolmen have been worried by this fact when considering individuation? After all, at any given time every substance has some matter, and that matter is simultaneously unshareable in its entirety with any other substance (or so I have claimed). So why be concerned about variation? Surely it must have something to do with the fact that the principle of individuation should not just capture what obtains at a slice or slices of the history of the universe, but also what happens during an *interval* or intervals in the history of the universe. To be sure, a candidate *p/i* is a non-starter if it cannot, at any given moment in the history of the universe, capture what it is, metaphysically, which distinguishes every substance existing at that moment from every other one existing at that moment; or what distinguishes what exists at one moment from what exists at some other moment. But one would have thought that another requirement was for it to be able to capture what it is, *during a given interval,* which distinguishes every substance persisting during that interval from every other substance persisting during that interval; and what distinguishes that which exists during one interval from that which exists at some other interval. Now, during an interval, a substance simply may not *have* determinate dimensions. So if we want to be able to say what it is that numerically distinguished, say, Churchill during 1940–45 from Stalin during 1947–50, or what distinguished Churchill from Roosevelt during the interval in which their lives overlapped, we cannot appeal to determinate dimensions but rather must speak of *ranges* of determinate dimensions; and this, both the modal and temporal variability of dimensions, is what St Thomas and others mean by *indeterminate* dimensions, which is why they often do so in the context of the phenomenon of variation. Naturally, when the moments or intervals being compared are the same, we cannot appeal to distinct temporal dimensions, but will have to appeal to spatial ones: Churchill and Roosevelt (rather, their matters) occupied distinct spatial ranges during the time their lives overlapped. Further, since a substance can change its matter over time, we cannot speak of a single parcel of matter designated by indeterminate dimensions as the *p/i*.

Fine proposes the idea of Plural Composition as another possible response to his puzzles, and I submit that we can adapt this to the question of individuation by saying that individuation is sometimes grounded in the several matters which a substance possesses over time; but since dimensionality is crucial, those matters must be indexed just as a single parcel of matter is indexed according to Relative Composition. And what we end up with, as Fine notes, is *Plural Relative Composition,* where (to adapt his proposal again), we take individuation throughout an interval as grounded in the series of temporally indexed matters which a substance possesses during that interval—its several matters, in order of appearance, during that interval. So, what distinguished Churchill during 1940–45 from Stalin during 1947–50 was their possession of distinct matters during distinct intervals. In fact, the approach in terms of Plural Relative Composition is almost certainly too strict, because it is clear that, whatever the changes of non-proximate matter in, say, a living body over time, the body itself remains numerically the same, and it is just about as clear that, on the Thomist (and general scholastic) view, what individuates a man is his proximate matter, which is his body; mutatis mutandis for other organisms and possibly even some inanimate objects to the extent that they are not mere lumps of matter. In which case, we can leave Plural Relative Composition to one side as a useful adjunct elaboration of our general *p/i,* and speak solely of Relative Composition, where the temporal relativization is either to a moment or an interval, as the case may be.

Despite all that has just been said, however, we are still no closer to being able to employ the *p/i* to specify what it is that grounds the identity of a given substance *over time.* The *p/i* must, as has been claimed, state in virtue of what a substance at a time or over time is distinguished from every other substance at every other time or over every other time.

The glaring exception to this, however, seems to be the substance itself. Can we say, in terms of the p/i, what it is that ensures that Churchill at a given moment in 1947, or over a given interval during 1947, is *not* distinguished numerically from Churchill at a given moment, or over a given interval, in 1960? It seems we cannot. All of the dimensions are different. By the p/i, then, they should be two distinct people; but they are not. So, it is argued, Gracia and Kronen are at least prima facie correct to distinguish the principle of individuation from the principle of diachronic identity, whatever it may be (which we cannot, of course, canvass here).[28] The p/i only applies on the assumption that we have a separate principle of diachronic identity, one which secures the persistence of a substance such as Churchill from one moment to the next. Assuming this, we can say that it is substance S's matter, under indeterminate dimensions, which individuates it. For any *given* moments t_1 and t_2, we must appeal to the principle of diachronic identity, rather than individuation, in order to state that whereby S at t_1 is the same as S at t_2. In other words, once given our individuals at a time (through actuation by substantial form) and over time (through a principle, no doubt form-invoking, which secures persistence), we can state how the principle of individuation applies for both synchronic and diachronic individuation. A certain amount of unpacking, then, is needed in order to have at least a plausible understanding of why John of St Thomas and so many other schoolmen speak of the need for individuation by indeterminate dimensions in contexts in which they also speak of variation over time. Variation does indeed require that the dimensionality of individuating matter be indeterminate (though of course determinate at any specific moment), but this does not imply that matter designated by indeterminate dimensions is just what secures substantial identity through variation in the first place.

5. Conclusion

I do not pretend to have given an incontestable interpretation of Thomistic thought on the principle of individuation. There are many more things that need to be said, and difficulties to be solved. When trying, as we should, to make of the philosophy of the School more than mere material for the museum of intellectual history, we are faced both with problems of exegesis and of evaluation. Sometimes it is the former problem which is greater, a result, among other things, of the sometimes alien vocabulary and thought patterns of the schoolmen. With work, however, we can and should try to make sense of them, and to use whatever tools have been made available to us by analytical philosophy to accomplish the task. Such a task is what has been attempted here, and if the theory I have outlined is at least arguable it can then serve as the basis for further investigation of one of philosophy's most difficult problems. If it is correct it can, I believe, solve a number of related problems raised in recent literature.[29] But that is a matter which will have to be addressed elsewhere.

Notes

1. See, for instance, the suggestive remarks by Joseph Owens in his "Thomas Aquinas," in Jorge J. E. Gracia, ed., *Individuation in Scholasticism, the Later Middle Ages and the Counter-Reformation, 1150–1650* (Albany: SUNY Press, 1994; hereafter Gracia), pp. 173–94, at p. 188. The School's other fate, on the Continent, was to be filtered through the Rationalists, Kant, the Idealists, and finally Brentano, Husserl, et al. to become what are now the various branches of Continental philosophy. While there is important material in the early phenomenologists, I do not believe that the School can or should be revived by doing philosophy the Continental way.

2. For the variety of views, see Gracia, a uniquely important collection for obtaining an overview of the question.

3. See, e.g., St Albert the Great (as expounded by J. M. G. Hackett, in Gracia, pp. 97–99, and references therein); St Thomas, *S. Theol.* q.11, a.3, *responsio*. See also Gracia, "Individuals as Instances," *Review of Metaphysics* 37 (1983), pp. 39–59.

4. E. J. Lowe, *Kinds of Being* (Oxford: Blackwell, 1989), p. 38. The left conjunct is included since our examination is confined to material individuals. It does not apply to immaterial substances such as God and the angels, which are identical with their own species. Note also that Lowe's formulation is non-modal—x has no instances other than itself—but I have changed this to a modal claim—x can have no instances other than itself—so as to capture better the essence of individuality and to forestall possible Platonist ripostes concerning uninstantiated universals.

5. D. Wiggins, *Sameness and Substance* (Oxford: Blackwell, 1980), passim, esp. ch. 1.

6. More precisely, *synchronically* identical: for reasons to be given, the p/i is not a principle of identity *over* time (diachronic identity).

7. Aristotle, *De Anima* II.i, 412a6–10. My translation is taken from Thomas Harper, S.J., *The Metaphysics of the School*, vol. 1 (London: Macmillan, 1879), from whose important work much of the present outline is derived (with modifications).

8. *Commentary on De Anima* (passage cited in n. 7), trans. Foster and Humphries (Notre Dame: Dumb Ox Books, 1994; reprint of 1951 Yale edition), s. 215, p. 73.

9. See Gracia, "Francis Suarez," in Gracia, pp. 475–510, and references therein; also Harper, vol. 1, proposition xlvi ff.

10. Owens admirably emphasizes the neglected role of form in individuation: see esp. sec. II of "Thomas Aquinas" in Gracia.

11. Following Harper, vol.1, prop. xlviii.

12. *S.Theol.* I, q.29, a.4: "Individuum autem est quod est in se indistinctum, ab aliis vero distinctum." Needless to say, 'indistinct' does not have its current meaning, but means 'having the character of an undivided unity'.

13. See Owens in Gracia, esp. pp. 182–83 and references, for St Thomas's espousal of this position. A cursory glance at the work of Thomists (e.g. John of St Thomas, and latterly Harper) shows that indeterminate quantity is accepted as the designation of individuating matter.

14. See, e.g., Harper, echoing John of St Thomas.

15. See further Wiggins, *Sameness and Substance* .

16. Harper, vol. 1, prop. xlviii.

17. Opusculum *De Natura Materiae et Dimensionibus Interminatis*, c.3; passage trans. Harper, p. 254; my emphasis in last line.

18. Opusculum *De Principio Individuationis*; passage trans. Harper; my emphasis.

19. There is no question but that, *epistemologically* speaking, accidents play a crucial role in individuation.

20. Since the temporal dimension is rarely mentioned by the schoolmen in connection with individuation, the objections raised in my general survey to the idea of the *p/i* being matter under determinate quantity were implicitly restricted to spatial quantity, but it can be readily seen how they apply to determinate temporal quantity: a change in determinate temporal quantity would change the individual; and determinate temporal quantity is also accidental, which raises the circularity problem again.

21. Fine, "A Puzzle concerning Matter and Form," in T. Scaltsas, D. Charles, and M. L. Gill, eds., *Unity, Identity, and Explanation in Aristotle's Metaphysics* (Oxford: Clarendon Press, 1994), pp. 13–40, at p. 32ff.

22. Ibid., p. 14.

23. D. S. Oderberg, "Coincidence under a Sortal," *Philosophical Review* 105 (1996), pp. 145–71. I did not consider whether substances of different kinds can coincide in space and time, but the general considerations advanced here lend obvious support to the idea that they cannot. Which does not mean

distinct *material objects* cannot coincide; only that if they did, at least one of them would not be a substance.

24. Fine, "A Puzzle," p. 34.

25. We should say that it *fises*, by analogy with *fusion/to fuse*.

26. See C. Hughes, "Aquinas on Continuity and Identity," *Medieval Philosophy and Theology* 6 (1997), pp. 93–108, at pp. 98–9. Of course a miraculous intervention could reinstate a corrupted substance, but even then its essential principles (matter and form) would have to have survived the period of non-existence, which they do in the case of man.

27. Gracia and Kronen, "John of St Thomas," in Gracia, pp. 511–33, at p. 526.

28. In *The Metaphysics of Identity Over Time* (New York: St Martin's Press, 1993), I at least say what the principle of diachronic identity could *not* be.

29. I have in mind the interesting work of Christopher Hughes on identity and individuation in St Thomas: see his "Matter and Individuation in Aquinas," *History of Philosophy Quarterly* 13 (1996): pp. 1–16; and "Aquinas on Continuity and Identity," cited above.

CHAPTER NINE

Aquinas on God's Knowledge of Future Contingents

Christopher Hughes

I

Thomas Aquinas held that there are future contingent events and states of affairs. If there were not future contingents, he believed, none of our future acts would be free, or deserving of punishment or reward, and deliberation would be needless.[1] Aquinas also believed that God knows future contingents. By his lights, to recognize the existence of future contingents, but to deny that God knows them, would be to deny God's omniscience and to place unacceptable limitations on his providential government of human affairs.[2]

Although Aquinas thought that God's knowledge of future contingents was compatible with their contingency, he did not think that this compatibility was immediately obvious. He was familiar with, and took very seriously, a variety of arguments purporting to show the incompatibility of God's knowledge with the contingency of its object.

In what follows, I shall consider two such arguments, together with Aquinas's responses to them. Aquinas's response to the first argument is straightforward, and I shall accordingly discuss it only briefly. His response to the second argument is much more detailed, but also much more obscure. I shall attempt to determine how that response should be understood, and raise some questions about its adequacy.

II

At *Summa Contra Gentiles,* I, 63, Aquinas sets out the following argument for the impossibility of God's knowing future contingents:

> Knowledge that is certain is knowledge that can not be deceived. But all knowledge of what is contingent can be deceived, when the contingent is future, since the opposite of what is held by knowledge can be known; for, if the opposite could not happen, it would be necessary. So we cannot have knowledge of future contingents, but only a certain conjectural estimation. But it must be supposed that all of God's knowledge is certain and infallible. . . . And, because of His immutability, it is impossible for God to begin to know something. From all this it seems to follow that God does not know future contingents.

The argument has the following structure: since future contingents are not subject to certain knowledge when they are future, and all of God's knowledge is certain, God cannot know future contingents when they are future. Nor can he know them at any other time, lest his knowledge be mutable. So God does not (ever) have knowledge of future contingents.

Aquinas responds to this argument as follows:

> The contingent is opposed to the certainty of knowledge only insofar as it is future, not insofar as it is present. For when the contingent is future, it can not-be. Thus the knowledge of one who conjectures that it will be, can be mistaken. . . . But insofar as the contingent is present, at that time it can not not-be. It can not-be in the future, but this affects the contingent not insofar as it is present, but insofar as it is future. Thus nothing is lost to the certainty of sense when someone sees a man running, even though this judgment is contingent. All knowledge, then, that bears on something contingent as present can be certain. But the vision of the divine intellect from all eternity is directed to each of the things that takes place in the course of time, insofar as it is present. It seems, then, that nothing stands in the way of God's having from all eternity knowledge of future contingents. (*Summa Contra Gentiles,* I, 67)

Here Aquinas presupposes the Boethian view that God and his knowledge are not sempiternal (that is, omnitemporal), but timeless. Because only changeable things exist in time, and eternity is entirely unchangeable, eternity does not "overlap with" or include time, any more than the center of a circle overlaps with or includes its circumference (cf. *SCG*, I, 66). Nevertheless, any event happening at any time is "present to" eternity, even if it is past or future with respect to other times. (In terms of Aquinas's geometrical analogy: any point on the circumference is at the same distance from the center of the circle, even if different pairs of points on the circumference are at different distances from each other.) Thus God sees, as present, any event that takes place in the whole course of time.[3]

The gist of Aquinas's response could be put this way:

Since *being a future contingent event* and *being an event whose occurrence is (then) subject to certain and infallible knowledge* are incompatible properties, nothing can have both of these properties at the same time. But nothing prevents an event from having the first of these properties at one time (when the event is future), and having the second at another time (when the event is present). Similarly, nothing prevents an event from having the first property at one time, and the second at the "un-time" that is God's eternity. So there are (now) future contingents, and God has certain and infallible knowledge of them—not now (when they are future), but in eternity ("when" they are eternally present).

Aquinas's response, like the argument itself, is very clear. It also seems successful, at least in a limited sense. I don't mean to suggest that Aquinas has demonstrated that God does, or even could, know future contingents. Nor do I mean to suggest that Aquinas has shown that the argument under consideration could not be turned into a cogent argument against (the possibility of) God's knowing future contingents. Perhaps the argument could be supplemented by considerations establishing that if God has knowledge of future contingents, he must have knowledge of future contingents *as* future. If it could, the resulting argument would, I take it, be a cogent argument against the possibility of God's knowing future contingents. Be that as it may, I think Aquinas succeeds in showing that the argument at issue, as it stands, is incogent.

III

At *Summa Theologiae*, Ia, 14, 13, and *De Veritate*, 2, 12, Aquinas devotes a great deal of attention to the following argument against God's knowledge of future contingents:

> If a true conditional proposition has an absolutely necessary antecedent, it has an absolutely necessary consequent. The conditional, *If God knew this will be, it will be*, is true. Moreover, its antecedent is absolutely necessary, since it is eternal, and concerns the past.[4] So its consequent is absolutely necessary. Thus whatever God knows is absolutely necessary, and God's knowledge is never of contingent things.

Since *God knew that this will be* entails *This will be*, it looks as though both of these propositions are absolutely necessary, or neither one is: whatever exactly absolute necessity consists in, it will presumably be closed under entailment. We might accordingly expect Aquinas to respond to the above argument by flatly denying that statements of the form *God knew that this will be* are (in every case) absolutely necessary.

In fact, Aquinas addresses the argument in a very different way. At both *De Veritate*, 2, 12, ad 7um, and *Summa Theologiae*, Ia, 14, 13, ad 2um, he notes that, for a variety of reasons, some have denied the necessity of *God knew that this will be*. Some have supposed that that proposition was contingent, on the grounds that it imports a relation to the future. This is no good, Aquinas says, because whatever has had a certain relation to the future, (now) must have had it. Some have supposed it was contingent, on the grounds that it is a contingent compound of the necessary and the contingent (inasmuch as God's knowledge is necessary, but its object is contingent). This again is no good, Aquinas argues: the contingency of *Peter is reading* does not entail the contingency of *God knows that Peter is reading*, any more than the contingency of *Peter is running* entails the contingency of *I think Peter is running* (*DV*, 2, 12, ad 7um; see also *ST*, Ia, 14, 13, ad 2um).[5]

Aquinas appears to conclude that the antecedent of the conditional, *If God knew this will be, it will be*, is absolutely necessary (as he puts it at *ST*, Ia, 14, 13, ad 2um) or simply necessary (as he puts it at *DV*, 2, 12, ad 7um).[6]

If we cannot block the argument of objection 2 by denying the absolute necessity of the conditional, *If God knew this will be, it will be*, how can we block it? Aquinas offers his own response to that argument, and concludes his discussion of objection 2, as follows:

> When there is in the antecedent something pertaining to an act of the soul, the consequent must be understood, not as it is in itself, but as it is in the soul, since the being of a thing in itself is different from the being of a thing in the soul. For instance, if I say, *If the soul understands something, it is immaterial*, it must be understood that that thing is immaterial as it is in the understanding, but not as it is in itself. Similarly, if I say, *If God knew something, it will be*, the consequent must be understood as it is subject to divine knowledge, that is, as it is in its presentiality. Understood that way, it is necessary, like its antecedent: for everything which is, necessarily is, when it is, as Aristotle says in *Peri Hermaneias* I.

Because Aquinas's response is compressed, and does not explicitly contradict anything said in objection 2, it is not immediately clear just how the response is meant to address the objection. I think it works like this: most of objection 2 is devoted to trying to establish that if God knew that this will be, that it will be is absolutely necessary. From this claim the inference is drawn that God does not know future contingents. Aquinas's strategy, I think, is to concede that if God knew that something will be, its being so, *considered in a certain way*, is necessary, but to deny that if God knew that something will be, its being so (considered in itself) is absolutely necessary. Aquinas does not make this denial explicitly in the passage just cited, but I think we are meant to infer it from what he does say explicitly, and the nature of the objection he is answering.

As Aquinas sees it,

(1) If the soul understands a thing, that thing is immaterial.

means

(1a) If the soul understands a thing, that thing, as it is in the soul, is immaterial.

and not

(1b) If the soul understands a thing, that thing, as it is in itself, is immaterial.

Thus, for Aquinas (1a) can be (and is) true, in virtue of the truth of (1a), even if (1b) is false (because, say, the thing understood is a stone).
Similarly, for Aquinas,

(2) If God knew that this will be, its being so is necessary.

means

(2a) If God knew that this will be, its being so, as it is known by God, is necessary.

and not

(2b) If God knew that this will be, its being so, as it is in itself, is necessary.

So again (2) will be true if (2a) is true, even if (2b) is false. And, Aquinas holds, (2a) is true. Since this thing's being so, as (or "when") it is known by God, is present, and whatever is present is (then) necessary, this thing's being so, as it is known by God, is necessary. But, Aquinas thinks, this provides no reason to suppose that this thing's being so *as it is in itself* is necessary. Hence it provides no reason to suppose that this thing's being so is absolutely or simply necessary (that is, necessary as it is in itself, as opposed to necessary as known by God).

In this context it is interesting to look at the contrast Aquinas goes on to draw (in his response to the next objection) between our knowledge of future contingents, and God's. For Aquinas,

(3) If we know that something will be, its being so is necessary.

means

(3a) If we know that something will be, its being so, as it is known by us, is necessary.

and not

(3b) If we know that something will be, its being so, as it is in itself, is necessary.

Nevertheless, Aquinas thinks that (3b), like (3a), is true: for what is known by us must be necessary, even as it is in itself.[7] It is otherwise with God: what is known by God must be necessary as it is subject to God's knowledge, but need not be absolutely necessary.[8] Here Aquinas explicitly denies what (I take it) he is implicitly denying in his response to objection 2—that what God knows is necessary, not just as it is subject to God's knowledge, but as it is simply or absolutely, as it is in itself.

Aquinas's response to objection 2, understood in the way I have suggested, is clearly relevant to that objection. At the same time, it does not seem to engage with it in a fully satisfactory way. Objection 2 rests on the following claims: (a) facts about what God knew are always absolutely necessary, and (b) absolute necessity is closed under entailment. If (a) and (b) are conceded, there is surely no hope of denying the absolute necessity of whatever God knows. But Aquinas's rebuttal of objection 2 is mute on which of these two claims should be rejected. Which one would he deny?

There is some evidence that Aquinas accepts (a) and denies (b). As we have seen, in his discussion of other attempted rebuttals of objection 2, he appears to say that the antecedent, *God knew that this will be* is absolutely necessary (see note 6). And, as we have also seen, he appears to say at *De Veritate*, 2, 12, ad 7um, that *God knows that Peter is reading* can be necessary, even if *Peter is reading* is not (see note 5). True, Aquinas does not say explicitly in that context that the necessity under discussion is absolute; but it is hard to see why absolute necessity should be less fit than any other kind not to be closed under entailment.

We need to be careful here. In answering objection 2, Aquinas never says explicitly that *God knew that this will be* is necessary as subject to God's knowledge, but not necessary absolutely. On the other hand, neither does he say explicitly that *This will be* is necessary as subject to God's knowledge, but not necessary absolutely. He concludes his response by saying that both *God knew that this will be* and *This will be* are necessary as subject to God's knowledge; perhaps he means us to conclude that neither proposition is necessary absolutely.

Perhaps. But although—as we have seen—Aquinas goes on in his response to objection 3 to explicitly deny that what God knows is (in every case) absolutely necessary, he does not deny there that God's knowing it is (in every case) absolutely necessary. Nor does he explicitly deny it at *De Veritate*, 2, 12, or *Summa Contra Gentiles*, I, 67, or in various other places where one might expect him to deny it, if he disbelieved it.[9] As far as I know, the closest he comes to an explicit denial is at *De Veritate*, 2, 13, ad 5um, where he says that, as long as God's knowledge of vision is at issue, it is true (*in sensu diviso*, though not *in sensu composito*) that God could know what he does not know (*potest scire quod nescit*).

Even if Aquinas does not explicitly deny that (all) the facts about what God knew are absolutely necessary, it seems clear that he should deny it, given that he wants to defend God's knowledge of future contingents against objection 2. The only other way to block that objection is to insist that absolute necessity is not closed under entailment. But, as Aristotle says,[10] (any kind of) necessity is closed under entailment. *P* is necessarily true if and only if all the possible worlds of a certain kind are worlds in which *P* is true (*P*-worlds, for short). (If the necessity in question is unrestricted, the modifier "of a certain kind" may be dropped.) *P* entails *Q* only if every *P*-world is a *Q*-world. So if *P* is necessary, and *P* entails *Q*, then all the worlds of a certain kind are *P*-worlds, and all *P*-worlds are *Q*-worlds. In that case all the worlds of that kind are *Q*-worlds, and *Q* is necessarily true.

But does Aquinas have good reasons to suppose that *God knew that this will be* can be true, without being absolutely necessary? That will obviously depend on what absolute necessity consists in—a matter not addressed in either objection 2 or Aquinas's response to it.

Since Aquinas takes "simply necessary" and "absolutely necessary" to be equivalent, it is natural to suppose that "absolutely necessary" means "necessary *sans phrase*" (as opposed, say, to necessary on some condition, or necessary "according to the mode of the knower," or necessary as subject to God's knowledge). In support of this, we may note that while objection 2 starts from the premiss that *God knew that this will be* is absolutely necessary, Aquinas begins his response to that objection by considering whether that proposition is contingent or necessary. This would be odd, if "absolutely necessary" meant something more than "necessary," and not at all odd, if it did not.

If "absolutely necessary" just means "necessary," how should the latter be understood? In different contexts, Aquinas understands necessity in different ways. When for example he argues at *ST,* Ia, 19, 3 that God wills his own goodness of (absolute) necessity, but does not will things other than himself of (absolute) necessity, the necessity in question appears to be what we would call metaphysical necessity (truth at all times in all possible worlds).[11] Presumably, though, this is not the sort of necessity at issue in objection 2 and Aquinas's response to it. After all, why should anyone suppose that, just because a proposition is about the past, it is true at all times in all possible worlds? If, as is assumed in objection 2, pastness is a guarantee of necessity, then necessity cannot be metaphysical necessity.

In fact, in the *De Veritate* article that parallels *Summa Theologiae,* Ia, 14, 13, Aquinas distinguishes the necessary from the contingent in a way that makes it clear that necessity should not be understood (there) as metaphysical necessity:

> The necessary can not be prevented before it comes about, inasmuch as its causes are immutably ordered to its occurrence.... The contingent can be prevented before it comes into being, because it does not exist save in its causes, which may be impeded from having their effect. (*DV,* 2, 12, *responsio*)

In a similar vein, he writes:

> The contingent differs from the necessary in the way it exists in its cause. The contingent is in its cause in such a way that it can both be and not-be from it; the necessary can not but be from its cause. (*SCG,* I, 67)

In each of these passages, the contingent and the necessary are thought of as partitioning the set of (actually occurring) caused events. For Aquinas, all caused events are metaphysically contingent. So necessity, as Aquinas understands it at *Summa Contra Gentiles,* I, 67, and *De Veritate,* 2, 12, and—presumably—*Summa Theologiae,* I, 14, 13, is not metaphysical necessity, but something more like predeterminedness: an event is necessary if its occurrence is determined or settled by its causes, before it occurs.

We might accordingly suppose that absolute necessity, as it figures in objection 2, and Aquinas's response to objection 2, is predeterminedness. The drawback of this interpretation is that it would again turn the argument of objection 2 into an obviously bad one. Why should anyone suppose that being a past event is a sufficient condition for being an event whose occurrence was predetermined by its causes?

Suppose on the other hand that an event is necessary if its occurrence is guaranteed either by its (present or past) causes, or by the actual history of the world (up to the present). And suppose that a statement is necessarily true if (the occurrence of) a necessary event is its truth-maker. Necessity so construed will be a property of all (actually occurring) past and present events, and there won't be a puzzle about what underwrites the inference in objection 2 from the pastness of God's knowledge to its necessity.

Is there a sense of "necessary" in which an event may be said to be necessary, simply because it is occurring, or has occurred? It seems so. Suppose that I plan to go to Mazzorbo, though it is not yet settled that I shall be able to. In those circumstances, I could (truly) say that the trip to Mazzorbo I have been planning to take might not happen. Once, however, I actually take the trip, I can no longer (truly) say of that trip that it might not happen, although I can of course (truly) say that it might not *have* happened. The non-occurrence of that event is no longer possible, although it remains true that its non-occurrence *was* once possible. Simply by happening, the event has become necessary—in the sense that its non-occurrence is impossible.

This sort of necessity, which often goes by the name of inevitability, is not unfamiliar to Aquinas. It is in fact just the sort of necessity he appeals to at *Summa Contra Gentiles,* I, 67 and elsewhere, in explaining why the same event that cannot be known *certitudinaliter* when it is a future contingent, may be so known when it is present. When the event is future and contingent, Aquinas says, it can both be and not-be; when it is actually occurring (and, presumably, when it has actually occurred), it can no longer not-be.

If the necessity ascribed to the past in objection 2 is inevitability, does this mean that Aquinas would concede to that objection that the past and present are absolutely necessary? It seems not. Although Aquinas does not flatly deny that the past and present have a kind of necessity, he appears to think that that necessity is not absolute, but *ex suppositione:*

> It is manifestly true that everything which is must be when it is, and that everything which is not, must not be at the time when it is not: and this is not absolute necessity, but necessity *ex suppositione.* Whence it cannot be said simply and absolutely that everything which is, necessarily is, and that everything which is not, necessarily is not. It is one thing to say that every being, when it is, is necessarily, and another to say that every being simply is necessarily. In the first case, necessity *ex suppositione* is signified; in the second, absolute necessity. (*In Peri Hermaneias, Lectio* 15, n. 200)

Whatever is, must be, when it is. So if I see Socrates running, both my seeing him and his running are necessary when they "are"—that is, when they occur.[12] Even so, if I see Socrates running, or sitting, his running or sitting is not necessary, but contingent.[13]

This is puzzling. The following argument is clearly valid:

Socrates heats up when he runs.
Socrates is running.
So, Socrates is heating up.

Pari ratione, one should think, so is this one:

Socrates' running is necessary when it occurs.
Socrates' running is occurring.
So *Socrates' running* is necessary.

If Socrates heats up when he runs, and he is running, then Socrates is heating up—absolutely, *simpliciter*, and not just *ex suppositione*. Similarly, it would seem, if Socrates' running is necessary when it happens, and it is happening, it is necessary absolutely, *simpliciter*, and not just *ex suppositione*. It may not have always *been* necessary *simpliciter*—just as Socrates may not have always been heating up—but it *is* necessary *simpliciter*. In short: if, as Aquinas seems to grant, everything that happens, is necessary when it happens, it seems to follow that everything happening is necessary *simpliciter*, so that the present—and, presumably, the past—are necessary absolutely, and not just *ex suppositione*.

Perhaps, though, this objection to Aquinas rests on a misunderstanding of Aquinas's views on the necessity of the present. As Aquinas often notes, a statement such as

(4) If *P,* then necessarily *Q.*

is ambiguous. It could be construed either as meaning

(4a) Necessarily: if *P,* then *Q.*

or as meaning

(4b) If *P,* it is a necessary truth that *Q.*

Whether or not we may deduce the necessity of Q from the truth of (4) and the truth of P depends on whether (4) is construed as (4a) or (4b).
Similarly, a statement such as

(5) When P, necessarily P.

could be construed either as meaning

(5A) Necessarily: when P, P.

or as meaning

(5B) When P, it is a necessary truth that P.

Again, whether or not we may deduce the necessity of P from the truth of (5) and the truth of P depends on whether (5) is construed as (5a) or (5b).
To reiterate: Aquinas tells us that

> It is manifestly true that everything which is, must be when it is, and everything which is not, must not be at the time when it is not; and this is not absolute necessity, but necessity *ex suppositione*.

The point of what follows the semi-colon may be that what precedes it—*viz.*, everything which is, must be, when it is—should be understood along the lines of (5A), and not along the lines of (5B). When Socrates is sitting, he is necessarily sitting. But from this, together with the claim that Socrates is sitting, we may not infer the necessity of Socrates' sitting. To do so would be fallaciously to infer the necessity of P from the truth of P, and the necessity of *When P, P*. So Socrates' sitting is contingent, and not necessary, even when it is present—as long as necessary means "absolutely necessary," rather than necessary *ex suppositione*, or conditionally necessary. To say that Socrates' sitting is necessary on the supposition or on the condition that he is sitting (or that I see him sitting) is just to say that necessarily: he is sitting when (or if) he is sitting (or, when (or if) I see him sitting).[14]
Suppose that all this is an adequate account of how Aquinas thinks the Aristotelian dictum "What is, necessarily is, when it is" should be understood. Then Aquinas is offering a profoundly deflationary account of the necessity of the present—one on which the fact that the

present is (after a fashion) necessary tells us nothing interesting about the present as such. Present events necessarily happen, on the supposition that they happen—but the same could be said, not just for past events, but also for future ones. The necessity of the present (together with the necessity of the past) collapses into the necessity of the law of non-contradiction.

If Aquinas does take a thoroughly deflationary view of the necessity of the past and present, that would certainly afford him a way of blocking objection 2. If neither the past, nor for that matter the eternal present, is as such absolutely necessary, then the argument of objection 2 falls at the first hurdle. At the same time, I think that there are good philosophical reasons, and good *Thomistic* reasons, to doubt that objection 2 can be satisfactorily met in this way.

To start with, as I have already suggested, past and present events appear to have a kind of (unconditional) necessity that (at least some) future events lack. If I went to Mazzorbo yesterday, my not going there yesterday is now impossible (no longer possible). By contrast, it does not seem true that if I will go to Mazzorbo tommorow, my not going there tomorrow is now impossible. (It is one thing to suppose that I will go to Mazzorbo tomorrow, and another to suppose I am bound to go to Mazzorbo tomorrow).

Moreover, we have seen that, for Aquinas, the same event that is not subject to certain knowledge when it is future contingent, is subject to certain knowledge when it is present. This is so, for Aquinas, because the same event that can both be and not-be, when it is future, can only be, when it is present. This explanation appears to presuppose that the present has a kind of unconditional or absolute necessity that the future lacks. If all it means to say that a presently occurring event can not but be, is that it cannot but happen, on the supposition that it happens— in other words, that necessarily, it happens (now) if it happens (now)— then the fact that a presently occurring event could not but be, could not explain that event's (current) knowability. To put the point another way, Aquinas wants to say that an initially future contingent event goes from being unknowable (before it occurs) to being knowable (when it occurs), because, in moving from the future to the present, it goes from being non-necessary to being necessary. This could not be true, if the only sort of necessity that presently occurring events had, was the conditional or *ex suppositione* necessity that does not discriminate between present and future events.

To recapitulate: in his response to objection 2, Aquinas does not explicitly deny that true statements of the form, *God knew this will be,* are always absolutely necessary. Nevertheless—I have argued—any viable answer to objection 2 will involve the denial of that claim. Someone might deny that claim on the grounds that, although the past, temporal present, and for that matter the eternal present are all conditionally necessary, neither the past, nor the temporal present, nor the eternal present, as such, is absolutely necessary. Indeed, some of Aquinas's remarks suggest that he held this kind of radically non-neces-sitarian view of the past and present. Still, I have tried to show, this kind of non-necessitarianism is not only philosophically problematic but also at variance with Aquinas's explanation of why contingents that are unknowable when they are future become knowable when they are present.

There is, however, another reason one might have for denying that truths of the form *God knew that this will be* are always absolutely nec-essary. Someone might concede that the past and temporal present are, as such, absolutely necessary (where, again, absolute necessity is inevitability, and not metaphysical necessity). Still, it might be said, this has no implications one way or the other for the absolute necessity of *God knew that this will be.* Grammatical appearances to the contrary, *God knew this will be* is not (genuinely) about the past or the tempo-ral present: it is about the eternal present, and the future. *God knew this will be* can accordingly be true, without being (absolutely) necessary, inasmuch as neither the future, nor the eternal present, is, as such, abso-lutely necessary.

This is, up to a point, not unlike what Aquinas says. As he sees it, the eternal present is not, as such, absolutely necessary. Some eter-nally present events or states of affairs—such as God's wiling his own goodness—are absolutely necessary (metaphysically necessary, and *a fortiori* inevitable). Other eternal events or states of affairs are not. It is true, in one sense, that everything eternal is necessary; but the necessity in question is *ex suppositione,* rather than unconditional or absolute.[15]

In another way, though, the response to objection 2 I have just sketched is quite unlike Aquinas's. My response concedes that every-thing happening now is unconditionally necessary, and denies that the same can be said of everything happening eternally-now. Aquinas appears to deny that everything happening now is unconditionally nec-essary, just as he denies that everything happening eternally-now is unconditionally necessary. In other words, while Aquinas's response appears to assimilate the eternal present to the temporal present, as far as its unconditional necessity is concerned, the alternative response distinguishes the eternal present and the temporal present on that score.

In sum, the response to objection 2 I have offered Aquinas is not Aquinas's own, as I understand it. Nor does it simply go beyond Aquinas's own response; it appears to conflict with it in important respects. Nevertheless, I think it is in certain respects more promising than Aquinas's own response, insofar as I understand the latter. It has the advantage of (clearly) allowing that the past and present have a kind of necessity the future lacks. Moreover, it is consonant with Aquinas's (Boethian) account of God's knowledge of future contingents. Finally, (apparently) unlike Aquinas's own response, it is clearly consonant with Aquinas's (Boethian) account of why future contingents are unknowable as future, but knowable as present.

Notes

A version of this paper was read to a conference on medieval logic and metaphysics at the University of St Andrews. Many thanks to the participants, and especially to John Marenbon, Stephen Read, and Eleonore Stump. Also thanks to Tony Dale, John Haldane, and Martin Stone.

1. See *De Veritate*, 2, 12, *responsio:* "Alii dixerunt quod Deus omnium futurorum scientiam habet, sed cuncta ex necessitate eveniunt. . . . Sed hoc esse etiam non potest, quia secundum hoc periret liberum arbitrium, nec esset necessarium consilium quaerere; iniustum esset etiam poenas vel praemia pro meritis reddere, ex quo cuncta aguntur."

2. See *Summa Theologiae*, Ia, 14, 13, *responsio* for the first point, and *De Veritate*, 2, 12, *responsio* for the second.

3. See again *SCG*, I, 66: "Quicquid . . . per totum decursum temporis agitur, divinus intellectus in tota sua aeternitate intuetur quasi praesens."

4. At *ST,* Ia, 14, 13, obj. 2, both of these considerations are advanced in support of the absolute necessity of *God knew that this will be;* at *DV*, 2, 12, obj. 7, only the latter one is.

5. "Veritas propositionis non variatur per necessitatem et contigentiam, ex eo quod materialiter in locutione ponitur, sed solum ex principali compositione in qua fundatur veritas propositionis, unde eadem ratio necessitatis et contingentiae est in utraque istarum: *Ego cogito hominem esse animal,* et *Ego cogito Petrum currere.* Et ideo, cum actus principalis qui significatur in hoc

antecedente, *Deus scit Petrum legere* sit necessarius, quantumcumque illud quod materialiter ponitur sit contingens, ex hoc non impeditur quin antecedens praedictum sit necessarium" (*DV*, 2, 12, ad 7um).

Aquinas's argument here is perplexing. Granting that the contingency of Q is compatible with the necessity of *I think that Q*, it is hard to see how the contingency of Q could be compatible with the necessity of *God knows that Q*, since *God knows that Q*, unlike *I think that Q*, entails Q, and only contingent propositions entail contingent propositions.

6. Aquinas seems to use *necessarium absolute* and *necessarium simpliciter* more or less interchangeably: see *DV*, 2, 12, ad 7um, and also *Quodlibetum* 11, q. 3, a. un., ad 2um.

7. "Illud quod scitur a nobis oportet esse necessarium etiam secundum quod in se est" (*ST*, Ia, 14, 13, ad 3um).

8. "Ea quae sunt scita a Deo, oportet esse necessaria secundum modum quo subsunt divine scientiae . . . non autem absolute" (ibid.).

9. At *ST*, Ia, 19, 8, Aquinas appears to say that whenever God knows something, his knowing it is (absolutely) necessary:

> God's knowledge bears a necessary relation to what is known, while God's will does not have such a relation to what is willed. This is because knowledge is related to things as they are in the knower, but will is related to things as they are in themselves. . . . For this reason, God knows necessarily whatever He knows, but does not will necessarily whatever He wills (*ST*, Ia, 19, 8, ad 6um).

When Aquinas says here that God knows necessarily whatever he knows, he cannot mean simply that necessarily, whatever God knows, he knows; for it is equally true that necessarily, whatever God wills, he wills. Moreover, the *responsio* makes it clear that the sort of necessity under discussion is absolute necessity, in at least as strong a sense of absolute necessity as the one in play at *ST*, Ia, 14, 13, and *DV*, 2, 12. So it might look as though Aquinas is saying here that whenever God knows that Q, his knowing that Q is absolutely necessary. In fact, though, I don't think he is making that claim, because I don't think he has in mind here God's knowledge of truths. I think he is saying instead that if it is true that God has knowledge of a possible individual or states of affairs (as possible, as subject to his power), it is absolutely necessary that he has knowledge of that possible individual or state of affairs (as possible, as subject to his power).

10. See *ST*, Ia, 14, 13, obj. 2: "Ex principiis autem necessariis non sequitur conclusio nisi necessaria, ut *Posterior*. I, 17."

11. See the *responsio* of that article, where Aquinas gives *man is an animal* and *a number is odd or even* as examples of (absolutely) necessary propositions, and *Socrates is sitting* as an example of a non-necessary proposition.

12. See *DV*, 2, 12, ad 7um: "Si ergo video Socratem currere, Socrates currit. . . . Utrumque est necessarium dum est."

13. "Visus meus non fallitur dum video Petrum sedere, quamvis hoc sit contingens" (*DV*, 2, 12, ad 2um).

14. See *ST*, Ia, 19, 3, *responsio:* "Socratem sedere . . . non est necessarium absolute, sed potest dici necessarium ex suppositione; supposito enim quod sedeat, necesse est eum sedere, dum sedet."

15. See *SCG*, I, 83: "Omne aeternum est necessarium. . . . Deum autem velle aliquid causatum esse est aeternum. . . . Est ergo necessarium. Sed non absolute consideratum. . . . Ergo est necessarium ex suppositione."

| CHAPTER TEN |

Ontology and the Art
of the Possible

Gerard J. Hughes, S.J.

Introduction

In this essay I intend to explore the twin concepts of necessity and possibility, as they appear in contemporary analytic philosophy, and as
they appear in the broadly Aristotelian tradition of which Aquinas is
one representative. I shall begin by giving my reasons for believing that
the recent approaches are in several ways unsatisfactory; they do not
solve all the problems which are posed even in their own terms; and
they are in a more general way unilluminating. In contrast, I believe
that there are at least some strands in the more traditional approach
which can provide a useful supplement and corrective to some of the
contemporary discussion.

In particular, I shall suggest that the ontology implicit in at least
some of the traditional views is an essential ingredient in any satisfactory treatment of possibility, and is at least an improvement on the
more strictly logical approach typical of recent discussion. On the other
hand, I shall also argue that the approach I favour, rather than facili-
tating an account of which states of affairs are possible, will lead to a
more agnostic assessment of what can and cannot be done.

I. The Logic of Existence

Uncontroversially, comparatively trivially, and quite ambiguously, what is possible is what can be, what is necessary is what must be, and what is impossible cannot be. As for the trivialities: the statement that what is possible is what can be, and so on, is trivial provided that one reads 'can' simply as an equivalent of 'is possible.' But of course, so understood, the claim is quite unilluminating. What is required if any light is to be thrown on these matters is some account of 'can' or 'is possible' which is at least not so narrowly circular, and which is in some sense genuinely explanatory.

The ambiguities have not, of course, escaped the attention of contemporary logicians. It is customary to distinguish between various uses of 'is', to express identity, predication, existence, and truth. To read the texts of Aristotle, or Aquinas, with these distinctions in mind, is to see at once that the correct interpretation of those texts is often far from clear; and that is surely progress. But the apparent clarity of contemporary logical systems itself disappears when questions are raised about their various possible interpretations. I shall be arguing in this essay that sometimes contemporary philosophers are tempted to suppose that properly metaphysical problems can be instantly solved by a simple invocation of the techniques of logic. It seems to me that they cannot.

The very term 'existential quantifier' used to describe '$(\exists x)$' is potentially misleading. Consider the simple sentence '$(\exists x)\emptyset x$' as it is customarily read: 'There is an x such that that x is $\emptyset$.' The first 'is' in this reading is often taken as 'exists'; and in Quine's dictum that 'to be is to be the value of a bound variable', the first 'to be' is usually interpreted in an existential sense. Hence the debate between Platonists and their opponents, or between nominalists and their opponents, is at least partially characterised in terms of the kinds of things over which they are willing to quantify. Platonists have no qualms about extending the domain of x to include properties, since they are prepared to say that properties (and not just property-instances) exist; others insist that x should range only over material individuals; and so on. A person's ontology, it is sometimes said, can be deduced from their quantificational practice. Practice, though, varies considerably. Quantification over such things as moments of time, sentences, propositions, persons, and actions is common, without it always being clear that those who quantify in this way are committed to the existence of all of these items. Nonetheless, since plainly '($\exists x$)' has a totally different logical function from 'ø', it is concluded that existence is not an attribute of things, or, perhaps, that 'exists' is a second-order predicate.

On this reading of the existential quantifier, it then becomes difficult to formalise such ordinary sentences as 'Pegasus exists' or 'King Arthur really did exist'. To deal with the first, the suggestion is that we write something like '($\exists x$)(Px)', where 'P' stands for 'Pegasises'; or else something like '($\exists x$)($x = $p)' where 'p' is the proper name of Pegasus. To deal with 'King Arthur really did exist' we have to perform one of the manoeuvres just mentioned, and in addition quantify over moments of time, while yet remembering to read both ($\exists x$) and ($\exists t$) in an atemporal, and yet existential, sense. This quantificational reading of 'exists' seems somewhat forced, though that in itself would hardly be a serious objection were there other compensating advantages. Nor perhaps is it impossible, though it is surely somewhat artificial, to suppose that there is a property such as Pegasising. More serious is the objection that such statements as 'Pegasus exists' or 'King Arthur really existed' surely ought to be taken as referring to Pegasus and to Arthur, rather than to some x which is an instance of the (universal?) property Pegasising, or to some x which was identical with Arthur. These artificialities are imposed by two assumptions: the first is that positive existential statements and negative existential statements ought to be structurally parallel: for it is the same thing which is being asserted or denied; and the second is that one may not use a sentence in which there occurs an 'empty' proper name. Hence the negative singular existential statements 'Pegasus does not exist' and 'King Arthur never existed' cannot be interpreted as referring to Pegasus or Arthur; and consequently, while '$\neg$ ($\exists x$) (Px)' is all right, since it asserts that the property of Pegasising is not instantiated, '$\neg$ ($\exists x$) ($x = $a)' is still problematic. For if '$\neg$ ($\exists x$) ($x = $a)' is to be intelligible, then the embedded '$x = $a' would also have to be, which it is not if 'a' has no bearer. On the other hand, Barry Miller has pointed out that there are reasons for denying the assumption that positive existential statements are in all respects parallel to negative ones. Existence might well be an attribute which an individual has, even if non-existence clearly is not an attribute of anything at all.[1] Alternatively, it might in some ways be less misleading to read the existential and universal quantifiers as 'It is sometimes true that . . .', and 'it is always true that . . .', respectively, provided 'sometimes' and 'always' are not taken temporally; or, even more clearly, to read them as 'It is true of at least one/all member(s) of the domain in question that. . . .' If they are read in that way, one is not automatically committed to the *existence* of properties, or of moments of time, or of bare particulars. But if this reading is adopted, then some additional strategy has to be adopted in order to deal with 'exists'.

Gareth Evans[2] is willing to introduce a concept-expression 'E', such that $(x)(x$ satisfies 'E'). 'Exists' is true of everything. He then deals with denials of existence indirectly, by explaining a 'make-believe' use of language in which we refer to, describe, and make inferences about objects just as we would do were they real. To deny that King Arthur exists is then to deny that he *really* exists, rather than a straightforward denial of the basic existential statement that King Arthur exists. Usually, however, as when someone is speaking about, say, Westminster Abbey, Evans maintains that there are *two* claims which can be made, 'Westminster Abbey exists' and 'Westminster Abbey *really* exists', which are in normal circumstances equivalent.

There are still some problems with this, though I believe that the introduction of a predicate such as 'E' is a considerable step in the right direction. The problems I have in mind concern the nature of the domain into which one is willing to quantify. If I understand him aright, Evans's suggestion is intended to be neutral so far as ontology is concerned. Everything exists; but that truth still leaves everything to be played for. Which is as it should be, since logic is simply the wrong kind of instrument to settle questions of ontology.

II. The Ontology of Existence

One need not be a Platonist in order to be unhappy with the suggestion that we quantify over x's which are *simply* individuals. Of course, nobody would dream of suggesting that there could exist an individual with no properties whatever. Nonetheless, the covert insinuation is that we are dealing with some kind of Lockean 'I-know-not-what', a property-less individual which is the bearer of all properties (and must be the bearer of at least some), including such exotic properties as pegasising or arthurising; the suggestion might also be that substances simply are bundles of properties. But suppose one wishes to offer a more Aristotelian view according to which substances are necessarily individuals of a kind. They have essential properties, as well as accidental properties, and their essential properties are shared only by individuals of that kind. This is intended to be a substantive ontological claim. It is therefore intended to be a claim about what can and cannot *really* exist, as distinct from a claim about the domain over which we are prepared to quantify and to whose members we are prepared, or make-believedly prepared, to refer.

Moreover, on an Aristotelian view of substances, substance-properties are not *predicated* of anything else,[3] nor do they belong to some property-less bearer; and finally, it is as yet unclear how we are to understand the sense in which essential properties are necessary and accidental properties are not (on which more later).[4] The point I wish to make is that one cannot readily adapt the logical notation to cope with the ontological thesis that to be without qualification an individual is necessarily to be an individual of a kind.

Aquinas once wrote,

> Existence is not part of the definition of any created thing, since it is neither a genus nor a differentia; and hence the questions 'Does it exist?' and 'What is it?' are different. Now, since whatever is not part of the essence can be called an accident, the 'is' which responds to the question 'Is there an X?' is an accident. So the Commentator on Aristotle's *Metaphysics* Book V states that 'Socrates exists' involves accidental predication since it concerns the existence of a thing, or the truth of a proposition. On the other hand, the word 'being', in so far as it means the thing to which existence belongs, refers to the essence of the thing, and is divided by the ten Categories. (*Quodl.* II,3c)

And again,

> The substantial being of a thing is not an accident, but rather the actuality of some existing form. . . . Thus, properly speaking, it is not an accident. Following Hilary, I claim that there is a broad sense of the term 'accident' which includes whatever is not part of the essence of something; and it is in this broad sense that existence is an accident of created things. (*Quodl.* XII,5)

A careful analysis of these two texts will, I hope, show a possible way of resolving some of the problems I have just mentioned.

Firstly, consider the relatively non-committal, a-temporal, reading of '($\exists x$)' as 'There is an x such that . . .', and forget about x's construed as bare particulars. It seems to me that the sense in which one should accept '($\exists x$)' is close to the sense in which Aquinas wishes to hold that existence is divided by the Aristotelian Categories. That is to say, the things that there are are essences, provided we remember that Aristotle also admits that in a secondary sense even accidents can be said to have essences (*Metaph Z* 5, 1031a10ff), and provided we leave on one side for the moment the ontological status of nominal essences. There is no difficulty, on this view, in quantifying over substances, or properties or relations, actions and affections, or propositions, or numbers. If '($\exists x$)' is read in this way, it is compatible with Evans's suggestion that some of the things there are do not *really* exist, and with a proper understanding of sentences such as 'The Equator is longer than any other line of latitude'.

Secondly, when Aquinas says that these are the 'things to which existence belongs' he has in mind real essences. His view here is therefore more restrictive than the one I have just outlined, in that nominal essences are excluded. Further, it is a matter of dispute exactly what Aristotle, or Aquinas, took to be the referent of the term 'real essence'.[5] It is clear that neither Aristotle nor Aquinas believe that real essences taken as universals *exist* in any straightforward sense of the term; that is precisely the Platonic theory they wished to reject. On the other hand, they would have wished to distinguish such putative essences as Chimaera or Goat-Stag (or, we may surmise, Winged Horse) from real essences such as Man, Lion, Goat, Stag, and Horse. The difference is that in their view some of these items *can* exist, and others cannot. How, then, is one to understand 'exist' as it applies to universals such as Man and to individuals such as John?

Aquinas and (I believe) Aristotle explain the relationship between species and individuals of that species in terms of the relationship of potentiality to actuality. This doctrine surely requires some account of what potentiality is. I suggest that at least a first shot at this can be made by saying that potentiality consists in the possession of the relevant disposition to enter into causal relationships (active or passive). Potentiality is thus a feature of actual things. That the species Horse exists whereas (we may suppose) the species Mermaid does not consists in the fact that there exist entities capable of producing individual horses, whereas there exist no entities capable of producing individual mermaids. That there exists such a colour as Red consists in the fact that it is causally possible to produce red objects. The species Dodo is perhaps a borderline case. Is it causally possible to produce a dodo? Clearly it once was, and hence the species Dodo did exist. And perhaps, given the resources of genetic technology, it is now, or will be, possible to produce dodos once again. In which case the species still does, or perhaps some day again will, exist. It is in this sense that Aquinas believes that actuality is prior to potentiality.

Thirdly, Aquinas explicitly concedes that 'exists' is not a predicate in the sense in which any species-term or genus-term is a predicate. Moreover, he is speaking of 'any created thing' which falls into any of the Categories, and hence is including accidents as well as substances. So he includes such terms as 'colour' or 'red', just as he includes 'animal' or 'rational'. 'Exists' is not like *any* of these terms, in that it is not part of the definition of any created thing at all. Just so, Kant denies that 'exists' is a real, 'determining' predicate, in the sense in which 'gold' or 'thaler' are determining predicates, and Evans introduces 'E' as a formal, logical predicate. Just as Hume and Kant deny that there is any contradiction involved in saying that John does not exist, or that the hundred thalers in my pocket need not exist, so Aquinas denies that there is any contradiction in saying that no humans exist or (we may surmise) no dodos exist either. Any existential sentence with a contingent being as its subject is only contingently true, if true at all.

Fourthly, since it need not be the case that John exists, just as it need not be the case that John is tired, though both happen to be true, there is a 'broad' sense in which both statements and the corresponding states of affairs are contingent—the propositions are contingently true, and the states of affairs contingently obtain. On the other hand, the second paragraph cited above makes it clear that, despite this parallel, existence is not an accident of John in the way in which his tiredness is; accidents in the strict sense are modifications of independently existing substances which persist through change. Aquinas therefore would quite accept that there is a difference between 'Some tigers are tame' and 'Some tigers exist'. The tricky question is how precisely this difference is best characterised. Aquinas would not, I think, accept that to say that John exists is to say nothing about John; it is to say of him that he is one particular actualisation of the potentiality for there to exist human beings; and to say that Fido exists is to say of Fido that he actualises the potentiality of there being dogs. To exist is to be an individual of a kind, and to say of something that it exists is (explicitly or implicitly, and excluding the special case of God) to state that it is an individual of a specific kind. It is further to state that the relationship between that individual and its kind is one of actuality to potentiality. To say that, surely, is a genuine description because of the species-content of what is said of the individual; and the description is 'accidental' in the broad sense because that species need not have been actualised in John or Fido.

It seems possible, then, that some such approach could provide a useful alternative to the ontological assumptions, or the deliberate avoidance of ontological assumptions, behind modern logical methods of dealing with existence. Some modifications would be required, however. If '$(\exists x)$' is to be read neutrally as 'There is . . . ', where in this case x ranges over species, then a set of fully existential predicates of the form 'E^n' will have to be introduced. 'John exists' could be expressed as '$(\exists M)(E^M j)$', to be read as 'There is a species man, such that John exists as a man'. Instead of taking 'existence' to be a real property, one should take 'existence-as-a-$\emptyset$' (where '$\emptyset$' is a species-term) to be the property which John has.[6] Second, one should not construe 'has' here in the way in which it is construed in connection with any accidental property in the strict sense. It is 'the actuality of a form', as Aquinas puts it.

I therefore wish to commend an important suggestion of Plato's (*Sophist*, 247d–e4, 248c4–5), that to exist just is to possess causal powers, and to take this last notion as ontologically primitive. There is, I believe, no way of establishing this claim by invoking some prior truths which support it. The most that can be done is to commend it by exhibiting some of the advantages which might follow from accepting it. Here are some of them.

First, if to exist is to possess causal powers, and if we are already disposed to accept the commonly expressed link between being an individual and existing, then it will follow that individuals are to be conceived of as the possessors of causal powers. Of course Plato, in making the suggestion that existence consisted in the possession of causal powers, was also quite happy to accept the existence of such individuals as The Same, Being, Difference, Rest, and Motion, and doubtless, the existence of numbers and universals. He did so because he believed that these entities were causally related both to one another and to items in the world. But the suggested account of what it is to exist is independent of Plato's views on which things in fact exist. One can still say, if one feels so inclined, that there *are* such things as Universals, or

Numbers, or the Equator, but deny that any of these things exists. Much the same goes for fictional characters, to which one can refer, but which one would not wish to say existed.

Existence, then, consists in the possession of causal powers; possible existents are just those things which it is causally possible to bring about; and possibility is a feature of the causal powers to act or to be acted upon possessed by actual things. In that sense, there exist real essences, but no putative essences. Real essences exist in that certain causal powers exist.[7]

III. Potentiality and Modality

Much ingenuity has been expended upon developing logical formalisations of the theory of possible worlds, and there has been some discussion of the ontological commitments which might be involved in possible-world semantics. As the previous argument will have suggested, I think that here again there has been an unfortunate tendency to allow logic to determine ontology rather than the other way round. 'Potentiality' as a term has largely been replaced by 'possibility'; and this shift in terminology has made it difficult to explain 'actuality' (the correlative of 'potentiality', but not of 'possibility'), as we have seen.

Of course one may construe 'is possible' by 'is true in some possible world', and one can provide logical characterisations for the relationships in such a world together with procedures for constructing such worlds. Nicholas Rescher and Ruth Barcan Marcus have both done so,[8] and in so doing have paid considerable attention to at least some of the underlying ontologies which might be assumed. Rescher in particular has been at pains to stress that the individuals in any possible world are to be constructed on the basis of individuals in the actual world, and to emphasise that possible worlds are constructs, rather than existing entities as they at least seem to be in the view of David Lewis.[9] It remains the case, though, that the notion of 'possibility' is less than clear.

I would insist on the importance of making a sharp distinction between logical and causal possibility (which latter is to be explained in terms of causal powers). To ask which worlds are logically possible is, so far as I can see, a question about which modal systems are consistent. The problems arise when one then proceeds to suggest possible interpretations of some such system, and to use these interpretations to draw ontological conclusions about what can and cannot be brought about. But one can, and should, question whether logical consistency or inconsistency is at all an adequate test for what is and is not causally possible.

Aquinas, in discussing God's omnipotence, seems to offer just such a criterion. Having dismissed the relational use of 'possible', on the grounds that to say that God can do everything which his nature enables him to do is narrowly circular, he continues,

> The only alternative, then, is to say that God is said to be omnipotent because he can do anything which is absolutely possible, which is the other use of 'possible'. Something is said to be possible or impossible depending on the relationship between terms: something is possible because the predicate is not incompatible with [repugnat] the subject, for instance, that Socrates is sitting down; and impossible because there is such an incompatibility, for instance that a man is an ass. (ST I,25,3)

The incompatibility test is explicitly spelt out in terms of non-contradiction, and the same criterion is invoked when Aquinas argues that God cannot undo the past (ibid., q.4). Some caution, however, is required in interpreting such texts, both in Aquinas and in Aristotle. Aristotle, as is well known, readily moves between discussing words and discussing things. It is not just that 'sitting' logically can be predicated of 'Socrates', but that sitting is an activity which Socrates is able to perform. It is not simply that the principle of non-contradiction is logically primitive, it is that things cannot exist with causally incompatible properties. Both in Aristotle and in Aquinas, discussions about the meanings of words are almost never simply about words, but are about the things which those words are used to stand for. That being said, though, it remains true that Aristotle and Aquinas in general give the impression that the match between what we say and the way things are is in general a close one. Several reasons might be thought to account for this assumption: both philosophers are on the whole untroubled with the epistemological problems connected with error, and hence with the possibility that we might have got the world seriously wrong; both philosophers seem to believe that induction plus the native ability of the intellect to see essential connections between apparently disparate items of information had actually led to a largely successful science based on the real essences of things: and this assumption might have been reinforced by the ontology of perception and of knowledge which they adopted, where the form of the thing known is present intentionally in the knower.

Be that as it may, we might well now be of the opinion that the assumption of a largely accurate match between the way we think about things and the way things are is at least somewhat over-optimistic. To the extent that that is so, the ways in which we classify things and the lexical relationships between the terms we use, are not reliable guides to the world. In other words, logical possibility is neither a necessary nor a sufficient condition for establishing whether or not something is causally possible. In general, our knowledge of causal possibility will be no better than, and might even be less comprehensive than, the empirical beliefs we have about our world, as those are expressed in the terms we use and in the causal laws which we take to describe the ways in which things of necessity interact. Descartes, whose discussion of omnipotence is often decried as an extreme and outlandish position seems, on the contrary, to have hit the nail on the head. He considers the objection that God could not be free to make it false that contra-dictories cannot both be true (the collection of negatives here is Des-cartes' own):

> It is easy to dispel this difficulty by considering that the power of God cannot have any limits, and that our mind is finite and so cre-ated as to be able to conceive as possible the things which God has wished to be in fact possible, but not to be able to conceive as pos-sible things which God could have made possible, but which he has nevertheless willed to make impossible.
> (Letter to Mesland, 2nd May 1644)

Descartes' point is not to make a wholesale attack on logic. He be-lieves that God made our minds in such a way that our understanding of this world can accurately reflect the way this world is. To that ex-tent, our conceptual apparatus, upon which contradiction and non-contradiction depends, is at least in principle a good guide to what is and is not possible given the way God has in fact created this world. It is perhaps unfortunate that, in applying this thought, he asserts that when the ideas we have of two things are clear and quite distinct, it is possible in this world for God to produce one without the other. For the clear distinction between concepts is not necessarily a good guide to the causal independence of the things those concepts stand for. Still, what he is intent upon denying is that this gives us any grip whatsoever on the infinite power of God. When Descartes says that what are contradictions to us need not be contradictions in some alternative creation which is in God's power, he is cautioning us against *defining* 'absolutely possible' in terms of our current terminology and the relationships between our current terms. In this he is surely right. Our knowledge of what is possible is based entirely upon our experience of the items in this world, and upon our assessments of their causal powers. But even in those terms our assessment is at best partial, and is doubtless also in some ways mistaken. When we discover such mistakes, we will then, of course, modify our concepts accordingly; it will no longer be a conceptual truth that all swans are white once we have discovered black swans.

Of course, all the foregoing bespeaks a realist view of things. There are real essences which at least in many cases we might hope to discover; things have, indeed consist of, the possession of causal powers which necessitate that they interact in specified ways, which our causal laws might hope to describe. Real essences are not definitions, and causation is not simply law-like behaviour, even though such behaviour is characteristic of causes. Causal possibility is not a logical matter, even if we will normally try to express it in logical terms. But where does such a realist view leave talk of possible worlds, and the proposed analysis of modal statements in terms of possible worlds?

It is a matter of ingenuity which consistent logical systems we can construct. It is a matter of definition and of the axioms which are adopted whether the angles of a triangle total two right angles or not. Similarly, it is a matter of ingenuity whether a consistent model can be constructed which might be given an interpretation in terms of a universe which obeyed laws quite different from the laws of the universe we know. Less formally, we can perhaps, as Hume does, imagine a version of this world with selective improvements which would eliminate most or all of this world's ills. But the limits of human ingenuity and imagination are little guide to what is or is not causally possible. Logically consistent models or appealing imaginative pictures may not be causally realisable, and there might well, for all we know, be causal possibilities which we, with our limited experience, cannot express at all.

Rescher is right, I believe, to start from the position that possible worlds are constructs, logical constructs; and that the items in possible worlds are based upon the individuals (whichever we take those to be) which are the individuals in this actual world. Logical possibility can then quite properly be analysed in terms of truth in some possible world, and logical necessity as truth in all possible worlds. I take these remarks to be broadly neutral, so far as ontology is concerned. What needs to be made explicit is that the ontology of possible worlds will depend on our identification of individuals in the actual world, and upon the causal powers which we ascribe to these individuals. Talk about the existence of possible worlds, then, is limited to talk about the causal powers of things as we take them to be. A causally possible world will then be a world in which those powers are exercised according to the laws of nature which govern the actual world, and will contain just those individuals which can be brought about in accordance with those laws. Our estimate of which worlds are causally possible will thus depend on the extent of our knowledge of the causal structure of the actual world, and will be mistaken or incomplete according as that knowledge is itself mistaken or incomplete. It is perhaps harmless, but also of limited value to suggest that '$\Diamond \phi x$' be read as 'There is a possible world in which ϕx', if 'possible world' here is read as 'logically possible world'; for while such a reading might be a useful pedagogical device, it affords no insight into whether such a world is or is not causally possible. Similarly, '$\Box \phi x$' can be harmlessly, but uninformatively, read as 'ϕx in all possible worlds in which x exists'. But for ontological necessity, it is not sufficient that x should *happen to be* ϕ if x exists at all, but rather that a world in which x exists and is not ϕ is not a causally possible world. Again, if one is willing at all to countenance such a truth as 'x necessarily exists', it cannot be explicated as 'x exists in all the logically possible worlds in which x exists', but should be read as 'A world in which it is not the case that x exists is not a causally possible world'.[10]

Conclusion

The logicisation of the notion of possibility goes back at least as far as Aristotle, and its roots are perhaps to be found in Plato and even in Parmenides. It persisted in the medieval philosophers until it was criticised head-on by Descartes; and it has reappeared in modern times with the development of more powerful logical systems. It is, to my mind,

regrettable that this development tended to obscure the equally Aristotelian notion of potentiality, which relates directly to the possession
of causal powers and only indirectly to logic. It is even more regrettable
that the notion of a causal power itself has commonly been analysed
in terms of what is fundamentally a Humean account in terms of
regular succession or law-like behaviour. This is to confuse what causal
powers are with the evidence we have for which causal powers individuals have, and it is therefore hardly surprising that wholly satisfactory accounts (in terms of counterfactuals, or INUS-conditions, for
example (INUS = insufficient but necessary part of a condition which
is itself unnecessary but sufficient) have not been forthcoming. I have
tried in this essay to argue that some recent developments in analytic
philosophy, now less rigidly empiricist, make it possible to return to
some aspects of the Aristotelian tradition which have been underesti-
mated. In particular, there is an important respect in which ontology is,
and should be seen to be, prior to logic. The most fundamental notion
of possibility is a causal notion. If this is accepted, the outcome will be
a view of possibility which is at once somewhat more agnostic and
more realist. And that is as it should be.

Notes

1. Barry Miller, *From Existence to God* (London: Routledge, 1992),
chap. 4, and the appendix to chap. 4.

2. In *The Varieties of Reference,* a posthumous collection of his papers
edited by John McDowell (Oxford: Clarendon Press, 1982). Evans discusses
existential statements in chapter 10.

3. It is at least a defensible view that the 'said in'/'said of' distinction in
the *Categories* is maintained also in the central books of the *Metaphysics;* and
it has often been remarked that statements such as 'Socrates is a man' are closer
to identity statements than to statements like 'Socrates is tired'.

4. Other essays in this volume deal with the comparisons and contrasts
between ancient and modern theories of essentialism, and I will not comment
further here.

5. It is a matter of dispute just how Aristotle, or Aquinas, understood the
term 'essence'. My preferred view is that both philosophers were willing to
speak of essences both as universals and as individuals in different contexts.
Socrates and Callias have the same essence, but it is also true that Socrates is
identical with *his* essence. Nor do they always make it entirely clear to which
of these they are referring at any given point.

6. All created things exist-as-a-*f*. God, on the classical view, exists without qualification. It may be for this reason that Aristotle thinks of the Prime Mover as alone fulfilling all the criteria for being a substance.

7. I am not here concerned with whether God can properly be said to have an essence. I take it that Aquinas speaks of the essence of God only in an analogous sense, in which no passive potentiality is involved.

8. Nicholas Rescher, *A Theory of Possiblity* (Oxford: Blackwell, 1975); Ruth Barcan Marcus, *Modalities: Philosophical Essays* (Oxford: Oxford University Press, 1993).

9. David Lewis, *Counterfactuals* (Cambridge: Cambridge University Press, 1973).

10. Quite in general, one cannot explain essential properties as those properties which some *x* has in all worlds in which *x* exists; and in particular, on that reading existence is always an essential property of everything. It is also important to notice that, at least on traditional views, God is the only absolutely necessarily existing being but is not a member of any kind. For that reason, 'exists' here cannot be expanded to 'exists-as-a', as I have argued it should be in all other cases.

CHAPTER ELEVEN

Contemporary "Essentialism" vs. Aristotelian Essentialism

Gyula Klima

1. The Principal Theses of Contemporary "Essentialism" vs. Aristotelian Essentialism

Contemporary "essentialism," if we want to provide a succinct yet sufficiently rigorous characterization, may be summarized in the thesis that some common terms are rigid designators.[1] By the quotation marks I intend to indicate that I regard this as a somewhat improper (though, of course, permitted) usage of the term (after all, *nomina significant ad placitum*). In contrast to this, *essentialism*, properly so-called, is the Aristotelian doctrine summarizable in the thesis—as we shall see, no less rigorous in its own theoretical context —that things have essences.

The two theses, although related, are by no means identical. In this essay I wish to show exactly how these theses differ in virtue of the radically different conceptual frameworks in which they acquire their proper meaning, yet without these conceptual differences rendering them logically "incommensurable." In these considerations, being primarily concerned with the distinction between them, I am going to treat both contemporary "essentialism" and Aristotelian essentialism very broadly and rather indistinctly in themselves, in the sense that I am not going to delve into otherwise important different versions of either of the two. For reasons of clarity and influence I have selected Kripke and Aquinas as paradigmatic representatives of their respective conceptual frameworks. Nevertheless, I will try to treat these frameworks in such general terms as to be able to cover the thought of a great number of similarly important thinkers

2. The Problems of Contemporary "Essentialism"

The most widely recognized framework of contemporary "essentialism" is possible-worlds semantics. That a common term is taken to be a rigid designator might be reflected in the formal system by stipulating that if an individual is an element of the extension of the corresponding predicate parameter in one possible world, then it is an element of the extension of the same predicate parameter in all other possible worlds in which that individual exists, i.e., the domain of which contains that individual as its element. Such a stipulation basically amounts to saying that rigid designators "stick with their individuals" ("their individuals" being the individuals that fall within their extension in a possible world) across all possible worlds in which those individuals exist.

Now, clearly, rigidity is an independent, additional stipulation on the possible-worlds framework. This stipulation is in no way part of the logical machinery of possible-worlds semantics itself, but something that may or may not be added to this machinery for independent reasons. This is how it comes about, then, that while various intuitions of several philosophers clash over admitting or omitting this additional essentialist stipulation, none of them can have decisive *logical* grounds for definitively proving their own position and/or definitively refuting the positions of others.

To be sure, there is nothing wrong *per se* in having recourse to extra-logical intuitions in philosophical debates. However, what renders using these extra-logical intuitions in the particular debates concerning "essentialism" highly dubious is that these intuitions are formulated and understood within the conceptual framework of a historically quite recent philosophical tradition, which for the most part evolved on the basis of a radically anti-essentialist, indeed, generally anti-metaphysical mentality. Perhaps a general characterization of what I take to be two main families of arguments in these debates—significantly, comprising arguments both from "essentialists" and anti-"essentialists"—will make clear what I have in mind.

2.1 "Opacity/Transparency" Arguments

The cluster of arguments I would gather under this heading range from Quine's cyclist mathematician and number-of-planets arguments, to Kripke's pain-argument, to Yablo's statue-argument, and many others.[2] All these arguments are based on the perceived inconsistency of three propositions of the following form:

1. d_1 is essentially P
2. d_2 is not essentially P
3. $d_1 = d_2$

In the various arguments, either these three propositions are used as premises to infer an inconsistent conclusion (e.g., Quine's cyclist mathematician argument follows this pattern), or two of them are used to infer the negation of the third (e.g., Quine's number-of-planets argument uses propositions exemplifying 1 and 2 to establish the allegedly absurd denial of 3;[3] while Kripke's and Yablo's above-mentioned arguments use propositions exemplifying 1 and 2 to establish the denial of 3, which in Kripke's case is hailed as a significant philosophical conclusion concerning the non-physical nature of pain, while in Yablo's case it is deemed to be an unacceptable conclusion, causing much philosophical pain).

The different uses to which these arguments are put by their "essentialist" or anti-"essentialist" proponents depend on the intuitions these philosophers have concerning the particular formulations of their premises and/or conclusions. Yet, what remains common in all these different arguments, despite their conflicting intents and various formulations, is the realization that 1–3 can be regarded as inconsistent only if 1 and 2 are taken to provide referentially transparent contexts for d_1 and d_2—or, what amounts to the same, if both d_1 and d_2 are treated as rigid designators of what they designate. Accordingly, whenever philosophers intend to neutralize the force of any of these arguments

(whether for or against some essentialist conclusion), they point out
that the proposition corresponding to either 1 or 2 has an equally (or
even more) intuitive opaque (or *de dicto*) reading or reformulation
which invalidates the argument in question, or correlatively, if they want
to preserve the validity of such an argument, they try to show why such
a reading or reformulation is unacceptable.

For example, consider Kripke's argument concerning heat and
molecular motion.

(H1) Molecular motion is essentially molecular motion
(H2) Heat is not essentially molecular motion
therefore,
(H3) Heat is not molecular motion

Provided that 'molecular motion' and 'heat' are "rigid designators," the
argument is valid, but the conclusion is scientifically false, hence a problem for "essentialism."[4] A "Kripkean reconstrual" accounting for the
alleged "strong intuition" for (H2), but invalidating the argument,
points out that 'heat' can be taken in two ways. It can be taken as referring to the physical phenomenon that actually causes in us the sensation of heat, which is nothing but molecular motion, and which,
therefore, is essentially molecular motion. On this reading 'heat' rigidly
refers to molecular motion, but then (H2) is false. The other reading,
however, takes 'heat' as referring non-rigidly to anything whatsoever
that may possibly cause in us the sensation of heat, which may back up
the intuition behind (H2), but then, since it renders 'heat' non-rigid, it
invalidates the argument.

Now, whatever one's reactions to particular formulations of this
type of argument may be, it should be clear that such moves merely
transform questions of intuitions about the essentiality of certain terms
into questions of intuitions about the essentiality of other terms. (In
this case, the question whether 'molecular motion' is an essential predicate of heat is transformed into the question whether 'heat' is a rigid
designator, that is, an essential predicate, of the phenomenon that it
actually designates.) This, again, would not be harmful in itself, if questions concerning terms about which our intuitions are uncertain could
in this way be transformed into questions about terms about which we
can be certain. However, given that the underlying logical framework
in these discussions not only fails to sort out which particular terms

should be deemed essential[5] but also fails to give any reason whatsoever why there should be *any* essential terms at all, arguments of this
sort within this framework are doomed to inconclusiveness.

Indeed, as the previous example shows, since *nomina significant ad
placitum*, to ask whether, for example, 'heat' is a rigid designator, is not
a very illuminating question. For the answer is that *it depends*. If we use
it as such, making it stick with the phenomenon it actually designates,
come what may, then of course it is rigid. But if we use it in another
way, making it stick with its actual conditions of applicability (perhaps
expressed in a nominal definition), whether in a possible situation these
conditions are satisfied by the same phenomenon that satisfies them
in the actual situation or not, then of course it is not rigid. But then it
seems that the whole issue about essential vs. non-essential predicates
boils down to determining the proper usage of certain terms, concerning which philosophers may have different intuitions, but certainly no
principled *metaphysical* reasons for preferring one usage over the other.

As a matter of fact, this last remark shows one of the most basic
problems with Kripke-style "essentialism," namely, that the modal approach to *essence* apparently puts the cart before the horse. Since it
seeks to explain essence in terms of essential properties, rather than the
other way around, it certainly cannot invoke essences in trying to cope
with its primary task presented by anti-essentialist criticisms: to offer
some reason why some common terms *have to* be regarded as essential
to the things they are actually true of. So while the issues in this framework could not be settled on *logical* grounds, in the same framework
they cannot be settled on principled *metaphysical* grounds either.

2.2 Insufficiency Arguments

This realization seems to be the main motivation for recent criticism of
the modal approach by Kit Fine. As he puts it, his objections to the
modal account "will be to the sufficiency of the proposed criterion, not
to its necessity."[6] These objections show that it is easy to find properties deemed essential by the modal criterion; that is, properties that in
the Kripkean parlance would be rigid designators of an object, which,
however, nobody would take to be essential in the stronger sense of
somehow characterizing or expressing the nature of the thing.

Take Socrates and the singleton whose only member is Socrates.
On the Kripkean account it would be essential both for the singleton

to contain Socrates and for Socrates to belong to the singleton. However, it is hard to see what it has to do with the nature of Socrates whether he belongs or not to any set whatsoever. Socrates would certainly be both the same thing and the same kind of thing, even if there were no sets at all.

In general, the Kripkean account renders any necessary property "essential" to anything, however extrinsic such a property to the thing in question may be. For example, the property $\lambda x[Px \lor {\sim}Px]$, or the property $\lambda x[Px \rightarrow Px]$ should be essential to any individual whatsoever. Consequently, it should be essential to you that you are either reading or not reading this essay, or that if you are reading it, then you are reading it, which on a stronger reading of 'essential' would mean that these properties, and along with them this essay, somehow belong to, and therefore constitute your nature, which is absurd.

Well, of course, these arguments can "work" only if someone is willing and able to recognize a sense of "nature" or "essence" that is somehow stronger than what can be reached on the basis of the modal account.

But then, again, it seems that we are left here with an appeal to intuition, which does not have much to do with the nature of things, but rather with a "feeling" as to linguistic usage, this time concerning the usage of 'nature'. However, especially nowadays, when every single philosopher seems to have their own "theory of meaning and/or reference" such an appeal cannot be expected to have a universally compelling force; and again, after all, *nomina significant ad placitum*.

But despite these and similar concerns, I assume that many philosophers are both willing and able to recognize a stronger sense of "essence" or "nature." Indeed, I think that many philosophers will also recognize the *need* for such a stronger sense, given the intuitive troubles with the modal approach. But the question then is what we should take as the standard for the *proper* expression of such a stronger sense.

Again, when it comes to *stipulating* a certain usage, anyone has the right to *introduce* any sorts of "strengthening" of the sense of this term *ad placitum*. But when it comes to the question of the *proper* usage of a technical term of a philosophical or scientific theory (as the term 'essence' and its equivalents, such as 'nature', 'quiddity', etc. clearly did function as such in the Aristotelian philosophical tradition), then we have to turn to the usage of those who used the term within the context of that theory within which it originally acquired its proper, intended meaning. Kit Fine, proposing in his alternative approach to recover the lost connection between the notions of essence and *real*, as opposed to *nominal, definition*, clearly moves in this direction. However, because of failing to reconstruct the traditional theoretical context of this distinction—which in fact is a comprehensive semantic theory connecting the notions of meaning, reference, predication, and being in a particular manner to the notion of essence—his approach, as we shall see, is still significantly different from this tradition. In any case, in the next section I will reconstruct precisely this proper theoretical context, thereby providing not only some ad hoc strengthening of the sense of the term 'essense', but also reconstructing the sense in which it was properly used in the medieval Aristotelian tradition.

3. The Conceptual Framework of Medieval Aristotelian Essentialism

In what follows I present a brief, summary reconstruction of the most basic, formal semantic principles that served as the theoretical background for the traditional Aristotelian concept of essence. For want of space, in this reconstruction I will proceed rather "dogmatically," without discussing the textual evidence backing the reconstruction. In a historical study such a procedure would be totally unjustifiable. However, what justifies it here is that in the present comparison it is only the reconstructed theory itself that will be relevant, not the historical verification of the reconstruction; and, in any case, I have already done the job of the historical verification in other papers.[7] So, instead of a piecemeal reconstruction based on the texts, I present here only some formal clauses describing (part of) the semantic theory in question, along with some brief explanatory comments on each.

3.1 Semantics

■ 1. Concrete common terms signify individualized forms of individual things.

Formally: $SGT(P)(u)(t) \in W \cup \{0\}$, in a model $<W,T,A,SGT,0>$, where $W \neq \emptyset$, $T \neq \emptyset$, $t \in T$, $A(t) \subseteq W$, $u \in W \cup \{0\}$, $0 \notin W$, and $SGT(P)(0)(t) = 0$; where W is the domain of discourse, comprising both actual and nonactual individuals, $A(t)$ is the set of actual individuals at time t, SGT is the signification function to be defined (in part) below,[8] and 0 is a zero-entity, a technical device used to indicate the case when a semantic function for a certain argument lacks a value from W.

Concrete common terms, such as 'man', 'stone', 'tall', 'runs', etc., which are predicable of several individuals, signify individualized forms of these individuals, that is, those individual features of these things in virtue of which these terms apply or may apply to these things, if they can apply to them at all. As this remark intends to make it clear, the term 'form' in this rule need not—indeed, must not—be interpreted with all the metaphysical weight it had in Aristotelian metaphysics.[9] Since this is a rule describing the *semantic function* of signification of common terms, it only serves to specify how their *significata*, as I will call the values of this function, are assigned, regardless of what the ontological status of these semantic values may be. For showing which semantic values of which expressions fall into which ontological categories can only be the task of a *subsequent metaphysical* inquiry, to be carried out in the language whose semantics has thus been specified. As can be seen, these significata, or "individualized forms," are assigned to concrete common terms in relation to two individualizing factors, namely, their subject and time, regardless of whether these "forms" are actual or not in these individuals at a given time. For example, the term 'sighted' in this framework is interpreted as signifying the individual sights of individual animals (that is, whatever it is in their constitution that enables them to see), at any given time; therefore, if in the formal clause above in an interpretation we let u range over the domain of the things and let t range over the dates of our actual universe, then we may get, say, the following instance of this clause:

$$SGT(\text{'sighted'})(\text{Socrates})(400 \text{ B.C.}) \in A(400 \text{ B.C.}),$$

which merely states that Socrates' sight was one of the actual things in this universe in 400 B.C. Of course, since u ranges over all things in the universe, it can take up values for which this term is not interpreted. It is such cases that are represented by assigning the term the zero-entity as its value. Thus, for example,

$$SGT(\text{'sighted'})(\text{the Statue of Liberty})(1996) = 0$$

As can be seen, in general, by picking up various individuals in the place of u, and various times (dates, time-points, or any other time-intervals, depending on the scale of the actual interpretation), we get the significata of a common term belonging to these individuals at these different times, whatever these semantic values are, regardless of whether they are actual or potential, or even whether the term can apply to the thing in question at all (for if not, then it simply gets 0 as its value).[10]

■ 2. A concrete common term, as the subject of a proposition, has the function to *supposit for* (refer to) the individuals in which its significata are actual at the time connoted by the copula of the proposition.

Formally: $SUP(S)(t) \in \{u: SGT(S)(u)(t) \in A(t)\}$, provided this set is not empty, otherwise $SUP(S)(t) = 0$.

If we say: 'A dinosaur is running', the term 'dinosaur' should refer to, or using the transcription of the medieval technical term, *supposit for*,[11] individual, actually existing dinosaurs at the present time of the actual use of the proposition. But of course only those things are actual dinosaurs in which the significate of the term 'dinosaur' is actual (i.e. those individual u's, for which it holds that $SGT('dinosaur')(u)(1996) \in A(1996)$). However, since at this time there is no such a thing in our actual universe, this term refers to nothing, that is, since $\{u: SGT('dinosaur')(u)(1996) \in A(1996)\} = \emptyset$, given that for any u, $SGT('dinosaur')(u)(1996) \notin A(1996)$, since nothing is a dinosaur at this time, $SUP('dinosaur')(1996) = 0$. On the other hand, if we say: 'A dinosaur was running', the term 'dinosaur' should, and actually does, refer to whatever *was* a dinosaur, that is, whatever *had* the significata of the term 'dinosaur' in actuality in the past relative to our present. That is to say, since $\{u: SGT('dinosaur')(u)(t<1996) \in A(t<1996)\} \neq \emptyset$ in our actual universe, this term will successfully refer to, or supposit for, things that were dinosaurs at some time in our past: $SUP('dinosaur')(t<1996) \in \{u: SGT('dinosaur')(u)(t<1996) \in A(t<1996)\}$. Aside from this contextual character of this theory of reference, another important thing to notice here is that as far as the semantic theory is concerned, there is no stipulation as to the identity or distinctness of the significata and supposita of the same term. So, anyone who is taken aback by the apparently "obscure" character of these significata is free to identify these semantic values *in their metaphysics.* Then, for example, a "dinosaurhood" will be no more "obscure" than a dinosaur is, but obviously such a position will have its own further *metaphysical* consequences. In fact, the possibility of identifying a concrete term's significata with its supposita is one of the most important conceptual tools in Aquinas's arsenal to express divine simplicity. For, expressed in terms of this reconstruction, Aquinas has proofs to the effect that SGT('God')(God)(t)=SUP ('God')(t), that is, that God's deity is God; or that SGT('good')(God) (t)=SUP('God')(t), that is, that God's goodness is God, etc. But note that these formulations are *not semantic stipulations* concerning the usage of the term 'God', but only metalinguistic expressions of what has to hold in the actual interpretation of the language in which Aquinas's conclusions are true. As can be seen, however, in these remarks I was already compelled to use the abstract counterparts of the concrete terms in order to be able to refer to the significata of these concrete terms. In fact, according to this theory, this is precisely the function of abstract terms, as stated in the next rule.

■ 3. The abstract counterpart of a concrete common term both signifies and supposits for the significata of the concrete common term.

Formally: SGT([P])(u)(t) = SGT(P)(u)(t), and SUP([P])(t) = SGT(P) (SUP(P)(t))(t), where [P] is the abstract counterpart of P.

As has been remarked above, the semantic rules concerning concrete terms do not stipulate anything concerning the identity or nonidentity of the supposita and significata of concrete terms. This semantic rule, however, does stipulate this identity concerning abstract terms, and it also stipulates that these semantic values of the abstract terms have to be identified with the significata of their concrete counterparts.

■ 4. The predication of a common term of an individual supposited for by the subject of the predication is true if and only if the significate of the common term in the individual thus supposited for is actual at the time connoted by the copula of the predication.

Formally: SGT(S—P)(SUP)(t) = 1 iff SGT(P)(SUP(S)(t))(t)∈A(t).[12]

Take, for instance, the proposition: 'Socrates is sighted'. According to this theory, the predication expressed by this proposition is true if and only if what is signified by 'sighted' in the *suppositum* of 'Socrates' at the time of the actual use of this proposition is actual at that time. That is, assuming that we are using (i.e. forming, asserting, or reading and actually understanding) this proposition at the date 1996, then

SGT('Socrates is sighted')(SUP)(1996) = 1 iff SGT('sighted')(SUP ('Socrates')(1996))(1996)∈A(1996).[13]

This, in our actual case, would evaluate this proposition as false, because Socrates' sight is certainly not among the actually existing things at this date, given the fact that now Socrates is dead, and only an actually living animal can have sight.

As can be seen, this formulation is just one possible way of putting what historians of medieval logic usually refer to as *the inherence theory of predication*. Even without going into its further technical details, I think it is clear that it is this theory which establishes the crucial conceptual connection between what may be called the *via antiqua* semantics of medieval Aristotelianism and the essentialist metaphysics of the pre-Ockhamist tradition.[14] For this is the theory that, by providing the truth conditions of simple predications in terms of the actuality of the *significata* of the predicates in the *supposita* of the subjects, connects the notion of the signification of forms of individual things to the central notion of this metaphysical tradition, the notion of being.

3.2 Metaphysics

Of course, there are many technical issues that would need to be clarified regarding exactly how this theory works. However, even this skeletal presentation of this semantics will be sufficient to deal with our central concern at the moment: the metaphysical payoff of this theory in handling the contemporary issues. To be sure, this payoff cannot be gained simply by deriving certain essentialist metaphysical principles from these semantic principles. On the contrary, as we could see, this semantics does not dictate to metaphysics any more than the contemporary framework does. However, by providing the above-described systematic connection between the semantic notions of the signification and supposition of both concrete and abstract terms and the central metaphysical notion of actual being, it provides a natural framework for formulating such plausible metaphysical principles from which the essentialist conclusions at issue are easily derivable.

To see this in detail, let us consider first how the semantics of the verb 'exists' and its abstract counterpart, the noun 'existence', as determined by the above semantic principles provides grounds for formulating some metaphysical principles. Let us take the proposition: 'Socrates exists'. In accordance with rule 4 above, this proposition is true if and only if the significate of its predicate in the suppositum of its subject is actual. But given that 'existence' is the abstract counterpart of 'exists', we can use the term 'existence' to refer to this significate, and so we can say that this proposition is true if and only if Socrates' existence is actual. Now, of course, as far as the above-described semantics is concerned, it would be possible to have models in which, say, Socrates is an element of the domain of actual things, while his existence is not, or vice versa, but such models would verify the metaphysical absurdity that Socrates would be actual while he would not exist, or that his existence would be actual while he himself would not be one of the actual things. Therefore, on the basis of these considerations it is reasonable to add the further rule concerning the metaphysically relevant notion of existence that

(E) $SGT('exists')(u)(t)A \in (t)$ iff $u \in A(t)$.

But this will immediately establish the predicate 'exists' as an essential predicate of anything in the contemporary sense, for, of course, on the basis of this rule the predicate 'exists' will necessarily be true of anything as long as it exists, that is, as long as it is actual.

In fact, Kit Fine has already drawn this conclusion concerning the modern theory, namely, that the predicate 'exists', interpreted as true on the basis of elementhood in the actual domain, will be one of the "trivial" essential predicates of things. However, he found this conclusion to be unacceptable, because on his reading this would mean that a contingent being, such as Socrates, essentially exists.

But in this framework we need not regard this conclusion as unacceptable at all. On the contrary, St. Thomas explicitly holds that existence in this sense has to be an essential predicate of all beings,[15] which, nevertheless, does not mean that he would identify the essence of any creature with its existence. In fact, this is precisely the point of

St. Thomas's famous metaphysical thesis of the real distinction between essence and existence in the creatures, which, for want of the required expressive resources, could not even be formulated in the contemporary framework, let alone be argued for or against.

To see this in more detail, having seen what the semantic values of 'existence' are, now we have to see what the semantic values of 'essence' are. To put it briefly, in accordance with what Aquinas says, the term 'essence' primarily stands for the significata of substantial predicates of substances (their *species, genera,* and *differentiae*). Now these substantial predicates are those terms the existence of the significata of which is identical with the existence of the things that have these significata. This criterion of the substantiality of a predicate (other than 'exists'), therefore, can be formulated in the semantics as follows:

(SP)   P is a substantial predicate if and only if SGT('exists')(SGT (P)(u)(t))(t) = SGT('exists')(u)(t)

and thus, if P is a substantial predicate, and in line with Aquinas's metaphysical theory we also assume that all substantial predicates have the same significata in the same individuals, then the semantic values of 'essence' can be assigned by the following rules:

(ES1)   SGT('essence')(u)(t) = SGT(P)(u)(t)

and

(ES2)   SUP('essence')(t) = SGT(P)(SUP(P)(t))(t)

So, for example, in this stronger, traditional sense, to say that Socrates is essentially a man means that what 'man' signifies in him, his humanity, is such a form that the actual existence of this form is nothing but the actual existence of Socrates, or, to put the same in perhaps more familiar terms, for Socrates to be is for him to be a man.

Now, of course, upon this understanding of 'essence', 'exists' and 'existence', it is clearly possible to hold that 'exists' is an essential predicate of everything in the modern sense, and yet, it is not an essential predicate in the stronger sense that it would signify every thing's essence. For although in virtue of (E) above, it will be necessary for the predicate 'exists' to be true of everything that exists, still, the significate of the predicate 'exists' in a thing need not be identical with the significate of any of the thing's substantial predicates. However, of course, this identity is not excluded by the semantic theory either; so, again, it takes separate metaphysical arguments to establish what the actual truth is, indeed arguments of the sort Aquinas used to establish the real distinction of these semantic values in the case of creatures, and their real identity in the case of God. But rather than going into these traditional metaphysical issues, it is time for us to see what we can gain from this approach in handling the contemporary issues outlined above.

4. Traditional Essentialism and the Problems of Contemporary "Essentialism"

First of all, even if the semantic apparatus sketched above does not in itself determine that there are any essential predicates, it allows us to formulate plausible *metaphysical* reasons for showing that there have to be some, since such predicates are those that signify the essences of things, and we have to concede that things have essences.

1. Suppose there is a substance that has no substantial predicates. This would mean that the existence of the *significata* of all predicates of this substance other than 'exists' would be distinct from the existence of the thing itself. This substance, therefore, would have existence, but no essence. So it would be possible for this substance to exist, but not to have any true predicates besides 'exists' at all. But then it should be possible that there is a substance which is neither material nor immaterial, that is, which is neither a body nor a non-body, and which is neither a man nor any kind of thing other than a man, etc., but this is impossible.

2. As the Philosopher says: *vivere viventibus est esse*—for a living thing to be is for it to live. Therefore, for a living thing to begin to live and to cease to live is for it to come to exist and to cease to exist; indeed, everybody would agree that the birth and the death of living things is their coming to be and passing away. However, if there were no essences, then, since it is the essence of a thing that constitutes it in its specific kind, determining what (kind of thing) it is, a living and a non-living thing would not differ as to what (kind of thing) the one and what (kind of thing) the other is. Consequently, a living thing could turn into

a non-living thing without ceasing to be what it is. However, whenever a thing changes, but without ceasing to be what it is, it can continue to exist. So, if things had no essences, a living thing could turn into a non-living thing without ceasing to exist, which contradicts what we have just conceded above.

3. Again, existence is nothing but the actuality of essence, since an essence is nothing but the determination of a certain kind of existence. But then, whenever a thing exists, there also has to be an essence, namely, this thing's essence in actual existence. So, if there exists anything at all, its essence also exists. But we know that there exist certain things in our actual reality (at least, nobody can reasonably doubt his or her own existence); therefore, we should also know that things actually have essences in our actual reality.

4. Furthermore, the essence of a thing, which determines what kind of a thing it is, determines what species of entities the thing in question belongs to. Therefore, whoever denies that things have essences has to deny that there is any specific difference between him or her and, say, an ass or a cabbage. But then such a person is no more worth talking to than an ass or a cabbage.[16]

So, on the basis of these and similar *metaphysical* reasons, it is safe to conclude that things in our actual reality do have essences. But then, since the essences of things are the significata of substantial predicates, it follows that there indeed *are* such predicates in our actual language(s) interpreted in our actual reality. Furthermore, since, as we have seen, such predicates are necessarily true of the things whose essences they signify, provided these things exist, these predicates will also be essential predicates of these things in the modern sense. Therefore, the Aristotelian position that things have essences implies the modern claim that things have essential predicates in the modern sense, thereby providing the required metaphysical underpinning for the modern claim. But the converse claim does not hold. Of course, all the "trivial" properties listed in the objections of Kit Fine are also necessary properties of anything in this semantics, yet in this semantics they need not signify the essences of anything; indeed, they are probably best handled as signifying some *entia rationis*, which do not have essences, given that essence is the determination of the act of existing of a real being.

However, even if we could in this way come up with principled metaphysical reasons to support the modern "essentialist" claim, neither these metaphysical reasons, nor the semantic rules that make their formulations intelligible are sufficient to sort out *which* predicates of our language(s) should be regarded as substantial. Indeed, this is how it should be. For *nomina significant ad placitum,* so just any term of any language can be used by anyone in any way, of course, under pain of occasionally making a fool of themselves. (Such occasions occur when their usage is blatantly divergent from the received usage without any acceptable justification for such a divergence.) But the really interesting cases are the subtle, hardly detectable deviations, or indeed cases where the established usage is underdetermined, allowing individual users leeway in stipulating usage as they please.

In any case, it is sometimes possible that users of the same language might disagree as to what should count as the correct specification of the proper usage of some term. While some user may insist that a certain term should stick with the things it normally designates, under whatever "abnormal" circumstances, another may insist that "the proper meaning" of the same term is correctly specified by some sort of nominal definition specifying the actual conditions of applicability of the term, no matter what may satisfy these conditions under various possible circumstances.

For example, take the term 'water' in English. On the former user's account the rule governing its use would be:

$$(U_1) \quad SGTU_1(\text{'water'})(SUP(\text{'water'})(t))(t) = SGTU_1(\text{'essence'})(SUP(\text{'water'})(t))(t)$$

On the other user's account, however,

$$(U_2) \quad SGTU_2(\text{'water'})(SUP(\text{'water'})(t))(t) = SGTU_2(\text{'TCDL'})(SUP(\text{'TCDL'})(t))(t),$$

where 'TCDL' is short for 'tasteless, colorless, drinkable liquid', or anything of that kind of nominal definition, the actual values of which should of course be determined compositionally on the basis of the values of its constituents, but we need not go into such technical details here. Now, the thing which under the present "normal" circumstances both users would identify as water could stay in existence without satisfying this definition under different circumstances. Therefore, under those different circumstances 'water' would still signify the actually existing essence of water according to the first user's usage, while according to the second user's it would signify some non-actual feature of the same thing (and thus he would no longer call it 'water').[17] Hence, clearly,

$$SGTU_1('water') \neq SGTU_2('water').$$

So, they are obviously using the same term with different significations, that is, equivocally, whence their disagreement is merely verbal, and can easily be settled by making this difference clear. In any case, the philosophically important point is that it is only after this issue of usage is settled that we can start the metaphysical inquiry into the natures of the things that are picked out by means of their essential terms. For in merely specifying the meaning (signification) of a term by means of a nominal definition, we simply cannot go wrong as to the nature of the thing actually referred to by the term. The nominal definition has nothing to do with the nature of the thing: it merely specifies the proper usage of the term (although, of course, we may have disagreements over what the proper usage is). However, when it comes to trying to characterize the nature of the thing referred to by the term by means of a real, essential, or quidditative definition, we definitely can, and very often do, go wrong.

In fact, among other things, it was precisely this type of error that discredited most of Aristotelian science in the late medieval and early modern period. But then it was not only particular Aristotelian claims concerning the natures of specific kinds of things that were called into doubt, but the whole Aristotelian conceptual apparatus with the entire metaphysical enterprise it defined. By now, however, we have come full circle. The originally anti-metaphysical trends of modern philosophy gave rise to analytic philosophical techniques which not only allowed, but more recently even demanded, metaphysical reflection. Furthermore, the development of modern science recently put us into a position from which we can quite safely provide the real definitions of several natural kinds. For example, the essence of water is by all probability correctly described by saying that water is a body of H_2O molecules. If this is indeed the correct essential definition of water, then (taking 'H_2O' short for 'body of H_2O molecules') what this means is the following:

$$SGT('water')(SUP('water')(t))(t) = SGT('essence')(SUP('water')(t))$$
$$(t) = SGT('H_2O')(SUP('water')(t))(t)$$

Of course, this move will make 'water' and 'H_2O' have the same signification, that is, synonymous. Yet, this need not imply that whoever knows the signification of 'water' would thereby know that water is H_2O. For one of course can have perfect possession of the concept of water without having any idea of chemistry whatsoever. What this person does not know is only that the chemical concept, which he or she does not have, picks out the same essence that his or her concept of water does.

So to acquire this knowledge is to acquire this chemical concept and to establish this quidditative definition in one's mind. Indeed, the *original* acquisition of this concept was precisely what happened in the history of chemistry, in the course of scientific research. Therefore, it should be clear that, contrary to the apparent practice of "essentialists," finding out what is essential to a given kind of thing is not a matter of personal intuitions, but rather a matter of experience, indeed, of scientific experiments, putting the thing in "abnormal" circumstances, making it interact with other things (after all, as St. Thomas says, the nature of the thing is the principle of its proper operation), precisely in the way in which modern science investigates the nature of things. In fact, this has also been the way in which we acquired our pre-scientific substantial concepts, but in a slow, uncontrolled, unsystematic accumulation of experience, getting encoded in, and passed down to generations by, language. (This is precisely the point Aristotle makes at the end of his *Posterior Analytics,* and, not by pure chance, also at the beginning of his *Metaphysics.*) So modern science in no way needs to undermine Aristotelian essentialism. On the contrary, if we manage to recover the adequate conceptual framework of traditional essentialism in the broadest, formal semantical terms, modern science can in principle just as well be integrated into the project of the traditional metaphysical enterprise as Aristotelian science could. All in all, it seems that the time is ripe for a *radical recovery* of our lost metaphysical tradition, yet this is possible only through recovering the language in which it is properly conveyed, uniting the formal rigor of contemporary logical techniques with the metaphysical vigor of the pre-modern tradition.

Notes

1. To be sure, this characterization by no means covers all versions of what goes by the name of "essentialism" in contemporary philosophy. Still,

this is arguably the most widespread notion of "essentialism" nowadays, and it certainly does serve as "the least common denominator" in discussions concerning "essentialism."

2. All these are conveniently brought together by Michael della Rocca in his "Recent Work on Essentialism," *Philosophical Books* 37 (1996), pp. 1–13 and 81–89.

3. Quite characteristically, "essentially" and "necessarily" are often used interchangeably in these arguments, so I am just following this practice here. Cf., however, R. B. Marcus, "Essential Attribution," in *Modalities: Philosophical Essays* (New York: Oxford University Press, 1993), p. 60.

4. A good example of a contrary use of the same type of argument, to establish an essentialist conclusion, is Kripke's argument against body-mind identity. Although in this case Kripke argues that a reformulation is unavailable, his critics' arguments are intended to show precisely this, thereby showing that one of the premises has to receive an opaque reading, which invalidates the argument.

5. To be sure, this is good; after all, if essential, or even "essential," terms should have to do something with the nature of things, such sorting out should not be simply a matter of logic.

6. Kit Fine: "Essence and modality," in J. E. Tomberlin, *Logic and Language*, Philosophical Perspectives 8 (Atascadero, Calif.: Ridgeview Publishing Company, 1994), pp. 1–15, p. 4.

7. G. Klima, "The Semantic Principles Underlying Saint Thomas Aquinas's Metaphysics of Being," *Medieval Philosophy and Theology* 5 (1996), pp. 87–141; G. Klima, "The Changing Role of *Entia Rationis* in Medieval Philosophy: A Comparative Study with a Reconstruction," *Synthese* 96 (1993), pp. 25–59.

8. A description of the complete technical apparatus can be found in essay 5 of G. Klima, *Ars Artium: Essays in Philosophical Semantics, Medieval and Modern* (Budapest: Institute of Philosophy of the Hungarian Academy of Sciences, 1988).

9. Cf. *QD. De Potentia*, q. 7, a. 10, ad 8.

10. We may also suggest that "in between" these two cases, that is, getting an actual form or o as its value, a predicate may get non-actual forms as its values, 'non-actual' covering several possible sorts of natural potentiality (or the lack thereof), which is a very rich field of further metaphysical inquiry, but which is irrelevant in our present analysis. For further technical details the reader should consult essay 5 of Klima, *Ars Artium*.

11. Medieval supposition theory is a topic deserving a book in itself. Here I reconstruct only one particular aspect of a tiny fragment of this theory. For further references, both to primary and secondary literature, and for further details of my reconstruction of the "core theory," see Klima, *Ars Artium*. To see how this theory of reference can be developed into a formal theory equivalent to generalized quantification theory, see especially essay 3, "General Terms

in Their Referring Function," in the same book, and Klima and G. G.-Sandu, "Numerical Quantifiers in Game-Theoretical Semantics," *Theoria* 56 (1990), pp. 173–92.

12. Since it is only the significata of predicates that are relevant in the present analysis, here I omit the reconstruction of Aquinas's theory of the copula altogether. The reconstruction of that theory can be found in the article referred to in n. 7.

13. Of course, for any t and any SUP, SUP('Socrates')(t) = Socrates, if Socrates ∈ A(t) and SUP('Socrates')(t) = 0 otherwise.

14. For more on these qualifications, see G. Klima, "Ockham's Semantics and Metaphysics of the Categories," in P. V. Spade, ed., *The Cambridge Companion to Ockham* (Cambridge: Cambridge University Press, 2000).

15. Cf. in *Metaphysics* 5, 9. n. 896.

16. Anyone who feels shocked by the apparently rude *ad hominem* character of this argument should consult Aquinas's discussion of Aristotle's instructions concerning the necessity to use *ad hominem* arguments against those who deny first principles, in book 4 of the *Metaphysics*.

17. Obviously, it is the first user's usage that follows actual English, for of course 'water' in English is used as a substantial term. So no wonder it cannot apply to Putnam's XYZ. In fact, the only reason why this otherwise trivial observation could be hailed as the harbinger of a "new theory of reference" was the tremendous influence of empiricism, which for its own epistemological reasons (in fact, going back to the original British empiricist program of trying to analyze all our mental contents ultimately in terms of simple sensible ideas), tied the meaning of all terms to their nominal definitions, ideally, ultimately analyzable in terms of simple sensible qualities. But since all such qualities are accidents, no wonder that in this (mostly programmatic) analysis all terms came out as non-rigid designators of their individuals. However, if we abandon the rather narrow-minded empiricist platform and the consequent philosophy of language (as most analytic philosophers by now have done), it is no longer a sacrilege to insist that some terms do designate "rigidly" their individuals, regardless of their accidental features. These features under "normal" circumstances may be useful indicators of what kind of thing we are actually dealing with, but under "abnormal" circumstances they may be deceptive, in that they may not belong to the kind of thing they normally belong to, and/or they may belong to some other kind of thing that they normally do not belong to.

CHAPTER TWELVE

Practical Reason and the Orders of Morals and Nature in Aquinas's Theory of the *Lex Naturae*

M. W. F. Stone

The recent past has witnessed a profusion of studies by English-speaking scholars that have contrived to consider most aspects of Thomas's theory of the natural law and its relation to his practical philosophy (*philosophia practica*).[1] A recurrent theme in these works has been the attempt to define the point and scope of Thomas's so-called 'ethical naturalism'.[2] At its strongest, ethical naturalism is the idea that goodness and rightness can be reduced to a set of natural properties, while at its weakest the theory holds that moral predicates can be identified, in some sense or other, with facts about the natural world. As is to be expected, contemporary ethical naturalism comes in many varieties. There are not only the aforementioned versions of theory, but also more intermediate positions that seek to straddle the dividing line between weak and strong versions of naturalism.[3] However, what all forms of ethical naturalism share, thus enabling us to speak of a relatively homogeneous class of theories within modern-day ethics, is a rejection of the thesis that moral properties are *sui generis*.

It is important to understand why the issue of naturalism has come to dominate present-day discussion of Thomistic *philosophia practica*. In the first place, there developed in some quarters the desire to liberate Thomas from the charge of a crude naturalism which had become associated with his work by virtue of a number of neo-Scholastic readings of natural law theory. These interpretations had argued that the theory of natural law was little more than an attempt to found normative principles upon a theoretical description of human nature and its needs and tendencies.[4] Such a view, it was held, simply missed the point of Thomas's writings on natural law, for it merely served to licence a series of restrictive moral norms that were supposed to derive their action-guiding force from a 'quasi-scientific' statement of the workings of nature. Not only was this view held to be morally unattractive in its own right, but it was also deemed to be philosophically unsatisfactory on grounds that it was far from obvious that a theory of human conduct could ever be founded upon an anthropology, let alone a particular biology.

The first to argue systematically against this view were Germain Grisez[5] and John Finnis.[6] Over the years they have argued that the Thomistic theory of the natural law can be extricated from the charge of crude naturalism. For them, Thomas's practical philosophy, of which the theory of natural law is one important component, is based upon the notion of 'practical reasonableness'. As Finnis has argued, no theoretical insight into human nature and its basic inclinations can tell us which moral goods we ought to pursue. It is only when we reason practically, that is, when we think about what to do, or be, or have, that questions about the goods of life become tractable and answerable.[7]

While the arguments of Grisez and Finnis have reinvigorated the study of the natural law tradition,[8] as well as providing a nuanced set of reflections on Thomas's ethical thought, a more general worry can be said to dominate present-day discussion of Thomistic natural law theory. This concerns the fact that even if Thomas's theory can be distinguished from the crude naturalism of his neo-Scholastic interpreters, it is difficult to determine in precise detail the *extent* of his ethical naturalism. This is the case for the simple reason that plausible yet contrary readings of the theory of natural law, readings which lend themselves to both naturalist and anti-naturalist interpretations, can be derived from important passages in the *Summa theologiae*. The *Summa*, it appears, offers conflicting advice as to how Thomas's putative naturalism in ethics is to be assessed.

This last claim can be illustrated as follows. In the much-cited article 2 of question 94 of the *Prima secundae*, we find Thomas explaining how it is that practical reason, starting from the first intuitive principle *bonum est faciendum* can formulate the following axiom: "all things to which men have a natural inclination are naturally apprehended by reason as being good, and consequently as objects of pursuit."[9] So it seems that practical reason considers so-called 'natural ends' (these being the objects of our natural inclinations), as goods to be pursued; that is, as 'moral ends'. But if practical reasoning ought to take as its starting points (*principia*) the ends predetermined by our natural inclinations, then this seems to suggest that the theory of natural law is part of a more general version of ethical naturalism.

This last thought, however, appears to sit uneasily next to Thomas's robust statement at Ia–IIae, q. 1, a.3 ad 3 that "moral ends are only accidentally related to a natural thing, and that the notion of a natural end is accidental to the moral end,"[10] a passage which suggests anything but the ethical naturalism described above. For here we meet the explicit denial that the 'object' of a moral end is supplied by anything that is, as such, within nature. For Thomas often distinguishes what he calls the *genus moris* or *genus morale* from the *genus naturae*. The former concerns human action while the latter encompasses the domain of natural actions.[11] Each genus has its own essential properties, its own specific differences, and its own principles that explain and regulate its operations. These set it apart from other genera. If the so-called order of nature and the domain of morality are distinguished as two separate genera, then it appears impossible that specifications of the one could explain those of the other. Thus, what is good or evil by the standards of nature is not necessarily so in the moral domain and vice versa. The distinction between the *genus naturae* and the *genus moris* seems to rule out any direct correspondence between the classes of natural goods and those of moral goods. Further to this, it appears to preclude the idea that one domain or order can have its foundation upon the other. So much, then, for ethical naturalism.

In what follows, I shall provide a series of suggestions that will argue that the ongoing attempt to make sense of Thomas's *philosophia practica* ought not to be hijacked by a concern to produce, once and for all, a consistent 'naturalist' or 'anti-naturalist' reading of Thomas's theory of the natural law. My argument will be that if it can be shown that the relevant passages in the *Summa theologiae* are equivocal, then that must be accepted as the starting point of any further enquiry, rather than as an issue that has to be settled in its own right. Going on from there, I shall suggest that if one is to make sense of the theory of natural law within the more general context of Thomas's system of *philosophia practica*, then we should direct our attention to an analysis of the roles of reason and will in his explanation of human action. In this sense, the theory of action, and its basis in Thomas's philosophy of mind, hold the key to understanding his ethics. The contemporary preoccupation with naturalism has caused many English-speaking commentators to lose sight of this fact.

The equivocal nature of Thomas's position can be made explicit by focusing on the distinction between moral and natural ends in his account of human action. Thomas states that the domain of morality can be distinguished from that of nature because it encompasses acts that are explicable by the causality of the will. He says:

> No action can be put in the *genus moris* unless it stands in relation to the will, which is the starting point of morals [*principium moralis*]; hence the *genus moris* begins where the reign of the will [*dominum voluntatis*] is first to be found.[12]

Thus the moral domain is distinguished from the domain of nature because the will exercises a type of causality that is entirely different from any kind of natural causality:

> For the will is distinguished from nature as one kind of cause from another. For some things occur naturally and some are done voluntarily. Therefore, there is another manner of causing that is proper to the will, which is mistress of its acts, besides the manner proper to nature, which is determined to one thing.[13]

One needs to be precise here because, for Thomas, there is no radical opposition between will and nature; both are *intrinsic* principles of action, and thus different from any other kind of causality where the principle of action is external. Further to this, both are directed in their causation toward an end. That is, finality is not an exclusive feature of voluntary action: all agents, be they human or otherwise, act for ends. Thus, finality can never suffice to set the will as a cause apart from nature. That said, it is only the will which is directed to an end as a *known* end. For the desire of the will always presupposes knowledge of its goals, whereas the inclinations by which natural phenomena are directed to their ends are spontaneous and non-cognitive.[14] Only agents that *know* the end they desire are self-moving and self-directing in a proper sense; since they apprehend the end as an *end* (*sub ratione finis*), they can intentionally organise and arrange their action in view of that end.

The point of significance, then, is that Aquinas considers what we now refer to as 'intentionality' to be characteristic of voluntary actions. As he so often says, "the good and the end" (*bonum et finis*) are the formal objects of the will, for the will desires something only insofar as that thing is apprehended as a good or an end, whereas no natural power, however much it may be directed to its own end, has the end as its formal object.[15] Although all agents act for an end, only voluntary action may be characterised by purposiveness or intentionality, since the end or the good is its proper object.

Because the will is a desire consequent upon knowledge of an end, it can never be determined by just one proper end as are all natural inclinations. In fact, beings endowed with knowledge grasp many different forms as desirable ends and bring about a variety of actions in their pursuit of them. A natural inclination, by contrast, is based upon a being's nature, upon its natural form and not upon intentionally present forms. For this reason a natural inclination is determined to one proper end: *natura determinatur ad unum*.[16] Natural acts receive their specification from the natural forms of which they are the expression, whereas human voluntary acts are specified by their relation to their intended ends.[17]

We have seen how the *genus moris* defines the domain of human action. Going on from there, we must now note that the agency of the will, for Aquinas, does not suffice to demarcate acts as moral acts. This can be explained as follows. When the will is defined as a desire consequent upon knowledge it must be connected to practical reason if any voluntary act is to be deserving of the epithet 'moral'. Reason, for Thomas, performs two functions with respect to the will. First, it specifies the will by presenting it with appropriate objects of desire, for an agent always wills *this* or *that*; and this specification does not come from the will itself, but from the rational apprehension of forms as desirable objects.[18] But reason not only specifies desirable ends, it also functions as the *regula* (rule) and measure that polices voluntary action. Therefore reason and not will is "the principle of human and moral acts" (*ratio enim principium est humanorum et moralium actuum*).[19] In point of fact, Thomas says "that which is the principle in any genus is the rule and the measure of that genus." He illustrates this point by use of the following examples: unity is the principle from which all numbers originate and is thus the measure of all numbers. Likewise, the movement of the first heavenly sphere is the principle of all movements in the universe and thus is the measure by which all movements can be measured.[20] But why should reason be considered the measure and rule of the moral sphere? Why should this measure not be the will itself, which is the principle of all voluntary actions encompassing the *genus morale*? Is not the principle of a genus always the measure regulating that genus? Why can the will itself not be the measure of its own willing?

In his answer to these questions, Thomas once more focuses on the difference between the moral and the natural orders.[21] Suppose that an active principle is itself the rule of the action it performs, then such a principle will always act rightly and never fail. For instance, if the engraver's hand were itself the rule that should direct his engraving, he would always engrave well. But the quality of his engravings is measured by a rule other than the power of his hand, and therefore he may engrave either well or badly. Now, in natural processes the rule regulating the action is the natural power of the agent that inclines it to a particular end: *ipsa virtus agentis est regula actionis*. For instance, in the development of an embryo, the sequence and order of all the different steps in this complex process are regulated by nature (the formative principle) that directs all intermediary processes to their end, viz. birth. Because nature is at the same time the teleological principle and the *regula* of its own action, a natural process is always 'right' (or nearly so, for there may be accidents); that is, a natural process does not deviate from the order of its active principle determining it to its end. But this does not hold in the case of voluntary or human acts, which as such are open to an infinite variety of ends and so are not determined by any one of them. Voluntary agents lack in themselves a *debita commensuratio*.[22] Only God's will is itself the *regula* of its own act of willing, because God's will is directed only to his own perfection and not to an end outside of, or superior to, himself. In all other cases of voluntary action, the will must be regulated by a principle different from the will itself; and this principle can only be reason: *ratio est measura voluntatis*.[23]

To understand just what Thomas means when he refers to the regulating function of reason, one should recall his view that voluntary agents are directed to their ends as *known ends*. It is precisely because they know their ends that agents can consider other things and acts as necessary or appropriate means to their ends. In a natural process, as in the aforementioned development of an embryo, the contrary pertains since the sequence of steps leading to the birth of a baby is unknown to the baby as a 'means' to that end; it would be ludicrous to claim that there existed a sense in which the baby can plan its own birth. Only rational agents, owing to their awareness of the end as an end, can organise or arrange their acts in proportion to the end they wish to realise. This is what Thomas means by the purposiveness or intentionality of human action. To order action is the proper function of reason,[24] only reason can understand the order in which things stand to one another, and particularly the architectonic relation of different things to a superior form that is their end. For it is only by considering the ends to which things are directed that one can understand such things as standing in a discernible order. Therefore, the notion of an end plays an important role both in metaphysical considerations about the order of the universe and in reflection about human action.

This last point receives extended attention in Thomas's introduction to his *Commentary on Aristotle's Ethics*. There, he argues that the organising function of reason is manifest in all four domains of knowledge. First, there is an order that reason discovers, but does not construct. This is the order of nature, which is the subject matter of speculative science, the culmination of which is metaphysics. Secondly, there is an order that reason introduces into the external world when it produces things by art and craftsmanship, such as the craft of making a house. Thirdly, there is an order that reason produces in the acts of thought, when it formulates propositions and syllogisms. This order is the subject matter of logic. And last, there is an order that reason extends to the operations of the will. This order concerns the practical activities of planning and deliberating in order to realise an end. This 'rational order in voluntary acts' is the subject matter of ethics.[25]

In this context we can see why Thomas argues that while the will is the 'universal motor' of all human acts,[26] since it seeks to obtain whatever appears as desirable to it, it is not as such the 'principle and rule' of the moral domain. This function belongs to reason, for reason alone can organise our voluntary acts in an order such that they can secure desirable ends. These ends are the first principles of all practical reasoning. To be sure, human reason is not the ultimate criterion of morality; this is provided by the eternal law. Nonetheless, Thomas contends, human reason alone can serve as the proximate rule and criterion of morality, since a 'rule' must always be a principle that is first within its genus, and it must be homogeneous within its genus.[27] The eternal rule, which is so to speak God's reason *quasi ratio Dei*, transcends the moral genus in every respect. Therefore, only a principle existing within that genus can serve as its proximate rule, and that is the *ratio humana*.[28]

The moral good, or the good of virtue, is "to be in accordance with reason," "in conformity with the rule of reason," as Thomas repeatedly says: "*secundum regulam rationis*," "*in ordine rationis*," "*in adaequatione ad mensuram rationis*," where 'reason' always stands for 'practical reason'. Nowhere does Thomas indicate 'nature' to be the proximate rule of morality. On the contrary, when at *ST* Ia–IIae, q. 54, a. 3 he wants to demonstrate that virtuous acts are suitable to human nature (*conveniunt naturae humanae*), he argues from reason to nature and not vice versa, saying: "Acts of virtue are suitable to human nature, since they are according to reason, whereas acts of vice are in discordance with human nature, since they are against reason."[29] A similar argument can be found at Ia–IIae q. 71, a. 2, where it is claimed that "whatever is in accord with reason is in accord with the nature of man *as man*. Thus vice is contrary to nature insofar as it is contrary to the order of reason" (*in tantum est contra naturam hominis, in quantum est contra ordinem rationis*).

Thus far, this essay has examined how Thomas distinguishes with some care the separate orders of morality and nature, explaining each by its own *principia*. This, however, is only an abstract distinction, for in reality a concrete human act can be described at the same time as a natural act explicable in terms of a natural process and as a moral act proceeding from a deliberate will. But how can the same act fall under two different descriptions? Or to put the question in another way, how can the same act fall under the same genera?

Thomas advances an answer to this question in the second book of his *Commentary on the Sentences of Peter Lombard*.[30] There, he says that an act or a thing may belong to a particular genus in one of two ways, either *per se* or *per accidens*. Consider the examples of whiteness and blackness. Both belong *per se* to the genus of 'colour', of which they are essential specifications. But a white thing and a black thing, e.g. a white cat and a black dog, do not belong *per se* to the genus colour. They belong to the genus 'animal' and only *per accidens*, because of some property present in it, to the genus colour. Now, the only acts that belong *per se* and directly to the *genus moris* are the interior acts elicited by the will: as such, they are either good or evil. On the other hand, all acts commanded by the will but carried out by other powers, such as thinking, imagining, cutting, drinking, walking, and having sexual intercourse, etc., belong only *per accidens* to the *genus moris*, namely and insofar as they possess voluntary character having been commanded by the will. Such acts belong *per se* to the *genus naturae;* they cannot be specified as morally good or bad on the basis of their ontological status. They receive their moral character *per accidens* on account of their dependence upon acts of will. Thus a sexual act (*concubitus*) is *per se* morally neutral and in its own natural order is even a good act. Only insofar as it is a voluntary act does the act assume a moral status: it is either an act of vice (adultery) or virtue (marital love). Likewise the physical act of cutting might be either a merciful surgical operation which saves someone's life, or a cruel act of murder. Apart from inner acts of the will, all other acts merely assume a moral character, a status which, as it were, "comes upon them": *sicut quoddam superveniens et accidentale sibi.*[31]

These last remarks put us in a much better position to understand what Thomas means when he says that "moral ends are only accidentally related to a natural thing and that the natural end is accidental to the moral end." This accidental relation must not be misconstrued as an external realisation, as though the imperated act of the will were only accidental to morality while the essence of morality was exclusively situated within the inner sphere of will, as Aberlard had claimed.[32] Thomas observes that the internal act of the will and the imperated act, although they differ *secundum genus naturae*, constitute one human act in the moral order because the imperated act receives its formal specification from the inner act.[33] A man who has *concubitus* with a woman, or a doctor who aborts a foetus, does not perform an act that is *per se* morally neutral and that becomes evil only owing to its relation to an evil intention of the will. The external sexual act is intended as an act of adultery, or the medical operation as such is intended as an act of abortion. In those texts where Thomas argues that the imperated act is only *per accidens* good or evil, his aim lies elsewhere; he intends to show that the specifications of the moral order—that which make this or that act virtuous or vicious—cannot be founded upon specifications of the natural order but must be determined by practical reason. At its most basic, with its natural principles tending towards ends, an imperated act remains essentially different from a command of the will. It is only under a description derived from the moral domain that it forms a unity with the internal act of will.[34]

A consequence of this view is that natural goods can never be characterised as ends specifying the moral order. As Thomas says, the good that is proposed to the will is good not by virtue of any natural goodness (*bonum bonitate naturae*) but is good because it is presented to the will by reason.

Only in so far as a good is in accord with reason does it enter into the moral order and cause moral goodness in the act of the will.[35]

The primary goodness of a moral act is derived from its *conveniens obiectum*. If this object is absent, then the act is intrinsically evil, whatever the circumstances or the intentions of the agent may be. Here again it must be stressed that the 'object' under discussion is not the external act taken in itself, but a certain relation to reason.[36] As examples of such acts, which are evil for lack of a suitable object, Thomas cites *tollere aliena* (taking what belongs to another) and adultery, examples that aim to show that the 'object' here does not mean the natural structure of the act (for in nature there is neither *alienum* nor adultery) but rather that which "is determined by the rule of reason."[37]

Having taken stock of these arguments, it might appear that we now possess good reasons for claiming that Thomas can be classified as an anti-naturalist. That said, we return again to the problem addressed by this essay, namely that other important passages and arguments in the *Summa Theologiae* suggest a very different interpretation of Thomas's theory of *philosophia practica*. Of the passages that are associated with a naturalist reading of Thomas's theory, the most important are those that are connected with his putative appropriation of Aristotelian moral philosophy.[38] Aristotle had observed in the *Nicomachean Ethics*, Book VI, that it is not enough to say that our moral conduct "should be in accordance with right reason" (κατὰ τὸν ὀρθὸν λόγον), for if a man had only this knowledge he would be none the wiser in matters relating to conduct. For this reason the philosopher must determine what right reason (ὀρθὸς λόγος) is, as well as its standard.[39] Aristotle goes on to clarify only what right reason is, defining it as φρόνησις or practical wisdom. On the question of the standard, or norm of practical wisdom, Aristotle remained vague, his view being that the normative foundation of practical wisdom is given by its connection with the moral virtues by which our desires are directed to good ends.

For Thomas, practical wisdom must be linked to the moral virtues, just as the virtues must accord with *recta ratio* or right reason. Tellingly, he goes beyond Aristotle by placing the foundation of practical reason in universal and self-evident principles.[40] He says: "human reason is not, of itself, the rule of conduct. But the principles that are imparted naturally (*naturaliter indita*) are the general rules and measures of human conduct."[41] He then goes on to subordinate Aristotelian φρόνησις to *synderesis,* the habit of the precepts of natural law from which all practical reasoning ought to proceed. He says, "as every judgement of the speculative reason proceeds from natural knowledge of the first principles, so every judgement of practical reason proceeds from naturally [*naturaliter*] known principles."[42]

Thomas's use of the term *naturaliter* here ought to be seen as a red herring. 'Naturally', in this context, simply means that these first principles are grasped immediately in virtue of the *nature* of the intellect; for this reason they precede all processes of reasoning. More questionable, however, is the fact that the first principles are specified and articulated in relation to the fundamental inclinations of human nature. As Thomas puts it in the much-cited article on natural law, *ST* Ia–IIae, q. 94, a. 4: "all things to which men have a natural inclination (such as self-preservation, procreation, the education of children, political life, etc.) are naturally apprehended by reason of being good." In this text we return again to the fundamental ambiguity in Thomas's account of *philosophia practica* with which this essay is concerned. In this context, however, the natural apprehension under discussion is not a theoretical insight into the facts of human nature, which would somehow function as a foundation of the precepts of how we ought to live. Rather, it is an immediate intuition of the practical intellect which enables us to understand that the ends towards which we are naturally inclined are 'goods' we ought to pursue. Without this practical understanding and its formulation by reason, there is no 'natural law' for human beings in the moral sense of that term. Natural law is "something constituted by reason," it is the work of reason (*opus rationis*).[43] The various ends of our natural inclinations as such are never human goods to be pursued; they must be integrated within a rational scheme. For this reason, the various inclinations of human nature belong to the natural law only and insofar as "they are ruled by reason."[44]

The point of importance here is Thomas's argument that the first principle of practical reason is not related to the basic desires of human nature, but is as an empty formal principle. Thus reason cannot exercise its function to order without taking into account the ends toward which our actions should be directed. But one often gets the impression that Thomas too readily identifies the fundamental 'ends' that we ought to pursue in a moral life with the ends that are predetermined by our nature, even by our biological nature. This implicit naturalism surfaces in his treatment of sexual morality. At the end of his discussion of *luxuria* (see *ST* IIa–IIae, q. 154, a. 12ff.) he poses the question whether the vice against nature, i.e. homosexuality, is the worst kind of all *luxuria*, including rape and incest. Thomas argues that in each genus the worst is always the corruption of the principle upon which all the rest depend. Now, as we have seen, all reasoning must start from the principles "that are determined by nature," and this holds for theoretical as well as for practical reasoning. Thus far, Thomas's argument can be interpreted as though he simply wants to remind us that all moral arguments must be based upon self-evident first principles, which are known by the intellect *naturaliter*. However, when he applies this argument to the question about unnatural acts, something like the type of ethical naturalism of standard textbooks in contemporary moral philosophy seems to emerge. For it appears that the first normative principles are nothing but the ends determined by our natural inclinations. Homosexuality, it is argued, is worse than rape because, in the former, human beings transgress "what has been determined by nature," whereas in the latter they transgress only "the rules determined by right reason" which always presuppose the principles of nature.[45]

Prima facie, it seems that so-called immoral sexual behaviour is evil primarily because it does not accord with nature and secondarily because it does not conform with *recta ratio*. From a reading of this text—where Thomas clearly subordinates practical reasoning to the finality in nature—it becomes clearer that the reference to "naturally imparted principles" is not quite as innocent as an anti-naturalistic interpretation of Thomas's *philosophia practica* would suggest. Of course, it is possible to discuss the morality or immorality of homosexual behaviour. But the discussion should not commence with considerations of predetermined ends of human nature. Rather, it should pose the question whether the mode of behaviour is appropriate to the finality of human life, which is a "finality in accordance with reason."[46] For that matter, Thomas himself clearly states that an act of *luxuria* is sinful because "it exceeds the order and manner of reason in sexual acts."[47] Still, as we have noted, he views the 'order of reason' as more than simply a formal principle of coherence because the "order of reason requires that each thing (or act) be ordered to its own end."[48] Reason, which introduces order into human actions, must respect the finality of human nature. However, in his discussion of sexual acts, Thomas far too readily departs from this view and interprets this finality in an overtly naturalistic sense, namely, as the preservation of the human species. But in another text (e.g., where he discusses virginity), he emphasises that biological finality must always be subordinated to and integrated within a rational project of life.[49]

Like Aristotle, then, Thomas locates the proximate standard of morality in the deliberation or judgement of *recta ratio:* to live morally means to live in accordance with reason. As Thomas writes, "the standard in moral matters is reason." Therefore it must be from the end of reason that acts in the moral domain are called good or bad. Nonetheless, when Thomas goes beyond Aristotle in an attempt to establish the first universal principles of morality, he often takes the ends of nature (*fines naturae*) as first principles of practical reasoning. The ambiguity of his position surfaces in his formulation of the one of the principles of natural law: "natural reason dictates to everyone to live in accordance with reason" (*naturalis ratio dictat unicuique ut secundum rationem operetur*).[50] It is for this reason that Thomas's relation to ethical naturalism—as that position is defined by contemporary English-speaking philosophy—is ambiguous; the relevant texts offer nothing more than a set of equivocal readings.

The argument of this essay has been to show that the attempt to determine, in one way or the other, the extent of Thomas's ethical naturalism in his account of the natural law is of little help in the more general activity of considering the overall coherence of his practical philosophy. By the standards of modern ethical naturalism, what Thomas actually says appears ambiguous. In many respects this remark really ought not to cause us much surprise. For the modern preoccupation with 'naturalism', in terms of a theory of morality that seeks to reduce goodness and rightness to facts about the natural world, is one which more properly belongs to the world of modern moral philosophy and not to the Middle Ages. Indeed, philosophers at Thomas's time would not recognise the issue of naturalism in ethics in the manner in which philosophers labouring in the tradition of G. E. Moore and his opponents have done for most of the twentieth century.[51] For the medievals were concerned to develop a theory of practical conduct in which an agent's actions would be assessed from the perspective of an ultimate end or purpose. In this sense, what we now refer to as 'moral psychology' or the study of the so-called 'propositional attitudes', was for the medievals indispensable to understanding action. Thus, if one wanted to understand what an agent does, one had to understand what that agent intended to do, and this would cause one to speculate yet further as to the causes of the action within the workings of his rational soul.

Thomas is no different from other medievals in this respect. Therefore, if we want to understand the aim and point of his theory of natural law, we must devote more time and attention specifically to his theory of action, and more generally to his philosophy of mind. Determining the extent or otherwise of his so-called 'naturalism' will throw little light upon these important issues.

Notes

1. A representative sample of these works would include: Anthony Battaglia, *Toward a Reformulation of Natural Law* (New York: Seabury Press, 1981); Jean Porter, *The Recovery of Virtue: The Relevance of Aquinas for Christian Ethics* (Louisville, Ky.: Westminster/John Knox Press, 1990); James F. Kennan, S.J., *Goodness and Rightness in Thomas Aquinas's Summa Theologiae* (Washington, D.C.: Georgetown University Press, 1992); Daniel Mark Nelson, *The Priority of Prudence: Virtue and Natural Law in Thomas Aquinas and the Implications for Modern Ethics* (University Park: Pennsylvania State University Press, 1992); Daniel Westberg, *Right Practical Reason: Aristotle, Action, and Prudence in Aquinas* (Oxford: Clarendon Press, 1994); Pamela M. Hall, *Narrative and Natural Law: An Interpretation of Thomistic Ethics* (Notre Dame, Ind.: University of Notre Dame Press, 1994); Anthony J. Lisska, *Aquinas's Theory of Natural Law: An Analytic Reconstruction* (Oxford: Clarendon Press, 1996); and John Finnis, *Aquinas* (Oxford: Oxford University Press, 1998). For a recent survey article which assesses the respective contributions of these works, with the exception of Lisska and Finnis, see Jean Porter, "Recent Studies in Aquinas's Virtue Ethics: A Review Essay," *Journal of Religious Ethics* 26 (1998): 191–215. The important study by Denis J. M. Bradley, *Aquinas on the Twofold Human Good: Reason and Human Happi-*

ness in Aquinas's Moral Science (Washington, D.C.: The Catholic University of America Press, 1997), came to my attention after this paper was completed.

2. For contemporary writers, discussion of these issues might be said to have begun with the article by Vernon Bourke, "Is Aquinas a Natural Law Ethicist?," *Monist* 18 (1974): 52–66.

3. A useful, if limited survey, of the doctrine is by Charles Pigden, "Naturalism," in Peter Singer, ed., *A Companion to Ethics,* Blackwell Companions to Philosophy (Oxford: Basil Blackwell, 1991), pp. 421–31. A more substantive discussion of the prospects for ethical naturalism within contemporary ethics can be found in the exchange between Peter Railton and David Wiggins in John Haldane and Crispin Wright, eds., *Reality, Representation, and Projection* (Oxford: Oxford University Press, 1993), pp. 279–336.

4. For accessible examples of this mode of interpretation see Etienne Gilson, *Le Thomisme* (Paris: Vrin, 1964), Part III; and Dom Odon Lottin, "Pour un commentaire historique de la morale de saint Thomas d'Aquin," in his *Psychologie et morale aux Xiie et Xiiie,* 6 vols. (Louvain: Abbaye de Mont Cesar, 1942–1963), see vol. 3, part 2, pp. 576–601; and *Études de morale: histoire et doctrine* (Gembloux: J. Duculot, 1961), pp. 56ff. In many ways this tradition of commentary can be said to continue up to the present moment. For a recent example, see Leo Elders, *The Philosophy of Nature of St. Thomas Aquinas: Nature, the Universe, and Man* (New York/Berlin: Peter Lang, 1997).

5. G. Grisez, "The First Principles of Practical Reason," *Natural Law Forum* 10 (1965): 168–95; reprinted in an abridged form in Anthony Kenny, ed., *Aquinas: A Collection of Critical Essays* (London: Macmillan, pp. 340–82). Rightly or wrongly, Grisez is more often than not acknowledged to be the first to have debunked the older neo-Scholastic in English-speaking circles. In many ways, Francophone Thomistic studies had been aware of these errors much earlier. For an excellent and illuminating discussion of Thomas's ethics from a distinctly anti-naturalist perspective, see Léonard Lehu, *La Raison, règle de moralité d'après Saint Thomas* (Paris: Librairie Lecoffre, 1930).

6. The works by Finnis of most relevance are his *Natural Law and Natural Rights* (Oxford: Clarendon Press, 1980), and *Fundamentals of Ethics* (Oxford: Oxford University Press, 1983). Finnis, *Aquinas,* can be said to reiterate many of the arguments advanced in these works, while offering more detailed exegetical support by way of extensive use of extracts from Thomas's philosophical and theological corpus.

7. See Finnis, *Fundamentals of Ethics,* p. 12ff.

8. For a very confident exposition of modern natural law theory see Finnis, *Natural Law,* and Robert George, ed., *Natural Law Theory* (Oxford: Clarendon Press, 1992).

9. *ST* Ia–IIae, q. 94, a. 2: "omnia illa ad quae homo habet naturalem inclinationem, ratio naturaliter apprehendit ut bona, et per consequens ut opere prosequenda."

10. *ST* Ia–IIae, q. 1, a. 3, ad. 3: "Fines autem morales accidunt rei naturali, et e converso ratio naturalis fini accidit morali."

11. See the references in the *Index Thomisticus*, s.v. 'morale' and 'moris'.

12. *II Sent.*, d. 24, q. 3, a.2: "nullus autem ponitur in genere moris nisi habita comparatione ad voluntatem quae est principium moralium et ideo ibi incipit genus moris ubi primo dominum voluntatis invenitur." Cf. d. 42, q. 1, a. 1: "actus non ponitur in genere moris nisi propter voluntatem, secundum quod est a voluntate elicitus vel imperatus."

13. *ST* Ia–IIae, q. 10, a. 1, ad. 1: "... voluntas dividitur contra naturam, sicut una causa contra aliam: quaedam enim fiunt naturaliter, et quaedam fiunt voluntarie. Est autem alius modus causandi proprius voluntati quae est domina sui actus, praeter modum qui convenit naturae, quae est determinata ad unum."

14. *ST* Ia–IIae, q. 6, a. 4: "Actus voluntatis nihil est aliud quam inclinatio quaedam procedens ab interiori principio cognoscente, sicut appetitus naturalis est quaedam inclinatio ab interiori principio et sine cognitione." Cf. q. 6, a. 1.

15. Aquinas frequently invokes this principle using a formula such as "finis est obiectum voluntatis"; or "obiectum voluntatis est bonum (universale, apprehensum)."

16. Cf. *ST* Ia, q. 41, a. 2; q. 80, a. 1; Ia–IIae, q. 10, a. 1, ad 3.

17. See *ST* Ia–IIae, q. 1, a.3: "utrum humani actus recipiant speciem ex fine?" Cf. also q. 18, aa. 2–3 and 4, and q. 72, a. 1 ad 3.

18. *ST* Ia–IIae, q. 19, a. 3: "obiectum autem voluntatis proponitur ei per rationem. Nam bonum intellectum est obiectum voluntatis proportionatum ei." On the specification of the will, see Ia–IIae, a. 1: "intellectus movet voluntatem sicut praesentans ei objectum suum." Of further relevance is *De malo*, q. 4, a.2 and 13.

19. *ST* Ia–IIae, q. 18, a. 5. Cf. q. 19, a. 1, ad 3, q. 58, a.2; q. 100, a.1.

20. See *ST* Ia–IIae, q. 90, a. 1.

21. See *ST* Ia–IIae, q. 21, a. 1; q. 63, a. 1.

22. See *ST* Ia–IIae, q. 71, a. 6.

23. *ST* Ia–IIae, q. 19, a. 4: "Ratio humana regula voluntatis humanae sit ex qua bonitas mensuratur." Cf. q. 60, a. 1: "mensura et regula appetitivi motus circa appetibilia est ipsa ratio."

24. "Rationis est ordinare" is one of Thomas's most cited principles. See, for example, *Summa contra gentiles*, II, c. 34. The principle can be traced back to Aristotle, see *Metaphysics*, I. 2, 982a18 and Thomas's *Commentary*, ad locum.

25. *In Ethicorum*, Lect. I, 1. I.

26. Cf. *ST* Ia–IIae, q. 17, a. 1: "primum movens in virbus animae ad exceritium actus est voluntas."

27. Cf. *ST* Ia, q. 3, a. 5, ad 2: "unumquodque mensuratur per aliquid sui generis"; Ia–IIae, q. 19, a. 4, ad 2: "mensura proxima est homogenea mensurato, non autem mensura remota." Cf. Aristotle, *Metaphysics*, X, 1, 1053a25.

28. *ST* Ia–IIae, q. 21, a. 1: "regula voluntatis humanae duplex: una est homogenea, humana ratio, alia remota et heterogenea, lex aeterna, quasi ratio Dei." Cf. q. 71, a. 6.

29. *ST* Ia–IIae, q. 54, a. 3: "Sicut actus virtutum naturae humanae conveniunt, eo quod sunt secundum rationem: actus vero vitiorum, cum sint contra rationem, a natura humana discordant."

30. In this argument I follow Thomas's exposition at *II Sent* d. 40, q. 1, a. 1ff.

31. *In II Sent* d. 40, q. 1, a. 4: "actus exteriores participant bonitatem et malitiam moralem sicut quoddam superveniens et accidentale sibi, in quantum tales actus sunt imperati a voluntate." Cf. *ST* Ia–IIae, q. 18, a. 7, ad 1: "secundum conditiones morales supervenientes."

32. See Peter Aberlard, *Ethica*, David Luscombe, ed. (Oxford: Oxford University Press, 1971), pp. 5–37.

33. *ST* Ia–IIae, q. 17, a. 4: "imperium et actus imperatus sunt unus actus humanus."

34. *ST* Ia–IIae, q. 20, a. 3: "actus interior voluntatis et actus exterior, prout considerantur in genere moris, sunt unus actus."

35. *ST* Ia–IIae, q. 19, a. 1, ad 3: "bonum per rationem repraesentatur voluntat ut obiectum; et in quantum cadit sub ordine rationis, pertinet ad genus moris; et causat bonitatem moralem in actu voluntatis."

36. *ST* Ia–IIae, q. 19, a. 5: "obiectum a quo bonitas vel malitia voluntatis dependet non autem propter obiectum secundum sui naturam, sed secundum quod *per accidens* a ratione apprehenditur ut bonum vel malum, ad faciendum vel ad vitandum." The context here concerns an argument about indifferent acts. As Thomas continues, however, he shows that the same argument serves for acts that are in themselves good or evil. See also Ia–IIae, q. 18, a. 2 and 3; q. 19, a. 1 and 2.

37. *De malo*, q. 2, a. 5: "sicut cognoscere mulierem suam et cognoscere mulierem non suam sunt actus habentes obiecta differentia secundum aliquid ad rationem pertinens; nam suum et non suum determinatur secundum regulam rationis."

38. For further discussion of Thomas's complicated relation to Aristotelian moral philosophy, see my *The Subtle Arts of Casuistry*, vol. 1: *The Casuistical Tradition from Aristotle to Kant* (Oxford: Clarendon Press, forthcoming 2003), chap. 4.

39. See *Nicomachean Ethics*, VI, 1. 1138b25–34.

40. For a discussion of Thomas's attempts to go beyond many of the strictures of Aristotelian practical philosophy, see my *The Subtle Art of Casuistry*, vol. 1, chaps. 3 and 5.

41. *ST* Ia–IIae, q. 91, a. 3, ad 2: "ratio humana secundum se non est regula rerum, sed principia ei naturaliter indita sunt regulae quaedam generales et mensurae omnium eorum quae sunt per hominem agenda."

42. See *ST* Ia–IIae, q. 100, a. 1.

43. Cf. *ST* Ia–IIae, q. 94, a. 1: "lex naturalis est aliquid per rationem constitutum, sicut etiam propositio est quoddam opus rationis."

44. Ibid., a. 2 ad 2: "inclinationes quarumcumque partium naturae humanae . . . secundum quod regulantur a ratione, pertinent ad legem naturalem."

45. *ST* IIa–IIae, q. 154, a. 12: "in vitiis quae sunt contra naturam transgreditur homo id quod est secundum naturam determinatum . . . ; in aliis praeteritur solum id quod est secundum rationem rectam determinatum, ex praesuppositione tamen naturalium principorum."

46. *Summa contra gentiles*, III, c. 9: "oportet igitur quod a fine rationis dicantur aliqua in moralibus bona vel mala."

47. Cf. *ST* IIa–IIae, q. 153, a. 3: "hoc autem pertinet ad rationem luxuriae ut ordinem et modum rationis excedat circa venera."

48. *ST* IIa–IIae, q. 153, a. 2: "habet hoc rationis ordo ut quaelibet convenienter ordinet in suum finem."

49. *ST* IIa–IIae, qq. 1–5; especially 9.2: "Et similiter si quis abstineat a delectationibus corporalibus ut liberius vacet contemplationi veritatis, per finet hoc ad rectitudinem rationis."

50. IIa–IIae, q. 47, a. 7.

51. For a discussion of Moore's attack on naturalism and its subsequent influence upon English-speaking moral philosophy, see Thomas Baldwin, *G. E. Moore* (London: Routledge, 1990), pp. 67–110. It should be remembered that Moore's 'naturalistic fallacy' argument is directed against all those who seek a reductive definition of the Good. In this respect, metaphysicians such as Bradley are just as guilty of committing the 'error' as contemporary naturalists

CONTRIBUTORS

DAVID BRAINE is Honorary Lecturer in Philosophy at the University of Aberdeen. He studied physics, history, and philosophy at Oxford, the latter under Gilbert Ryle, and now works in the areas of metaphysics, philosophy of religion, and ethics. He is the author of *The Reality of Time and the Existence of God* (Oxford University Press, 1988) and *The Human Person: Animal and Spirit* (University of Notre Dame Press, 1992). He is also co-editor of *Ethics, Technology and Medicine* (Avebury, 1988).

RICHARD CROSS is Tutorial Fellow in Theology, Oriel College, University of Oxford. He writes on medieval philosophy and theology. His recent publications include *The Physics of Duns Scotus: The Scientific Context of a Theological Vision* (Oxford University Press, 1998), *Duns Scotus* (Oxford University Press, 1999), and *The Metaphysics of the Incarnation: Thomas Aquinas to Duns Scotus* (Oxford University Press, 2002).

STEFAAN E. CUYPERS is Associate Professor of Philosophy at the Catholic University of Leuven, Belgium . His interests are in the philosophy of mind and the social sciences. He is the author of "Autonomy beyond Voluntarism: In Defense of Hierarchy," *Canadian Journal of Philosophy* (2000), and *Self-Identity and Personal Autonomy: An Analytical Anthropology* (Ashgate, 2001).

JOHN HALDANE is Professor of Philosophy at the University of St Andrews. Currently he is also Royden Davis Professor of Humanities at Georgetown University, and Stanton Lecturer in Divinity in the

University of Cambridge. He has published widely and extensively in several areas of philosophy. He is co-author, with J. J. C. Smart, of *Atheism and Theism* (Blackwell, 1996, 2nd edition 2002) and of *Faithful Reason* (Routledge, forthcoming).

CHRISTOPHER HUGHES is Reader in Philosophy at King's College, London. He works in metaphysics, medieval philosophy, and the philosophy of religion. He is the author of *A Complex Theory of a Simple God* (Cornell University Press, 1990). Recent publications include "Matter and Actuality in Aquinas," *Revue Internationale de Philosophie* (1998), and "Negative Existentials, Omniscience, and Cosmic Luck," *Religious Studies* (1998).

GERARD J. HUGHES, S.J., is the Master of Campion Hall in the University of Oxford, having previously been Head of the Department of Philosophy and Vice-Principal of Heythrop College in the University of London. He has published many papers on ethics and on philosophy of religion, and is the author of *The Nature of God* (Routledge, 1995) and *Aristotle on Ethics* (Routledge, 2001).

JONATHAN JACOBS is Professor of Philosophy and Chair of the Department of Philosophy and Religion at Colgate University. He writes on moral psychology, metaethics, and metaphysics. His recent publications include *Choosing Character* (Cornell University Press, 2001) and *A Philosopher's Compass* (Harcourt, 2001).

FERGUS KERR, O.P., is Regent of Blackfriars Hall, Oxford, and an Honorary Fellow of the Divinity Faculty in the University of Edinburgh. His publications include *Theology after Wittgenstein* (SPCK, 1997) and *Immortal Longings: Versions of Transcending Humanity* (University of Notre Dame Press, 1997). His *After Aquinas: Versions of Thomisms* is due for publication in 2002.

GYULA KLIMA is Associate Professor of Philosophy at Fordham University. His publications include several papers on medieval logic and metaphysics, primarily based on the works of Anselm, Aquinas, Ockham, and Buridan. His most recent publication is an annotated translation of John Buridan's *Summulae de dialectica* (Yale University Press, 2001).

C. F. J. MARTIN is Professor of Philosophy and a member of the Center for Thomistic Studies at the University of St. Thomas, Houston, prior to which he was Lecturer in Philosophy in the University of Glasgow. He writes in the fields of analytical and medieval philosophy. Recent publications include *An Introduction to Medieval Philosophy* (Edinburgh University Press, 1997) and *Thomas Aquinas: God and Explanations* (Edinburgh University Press, 1998).

DAVID S. ODERBERG is Reader in Philosophy at the University of Reading, England. He writes on metaphysics, philosophical logic, and moral philosophy, and his most recent books are *Moral Theory* and *Applied Ethics* (Blackwell, 2000). He is also the editor of *Form and Matter: Themes in Contemporary Metaphysics* (Blackwell, 1999).

M. W. F. STONE is Lecturer in the Philosophy of Religion at King's College, London. He is the author of several articles on medieval philosophy and early-modern scholasticism. His forthcoming treatment of the history of casuistry, *The Subtle Arts of Casuistry* (2 vols.), is to be published by Oxford University Press.

INDEX

Essays on the Active Powers of the Human Mind, 95
on volition, 95–98
Rescher, Nicholas, 168, 172
rigid designators, 70, 175–81, 193n.4, 194n.17
Rist, John, 5–6
Rowe, William, 94

scholasticism, ix–x, 39, 55–56, 62, 125–26, 140n.1
See also Aquinas, Thomas; John of St. Thomas; Thomism
skepticism, 7, 110, 111, 118, 119
soul. *See* mind, relationship between body and
Spengler, Oswald, 54
Stump, Eleonore, 51nn.11, 12
Suarez, Francis, 129, 131, 136
substances
    accidental properties of, 127, 131, 132, 133, 141nn.19, 20, 164, 165, 166, 202–3
    and agency, 96–98, 100
    Aristotle on, 39, 127–28, 163–64, 173n.3, 174n.6
    individuation of, 126–40
    substantial form, 37–50, 51nn.11, 12, 99, 114–18, 127–28, 129–30, 134–36, 139, 164–67, 182, 187–88, 189, 198–99
    See also essentialism
Summa Contra Gentiles, 21–22, 144–45, 149–50, 151, 152
Summa Theologiae, 7–8, 9, 20–21, 44, 52n.37, 72, 76, 80, 86, 114, 115, 116, 117, 123n.8, 124n.19, 146–47, 150, 151, 158n.9, 169, 196–98, 205, 206

"Teleology and Laws of Nature," 80, 81
Thomism, ix–x, 55–56, 59, 69, 71–73
    and analytical philosophy, x, 59, 71, 72–73, 125–26

See also Aquinas, Thomas; John of St. Thomas; scholasticism
Three Philosophers, 80

The Unity of Philosophical Experience, 54

Vico, Giambattista, 16
volition
    and agency, 94–106
    Aquinas on, 40–46, 52n.34, 76–77, 79–80, 91, 94, 98–106, 108n.32, 143, 198–204
    Aquinas on freedom of the will, 79–80, 91, 98, 100–106, 108n.32, 143
    Aquinas on the intellect and, 98–104, 106
    Reid on, 95–98

Wiggins, David, 56
Will, Freedom, and Power, 81
Williams, Bernard, 63
Williams, Christopher, 2
will. *See* agency; volition
Wittgenstein, Ludwig, 30, 59
    vs. Aquinas, 1–2, 4, 6–7, 8, 10, 14, 15–16
    and Augustine, 12–13, 14–15
    on following a rule, 14–15
    and induction, 2
    Kenny on, 1–2
    on language-use, 121
    on learning language, 7, 12–13
    on logical positivism, 2
    Philosophical Investigations, 7, 12–13, 58
    on private language, 2, 16n.5
    on understanding, 14, 15

Yablo, Stephen, 177

www.ingramcontent.com/pod-product-compliance
Lightning Source LLC
Chambersburg PA
CBHW030917150426
42812CB00045B/161